Annual Editions:
Human Development, 45/e

Claire N. Rubman

McGraw Hill Education

http://create.mheducation.com

ISBN-10: 1259661202   ISBN-13: 9781259661204

Contents

Unit 6   133

Detailed Table of Contents

ponders the effects of kids' "apps" on brain development, cognition, intelligence, and creativity. Digital media often functions as a baby-sitter during meals, car rides, and busy times. Will swiping become addictive for toddlers?

Unit: Development during Childhood: Cognition and Schooling

Food for Thought: Safe Brain Boosters for Kids, Michael T. Murray, *Better Nutrition*, 2014
Since the realization over 30 years ago that children can experience mental health issues such as depression, treatment has become a major focus. Natural alternatives including diet and herbal supplements are discussed.

Happy, Healthy Kids: Six Ways to Boost Mood, Calm ADHD, and Ease Anxiety, Lisa Turner, *Better Nutrition*, 2014
Eating healthily can increase brain activity in children. Certain foods can enhance attention and concentration. Deficiencies in vitamins, copper, iodine and other nutrients can adversely affect a child's brain development. Conversely, appropriate levels of EPA, DHA and PharaGABA have been shown in research studies to enhance brain development.

Are Exams Bad for Children? Stephanie Schneider and Matt Christison, *New Internationalist*, 2013
The benefits and disadvantages of standardized tests are debated in this article. Two teachers discuss academic performance, student evaluation and the effects of standardized tests on children.

Ritalin Gone Wrong, Alan L. Sroufe, *The New York Times*, 2012
The benefits of drugs such as Ritalin or Adderall are assessed for attention deficits or hyperactivity disorders. The history and initial success of such drugs is reviewed. This initial success is clouded by a study in 2009 of approximately 600 children that questioned any long term benefits of these medications on academic performance or behavior.

Giving ADHD a Rest: with Diagnosis Rates Exploding Wildly, Is the Disorder a Mental Health Crisis—or a Cultural One? Kate Lunau, *Maclean's*, 2014
The rates of ADHD seem to have risen in America and other countries. This article looks to the possible causes such as increased educational pressures. The criteria for ADHD in the Diagnostic and Statistical Manual of Mental Disorders (DSM) is discussed as well as the effects of stimulants on the brain.

Unit: Development during Childhood: Family and Culture

Do-It-(All)-Yourself Parents, Linda Perlstein, *Newsweek*, 2012
A popular approach called "attachment parenting" includes homeschooling. About 300,000 children and adolescents in the United States are now homeschooled. State laws vary; from no reporting to submission of plans and test scores. Advantages are flexible differentiated instruction, no bullying, family togetherness, and an enthusiastic welcome from colleges.

The Drugging of the American Boy, Ryan D'Agostino, *Esquire*, 2014
The prevalence of ADHD diagnosis in young boys is discussed in relation to their behavior and schooling. The DSM-5 criteria for diagnosis are discussed along with the funding for ADHD research.

Why Our Approach to Bullying Is Bad for Kids, Susan Porter, *Independent School*, 2013
Bullying is discussed in light of our understanding of preadolescent brain development. Porter suggests that increased rates of bullying are a result of the expansion of the term to include aggressive childhood behaviors such as name calling or unfriendliness. The perceived victims of bullying may suffer from a lack of resilience or self-esteem.

Time to Lower the Drinking Age, Mary Kate Cary, *U.S. News & World Report*, 2014
The author makes the case for lowering the drinking age back to 18 as it was in the Reagan era. Lowering the age, she claims, would reduce binge drinking, illegal prescription drug use and sexual assault on college campuses.

Unit: Development during Adolescence and Young Adulthood

The Incredible Shrinking Childhood: How Early Is Too Early for Puberty? Elizabeth Weil, *The New York Times Magazine*, 2012
Preadolescent girls with early puberty have more emotional health risks. One theory is that early puberty affects cognition, making the brain susceptible to depression. Another theory is that changed physical status may be due to environmental

estrogens. Parenting focused on exercise, nutrition, and self-esteem helps vulnerable girls.

***Rolling Stone* Article on Rape at University of Virginia Failed All Basics, Report Says**, Ravi Somaiya, *New York Times*, 2015
"Jackie" falsely reported that she had been brutally gang raped at a fraternity party at the University of Virginia. This alleged attack was reported in an article in the *Rolling Stone* magazine. Writer Sabrina Rubin Erdely reported a gang rape at a party that never took place. The reporting errors, lack of fact checking and poor editorial scrutiny that led to this erroneous article are discussed.

Will Your Marriage Last? Brooke Lea Foster, *Washingtonian*, 2012
Researchers have found many correlates of lasting marriages. This article reports that education, wives with career income or assets, peer friendships with other couples, good sex, and frequent positive interactions (playing nice) are advantageous. Children decrease happiness initially, but couples rebound as they grow up and leave home.

The Retro Wife, Lisa Miller, *New York Magazine*, 2013
Educated adult women with three roles (mother, wife/partner, and daughter) are rethinking the fourth role (independent career authority). Many meditate upon "A man's job is to earn money; a woman's job is to care for home and family." Are gender differences (females nurture, males assert) real, or just coming back into favor?

Kids Are Not Adults, Sarah Alice Brown, *Juvenile Justice Bulletin*, 2013
Juvenile justice policies in the United States, such as trying adolescents as adults within the criminal justice system are discussed. Recent research on brain development suggests that before the age of 25, the decision making processes in teens differ from that in adults. Adolescents are more likely to base their behavior on short-term consequences.

High-Tech Bullies, Ingrid Sturgis, *Diverse: Issues in Higher Education*, 2014
Bullying was once thought to be the domain of middle and high school students but it now appears to be a pervasive problem at the college level. Sites such as "College Wall of Shame" or "Juicy Campus" provide an ideal outlet for stalking, revealing secrets, or masquerading as somebody else.

Many Professors Say Their Students Lack Professional Qualities for Future Jobs, Ann Schnoebelen, *The Chronicle of Higher Education*, 2013
Multitasking is blamed for students' lack of professional qualities, which include good interpersonal skills, dependability, the ability to focus and pay attention, and complete a task.

Don't Leave Me Out! Catherine Sebastian, *The Psychologist*, 2012
This article pinpoints rejection as a form of relational aggression or bullying during adolescence. Adolescents are particularly sensitive to peer rejection due to brain development, in particular, the prefrontal cortex. Using Internet video games and MRI scans, the brain is tracked as it develops from early adolescence into adulthood.

Unit: Development during Middle and Late Adulthood

PICK Your PATH to Retirement, Jane Bennett Clark, *Kiplinger's Personal Finance*, 2015
Retirement has been redefined in the 21st Century as a result of increased life expectancy, more years in the work force, better health and higher levels of education.

The Switched-On Brain, Amy Barth, *Discover*, 2012
Optogenetics has stopped drug abuse in mice. It used opsins (light-sensitive microbes), inserted in mouse neurons, to control their brains with light. Creative scientists are motivated to get opsins into human cells. This technology could improve vision, heart health, and possibly neurological functioning. Will such mind control be deemed ethical?

Anxiety Nation, Sophie McBain, *New Statesman*, 2014
The mental illness, anxiety, is explored as a cultural concept. The relationship between anxiety and other emotions such as sadness or depression is discussed. Medications such as Prozac and Xanax are reviewed. There is a focus on the role of panic attacks, insomnia and phobias.

Preface

The authors of this collection of articles collectively challenge the notion of the status quo: They question overindulgent parenting, bullying in homes and across college campuses, standardized tests, and the pervasiveness of cheating in our educational system. They raise provocative questions such as:

- Is it possible to create artificial sperm or have a womb transplant?
- When an infant is left alone, forgotten and strapped into the infant seat in the rear of a car, is it because the parent was too busy multitasking, too emotionally and physically exhausted, or too absent-minded?
- Are we over-parenting our children?
- What is going on inside an adolescent's brain?
- Is technology such as Twitter, Snapchat, or other social media hurting us?
- Are our "virtual friends" on Facebook making us lonelier?

This Annual Editions anthology generates new perspectives on a wide range of topics from life for the infertile Iranian woman to the benefits and limitations of the ¡Pad for infants or toddlers. We will explore issues such as the potential benefits or disadvantages of iPads and technology for young children. We will explore the possible educational myths, especially in early childhood. You will read about what the creators of educational games and apps do with their own children—do they allow their children to play the very games that they created? We will ask you to think about how parents should address other prevalent issues with their children from poor attention skills to overcoming bullying and becoming a more resilient child. You might learn about the impact of positive parenting in adolescence and its impact on future employment. You can join in the "medication debate" with regard to Ritalin or Adderall as a potential cure for ADD/ADHD. Do you think that we are over-medicating our children? How should a twenty-first century parent discern between an active young son, for example, and a boy that requires medication? Is it possible that we are trying to medicate the very essence of childhood?

As we turn our attention to adolescence, you will read about current research on the pain associated with precocious, or early, puberty. We will share articles on the feelings of loneliness and isolation that the adolescent brain experiences as the prefrontal lobe and the "executive function" matures and is flooded with new hormonally charged experiences. You can learn about the myths and dangers of multitasking and why many professors say that their students are ill prepared for the workplace.

Our focus is, ultimately, on adulthood and aging. Find out what happens to the human brain as we age and discover techniques to keep our aging brains more dynamic. Think about life as we age. Who will take care of us? Think about your parents and how you will, potentially, take care of them in their retirement. We will look together at the potential dangers that lurk in some assisted living facilities or retirement homes with a view to avoiding physical or psychological abuse such as neglect or medication errors.

These articles were compiled to promote thought and discussion using the Socratic Method (Socrates, 470–399 BC) to generate critical thinking as a powerful tool for learning. They are the ideal catalyst for student-led discussions and student-centered learning. They can be used as the stimulus for a debate, student presentations, or small group discussions.

The topics were selected to motivate and inspire you to think, read, discuss, and learn in an interactive environment. Take ownership of these issues and themes in human lifespan development. Using Bronfenbrenner's Ecological model (1994), think about how they impact you as an individual as well as society at large.

Editor

Dr. Rubman is a Cognitive, Developmental Psychologist. She has numerous publications and radio interviews to her credit. She is frequently requested to present guest lectures, keynote addresses, and workshop presentations both within the United States and internationally.

Uniquely qualified to talk and write about cognitive development, Dr. Rubman has a refreshingly novel approach that appeals to students, teachers, parents, and experts in the field. Her conference presentations include titles such as:

- "What's Next: Calculus in Kindergarten?"
- "Youface and My Tube: Teens and Technology"
- "Time Out Doesn't Work"

- "Pixels in the Classroom"
- "The 21st Century Brain and Other Stories" and,
- "A Line in the Sandbox"

Magazine articles include such titles as:

- "Read-iculous: The Challenges of Reading Through the Eyes of a Child"
- "The Big Fat Question of Obesity," and
- "It's Never Too Soon to Plan for Kindergarten, Is It?"

Dr. Rubman is a Professor at Suffolk County Community College in Selden, NY, where she has taught for the past 14 years. She has also spent time in the classroom as a Kindergarten teacher in London, England and California, USA.

Born and raised in Glasgow, Scotland, she earned her PhD and MA degrees in Cognitive, Developmental Psychology from the State University of New York in Stony Brook. She holds a BA degree from Glasgow University and she also earned her FLCM, LLCM (Teacher's Diploma) degrees from the London College of Music in London, England, where she currently serves as an external examiner.

Dr. Rubman can be contacted through her website www.clairerubman.com or through her website "Education and Parenting Matters."

Academic Advisory Board

Members of the Academic Advisory Board are instrumental in the final selection of articles for each edition of ANNUAL EDITIONS. Their review of articles for content, level, and appropriateness provides critical direction to the editors and staff. We think that you will find their careful consideration well reflected in this volume.

Unit 1

UNIT

Prepared by: Claire N. Rubman,
Suffolk County Community College, Selden, NY

Genetics and Prenatal Influences on Development

Some women desperately want to have children but can't, while other women cringe at the very thought of motherhood. This collection of articles looks at parenthood from both perspectives. It takes into account the new technologies that are available to assist infertile couples both in the United States and around the world. It also addresses women who do not, for whatever reason, have children.

Perhaps you already have children and are wondering about how your pregnancy behavior impacted your child's development. Did you gain too much "baby weight"? Did that, somehow, affect your unborn child? Is it possible pregnancy behavior influences later development in your child's adolescent years? Some adolescents are already pregnant although teen pregnancy rates are declining.

Where does our twenty-first century knowledge about pregnancy originate? Do we learn about pregnancy-related issues such as contraceptives, abortion, technology assisted pregnancy, or childbirth from television and social media? Do teenagers, for example, learn from the vast array of wildly popular reality TV shows that have exploded onto our television screens? Shows on teenage pregnancy and motherhood such as *16 and Pregnant* or *Teen Mom* give viewers a closer look at the realities of pregnancy, birth, and motherhood. The first article in this unit focuses on the effect that shows like this have on teenagers. Is it possible that they are lured into pregnancy by the fame, attention, and "cuteness" of a new baby? Alternatively, is it more likely that the harsh realities of motherhood have actually reduced the number of teenage pregnancies in the USA?

The focus of our discussion shifts to prenatal development for the remainder of this unit. However, we pause to consider women who cannot have children or who choose not to procreate. "The No-Baby Boom" by Kingston allows us to think about the 1 in 5 woman who remain childless into their 40s. Why has this number doubled in just one generation? Why is this indicative of women in many developed countries around the world? The concept of "social infertility" is discussed.

For women who would like to become pregnant but experience difficulties along the way, "Making Babies" by Alexis Madrigal explores the many and varied options that today's technology has made possible, including a uterus transplant, artificial gametes, and the use of mitochondrial DNA.

These technological advances have created new possibilities for some women whose religion used to preclude this type of intervention. In Iran, for example, the issuing of a fatwa on donor eggs or sperm by the Ayatollah Ali Khamenei cleared the way for the 20% of that nation's infertile couples to try new reproductive techniques. Moaveni's "The Islamic Republic of Baby-Making" explores the growth of 70 fertility clinics and takes a closer look at the root causes including male infertility which he describes as "the hidden story of the Middle East."

With the advent of new technologies comes the potential for misuse including the sex-selection abortion in countries such as India, Taiwan, Azerbaijan, Albania, China, and the United States. Mara Hvistendahl explores the many and varied reasons for gender selection in her article "Unnatural Selection." Dowries, population control, and genetic diseases have contributed to sex selection in many countries around the world. Hvistendahl discusses the impact of these choices in many countries.

The final two articles in this section, "Beyond the Baby Weight" by Eric Reither, and "Maternal Obesity and the Development of Child Obesity" look at the impact of maternity weight gain or "baby weight" on the mother and child. The link between the weight gained during pregnancy and a child's potential for obesity are explored. Factors such as prenatal care and socioeconomic status are the basis of this study of Hawaiian and non-Hawaiian women. The relationship between maternal obesity, high birth weight, and obesity in adolescence is teased apart.

Article Prepared by: Claire N. Rubman, *Suffolk County Community College*

The No-Baby Boom

Social infertility, baby regret and what it means that shocking numbers of women aren't having children

ANNE KINGSTON

Learning Outcomes

After reading this article, you will be able to:

- Understand the nuances of social infertility.
- Explain the acronym "PANK."
- Describe how childless women are depicted in the media.

Catherine-Emmanuelle Delisle does not seem, at first glance, like a social firebrand. The 37-year-old school-teacher in Saint-Bruno, a Montreal suburb, is a thoughtful, sensitive woman who exudes gamine charm. She enjoys jewellery making, design, and cinema—and she really loves children, enough to devote her life to teaching drama and French in primary school. But Delisle knew as a teenager she couldn't have kids, a fact she was in denial about for years, she says. Grappling with never giving birth was painful, and required time to grieve. As she began to reframe her life as a **childless** woman, she observed a lack of role models or even discussion of the subject. "We are non-existent in the media, in cinema, in art, in magazines," she says. When **childless** women are depicted, it's characters like Breaking Bad's Marie, who deals with the unhappiness of her domestic situation by going to open houses and making up elaborate stories about herself, many involving fictional children. And of course there's 45-year-old actress Jennifer Aniston, the mother of all non-mothers, whose uterus is a chronic subject of tabloid fretting. (Last week, OK continued the "sad, barren Jen" narrative: "Jen agrees to fertility treatment to have kids," it claimed.)

Delisle is hell-bent on reframing the way women like her are depicted. "We're seen as selfish, or treated as if our lives lack meaning or value," she says with a bemused laugh, knowing well it's imagery that can be insidiously absorbed by women themselves.

Delisle's blog, FemmeSansEnfant.com, launched in 2012, provides a counterpoint, a place for women to connect and support one another. Interviewees share stories on video: the journalist Pénélope McQuade explains she never felt the "visceral" need for children; singer Marie Denise Pelletier speaks of dreaming of being a singer, not a mother. "My goal is to get women without children, whether by choice or circumstance, known and valued," Delisle says.

The schoolteacher is part of a growing global movement that's giving voice to a misunderstood phenomenon whose repercussions are personal and societal. "We think there is a room called childlessness with two doors: 'didn't want' or 'can't have,'" says Jody Day, the writer and social entrepreneur behind Gatway-Women.com, a network based in London, England, for the "**childless**-by-circumstance" (dubbed "NoMos"). "But there are many ways to end up not being a mother."

That millions of women are discovering this is reflected in statistics: one out of five women in the U.K., Ireland, the U.S., Canada, and Australia are reaching their mid-40s without having had children—twice as many as a generation ago. The 2010 U.S. census revealed 47.1 percent of women of child-bearing age don't have children—up from 35 percent in 1976.

To put those developments in historical context, Daly notes that the last time the **childless** rate was one in five, it was in a generation of so-called "surplus women" born at the turn of the 20th century. "The fact it took a war with unprecedented loss of life and global depression to cause such an increase in childlessness gives you some idea of the social change we're going through now," she says.

Yet discussion of childlessness remains mired in hand-wringing, pity and judgment—either concern over the consequences of a reduced tax base and diminishing social supports, as explored in Jonathan Last's "What to Expect When No One's Expecting: America's Coming Demographic Disaster," or coverage of the militant "child-free" movement seen in books like Jen Kirkman's *I Can Barely Take Care of Myself: Tales from a Happy Life without Kids.* Virtually ignored in the conversation is the impact of "social infertility"—Day's coinage for the growing number of women who don't have a partner or the right partner while they can have children. It's a big problem for women born in the '70s, says Day, who experienced social infertility herself: she married at 23 and tried to get pregnant in her late 20s; her 16-year marriage ended when she was 39 and considering IVF. "I couldn't find a suitable person to do IVF with," she says. "Now I know it was probably way too late by then anyway."

Social infertility is such a new concept that data are scarce. A 2013 study out of Australia's Deakin University published in the *Journal of Social Inclusion* reports there has been a "general failure to examine women's reasons for childlessness beyond [medical] infertility." It found that more than half of the surveyed women without children listed having never been in the "right" relationship, being in a relationship where the partner did not want to have children—what some bloggers call "infertility by marriage"—or never having wanted children as the reason.

The emerging topography of childlessness is also delineated in Melanie Notkin's new memoir, *Otherhood: Modern Women Finding a New Kind of Happiness,* an insightful, anecdotal account of the challenges facing professional Manhattan women who dream of finding the right partner and having children. (Think *Sex and the City* with IVF.) Notkin discusses the "dating Bermuda Triangle" faced by over-30 women and the fertility snatchers who end long-term relationships as a woman's reproductive life is ending.

The 44-year-old, Montreal-born, McGill-educated, New York City-based former marketing executive has made a career of focusing on **childless** women. In 2008, she launched the "multiplatform lifestyle brand" SavvyAuntie.com targeted at "PANKs" (her acronym for "professional aunt, no kids")—the 23 million **childless** American women who are invested both emotionally and financially in the children in their lives. Savvy Auntie suggests gifts, details activities from making dough animals to "Skype dance-offs," and even confers the "Savvy Auntie Best Toy Award" on worthy merchandise. **Childless** women, invisible to marketers in the past, are now appearing on the radar, Notkin says. A 2012 Weber Shandwick/KRC survey of 2000 women in U.S. and Canada, titled "The Power of the PANK," estimated total spending of $9 billion annually by PANKs on children in their lives, with an average of $387 per child. Thirty-four percent were also contributing to a child's education—hence the emergence of the "aunt" demographic. A commercial for Huggies released this month depicts a loving aunt being flown to meet her sister's newborn on the diaper-maker's dime.

Notkin's focus may be on tapping a new market, but she also exposes something more profound underlying it. Most women start out expecting to have children, she says, citing a recent Centers for Disease Control and Prevention study that found

80 percent of single women are **childless,** but that 81 percent of that group said they hope or plan to have children. She rejects the "career woman" label used to describe **childless** women: "It implies we have chosen work over love, marriage, children. I know no woman who has done that." Social infertility—or "circumstantial infertility" to use Notkin's term—forces women to recalibrate expectations in ways not discussed publicly, she says: "At 25, a woman expects to have children, at 35 she hopes to, and at 45 she says she's happy she doesn't."

Women don't broadcast wanting a child for fear of being lectured that they shouldn't wait, Notkin says. But they're well aware of the tick-tock, she says: "Every 28 days offers a reminder." The upshot is that women are being forced to make a tactical decision in their 30s: resort to solo motherhood, partner with someone simply to procreate, freeze their eggs, or rely on IVF. All are "choices" that are not fully choices. How many women have the resources to keep working while paying child care on a single salary—or to not work at all? How many can afford to freeze their eggs, and then pay for IVF too? Advances in fertility technology have created false perceptions, says Notkin, who writes that people talk about freezing eggs as if it's picking up a carton of milk. "The assumption is that if you wanted a kid, you would have a kid and go it alone. But that's not viable for a lot of women." People see Halle Berry giving birth at 47 and think it's the new norm, she notes. IVF is misrepresented in the media, says Day. "All we hear is miracle stories, not that it usually doesn't work over age 40."

The fact that discussion about childlessness is framed in terms of personal choice, failure and medical infertility shuts down conversation, says Day. So do the cultural narratives of motherhood and womanhood, a spectacle Notkin calls "mom-opia"—"seeing motherhood as the only normal, natural way to be a woman." It's a fixation reflected in manic coverage of celebrity "baby bumps" and loss of pregnancy weight—as well as photos of stars with their kids. We see it too in Michelle Obama's transformation from accomplished professional and activist to supermom, not only to her own kids, but to the nation—overseeing how it eats and encouraging it to exercise.

Women outside the maternal matrix are suspect—former Australian PM Julia Gillard was termed "deliberately barren" and unfit for leadership by a political opponent. In 2012, Wildrose Party Leader Danielle Smith's childlessness was questioned on Twitter by a PC staffer, who later resigned. Actress Helen Mirren's declaration that she has "no maternal instinct" was viewed as a salvo in an unnamed war. "**Childless** women represent a threat to the status quo," says Day. "We're seen as a destabilizing influence. If one does well in her career—and doesn't have children—she can do as well as a man." Against this grain, women don't speak up for fear of sounding shrill or pathetic or desperate or being defined by one aspect of their lives—disappointment in not having children.

But that is changing, particularly over the past year, as **childless** women are increasingly vocal, says Lisa Manterfield, the Los Angeles-based author of *I'm Taking My Eggs and Going Home: How One Woman Dared to Say No to Motherhood,* her 2011 memoir that chronicles how she was 34 by the time she met the man she wanted to raise a family with, then wrestled with infertility before coming to the difficult decision that motherhood wasn't in her future. When Manterfield launched LifeWithoutBaby.com 4 years ago, she says, there were only a few voices—Pamela Tsigdinos at SilentSorority.com and Tracey Cleantis at LaBeletteRouge.com—telling their personal stories to a small audience. Now more women are willing to talk about a loss others can't see, she says, one that forced her to confront how much of female identity is tied to motherhood. "The loss isn't tangible, so most women feel alone, their grief compounded by the attitude that they 'should be over it,' " she says. Adding to the isolation is the feeling of being "locked out of the Mommy Clubhouse," as one blogger put it on LifeWithoutBaby .com. "Women without children not only lose a future family," says Day, "but can lose their peer group who have moved to a country called motherhood where we don't speak the language."

The fact that the archetype of the most pitied and shamed woman has, in one generation, gone from single mother to single woman over 40 without children reflects fundamental societal shifts, says Day, who thinks it's not a coincidence that the "fetishization of motherhood"—from pregnancy studio shots to the ideal birth (at home! in water! without meds!)—comes at a time of rising childlessness. "There's so much cultural anxiety around what it means; there's reflexive nostalgia for a simpler time: women at home and gender roles more clearly defined." This isn't only societal pressure; some of it comes from women recognizing the increasing precariousness of motherhood. Day likens it to propaganda used to lure women home from the workforce after the Second World War. It can be seductive, she says. "It seems such a solid identity, being a mother; being **childless** is fluid, nebulous: 'What are you?' "

Rising childlessness is often blamed on feminism selling women a "bill of goods" about "having it all." But Betty Friedan's 1963 manifesto *The Feminine Mystique* presumed that women would continue to marry and have children. "The assumption of your own identity, equality and even political power does not mean you stop needing to love, and be loved by, a man, or that you stop caring for your kids," she wrote.

What no one could have predicted is that women born in the '60s and '70s would become what Day terms the "shock absorber" cohort, living through the most extraordinary changes in dating and mating in one generation. That's the result of a confluence of forces—the pill, women's access to higher education and professions—running headlong into a rigid corporate model that remains based on the husband-provider, male-fertility model—working hard in your 20s and 30s to establish a reputation, leaving kids to the stay-at-home

wife. "But that doesn't work for women," says Day. "If you make it work, it's as much luck as good judgment."

Today's "surplus women" are not war widows but young professional women for whom there aren't enough suitable male partners—a phenomenon referred to in China derisively as "A1 women and D4 men." Yet the blame invariably falls on them for being "too choosy," a motif of the booming advice-to-female-professionals book genre, the latest being Susan Patton's new *Marry Smart: Advice for Finding THE ONE,* in which the "Princeton Mom" advises women to snag their "MRS" in university as they'll never have access to such an elite dating pool again.

But the issue is more structural: we're transitioning from an old social model in which women are expected to "marry up" socially or economically that runs parallel to an emerging one examined in Lisa Mundy's *The Richer Sex: How the New Majority of Female Breadwinners Is Transforming Sex, Love and Family.* Mundy concludes that if successful millennial women want to marry and have children, they'll have to marry down. That's happening globally, but slowly, Mundy told *Maclean's.* Many women she spoke to admitted lying about what they did when they met a man, either fearing the truth would be intimidating or wanting to seem more feminine, she says. Notkin, too, chronicles how modern dating rituals can have one foot in traditional rom-com expectations: women want chivalry as well as a socially enlightened man. They have no problem "leaning in" at work, per Sheryl Sandberg's instruction, she says. "We lean in every day; we're almost falling over." Yet when dating, they want to lean back and let men do some of the heavy lifting. Notkin always envisioned "motherhood as part of the romantic wholeness of marriage and family," she writes, and was unwilling to settle for less.

Reconciling a new reality with the Vaseline-lens myth is the central theme of the **childless**-by-circumstance movement. Navigating unchartered waters requires a "plan B," Day writes in her 2013 book *Rocking the Life Unexpected.* **Childless** women feel pressure to have a big compensatory life, she says. "It's as though if you're not a mother, you have to become Mother Teresa. But you don't need a big life on the outside, just on the inside." Notkin describes her situation this way: "While it's not the life I expected, it's the life I directed."

But childlessness is not only a personal issue to be grappled with, it's a social one requiring new models, says Day—the most pressing being caregiving in old age. "It isn't just about childlessness," says Day. "The ratio of people around to take care of aging persons is changing, and daughters are not necessarily available to give that care because they're working." She'd like to see an intergenerational dialog among older women without children, mothers in her generation and their daughters. "We need to discuss not just what we did wrong but what we've learned, so it doesn't take them by surprise."

Looking around, there's no shortage of role models, including Aniston, who is finally voicing her frustration with the

childless stigma. When the actress interviewed the feminist activist Gloria Steinem at the Maker's Conference in California in February, Aniston noted that for women in the public eye, "our value and worth is dependent on our marital status and/ or if we've procreated." Steinem, who is also **childless,** shot back, "Well, I guess we're in deep s—t!" The audience laughed uproariously—with them, not at them.

Critical Thinking

1. Why has the rate of childlessness increased in recent years?
2. How has corporate America capitalized on the "childless" market?
3. How does feminism relate to the 21st-century woman and her childbearing choices?

Create Central

www.mhhe.com/createcentral

Internet References

CNN Health U.S. women having fewer children
   http://thechart.blogs.cnn.com/2013/12/06/u-s-women-having-fewer-children

Ranker.com Childless Celebrities | List of Famous People without Children
   http://www.ranker.com/list/childless-celebrities/celebrity-lists?var=2&utm_expid=16418821-48.w4XvOttHQz-Kl88l1iLzhA.1&utm_referrer=http%3A%2F%2Fwww.google.com%2Furl%3Fsa%3Dt%26rct%3Dj%26q%3D%26esrc%3Ds%26source%3Dweb%26cd%3D1%26sqi%3D2%26ved%3D0CB4QFjAA%26url%3Dhttp%253A%252F%252Fwww.ranker.com%252Flist%252Fchildless-celebrities%252Fcelebrity-lists%26ei%3DWrsYVJifJI_gsAS6y4KADg%26usg%3DAFQjCNFKy6rJjGCDAmm8CyU5dnhaYFriWA%26sig2%3Dzq8aq1kdh_mtMRsWRy2cHQ%26bvm%3Dbv.75097201%2Cd.cWc

savvyauntie.com PANK: Professional Aunt No Kids
   http://savvyauntie.com/About.aspx?GroupId=389&Name=PANK:%20Professional%20Aunt%20No%20Kids

Kingston, Anne. "The No-Baby Boom." *Maclean's* 127. 12 (March, 31, 2013): 48–50.

Article   Prepared by: Claire N. Rubman, *Suffolk County Community College*

Making Babies

Five predictions about the future of reproduction

ALEXIS MADRIGAL

Learning Outcomes

After reading this article, you will be able to:

- Explain how technology such as "GLOW" and "FETUS CARE" can enhance the reproductive process.

- Describe how stem cells may enhance reproduction in the future through the use of artificial gametes.

- Articulate the issue with the "slippage" that occurs as a result of screening and the potential paradox that may arise.

Forty years ago, there was exactly one way for humans to reproduce. A man's sperm would combine with a woman's egg, inside of her body. Together they would form a zygote, which would become an embryo, and then a fetus. With any luck, the woman would carry the fetus to term, and a baby would be born. The process had not changed since long before anyone could call us human. Until one day, after years of trial and error, Dr. Patrick Steptoe and Dr. Robert Edwards combined an egg from Lesley Brown with sperm from her husband, John, in a petri dish and implanted the resulting embryo in her uterus. On July 25, 1978, Louise Brown came squalling into the world, heralding a revolution not just in the mechanics of reproduction but in the surrounding culture.

At the time, James Watson, a co discoverer of DNA's double-helix structure, warned that if in vitro fertilization were allowed to proceed on a broader scale, "all hell will break loose, politically and morally, all over the world." Since then, not only has reproductive technology gone ahead, it has headed in previously unthinkable directions, and with little public scrutiny. For example, over the past 20 years, a new procedure called intracytoplasmic sperm injection has allowed fertility clinicians to select an individual sperm and insert it into an egg. It is the only reliable option for men with very low sperm counts or low-quality sperm, and for the hundreds of thousands of men it's enabled to have children, it's been life-changing. Happily, the procedure appears to cause only a relatively minor increase in the risk of birth defects.

Future reproductive innovations are likely to develop in similar ways—led by practitioners, with little U.S. government oversight. Few people, it seems, want to stand in the way of someone who desires a biological family. And so far, almost no one has. But some of the reproductive technologies on the horizon could test our flexibility. Here, drawn from interviews with scholars, doctors, and entrepreneurs are a handful of guesses about how the future may change what's involved in making a person—from the ease of getting pregnant, to the mechanics of procreation, to our very definition of family.

1 It Will Take a Village to Make a Child

Sperm and egg donation and surrogacy have already enabled unusual parental configurations. In some cases—say, a father contracting with an egg donor and a separate surrogate mother—a new baby could be said to have three biological parents. But this is only the beginning of what science may make possible in the near future. One new IVF procedure would combine the nucleus of a patient's egg with mitochondrial DNA from a donor's egg. The FDA is mulling approving the technique, which could prevent diseases that originate in mitochondrial DNA; it's already been successfully tested in monkeys.

Or take uterus transplants, in which one woman's healthy uterus is implanted in someone else's abdomen. Since 2012, nine Swedish women have received a uterus donation from a relative—in most cases their own mother. They're now under going IVF treatment, to see whether they can conceive and carry a baby. If successful, they'll be the first women to bear a child with another person's womb. Not only that: their children will in effect be sleeping in the same "room" that they once did. The implications are fascinating. As Charis Thompson, a sociologist at the London School of Economics who has written a book about IVF, observes, "Parenthood is multiplying."

2 Your Biological Clock Will Be Personalized . . .

One of the key problems in fertility research is how to help women who wish to start families later in life. Many women in their late 30s and beyond turn to IVF, usually with little sense of whether the physically demanding and expensive treatments are likely to work. Services like Univfy are trying to help women under stand their own fertility better. One of Univfy's co founders, the ob-gyn and fertility researcher Mylene Yao, says that women are entitled to a better read on their chances of conceiving through IVF than the rough age-based estimates that most fertility clinics provide. "There is no such thing as an average 38-year-old woman," Yao told me. Her company draws on detailed data from a 5-year study of IVF patients and other predictive models to provide personalized information about an individual's likelihood of conception. She compares the effort to those of Netflix and Amazon: "We're all, as consumers, getting better predictive information with online shopping than with health care."

3 . . . And Procreation Will Be Precisely Timed

Max Levchin is a co founder of Glow, a fertility-tracking app that helps users time sex for the greatest chance of conception. This isn't so revolutionary—solid knowledge of the menstrual cycle, a thermometer, a pen, and paper will let you do much the same thing—but by allowing users to pool data anonymously, it could lead to a better understanding of population-wide fertility patterns. There have been surprisingly few large-scale studies of couples' efforts to conceive; Levchin hopes that data from Glow can help change that.

The problem is, the data that people record are not very reliable. For example, slight temperature variations are key to predicting ovulation, and deviations in exactly when a woman takes her temperature can add noise to a data set. Down the road, Levchin sees simple sensors having a big effect on a couple's odds of conception and, ultimately, on our understanding of fertility patterns. He envisions a sticker-like thermometer that could "sit in some place, like the small of the back," he says. "You'll have a continuous feed of someone's temperature."

Such monitoring could be even more important for expectant mothers. Already, Taiwanese designers are working on an app called Fetus Care, which they say will use data from a sensor to detect worrisome uterine contractions or an abnormal fetal heart rate. Perhaps one day implantable sensors will track the interior state of the womb. After all, the FDA has approved ingestible data-logging sensors for use in other parts of the body.

4 Synthetic Sperm Will Save the Nuclear Family

As long as we're entertaining far-out but technically feasible scenarios, the most radical revision in reproduction could be the creation of artificial gametes, aka sperm, and egg cells. Researchers may ultimately be able to take a cell from an adult man or woman, turn it into a stem cell, then change that stem cell into a sperm or an egg. Doctors have already succeeded in breeding same-sex laboratory animals in this way.

Timothy Murphy is a philosophy professor at the University of Illinois College of Medicine at Chicago whose work focuses on the bioethical implications of reproductive technologies for gay, lesbian, and transgender people. He points out that creating artificial sperm and eggs could, rather than leading to radical social change, actually preserve a normative family structure. "For gay and lesbian couples, the synthetic gametes would eliminate the need for a third party," Murphy notes. This kind of assisted reproductive technology—"unnatural" as it might be—would allow same-sex couples to keep reproduction solely within the family.

5 Genotyping Will Breed Conformity

Here's a final paradox: even as reproductive freedom increases, enabling more types of parents to have children, these parents may choose children who ft a narrower and narrower notion of normal. Charis Thompson, the sociologist, told me about a conversation she recently had with a British in fertility doctor, who gave a disturbing preview of where we might be headed.

"You start out offering these prenatal screenings for certain conditions that everybody agrees are very severe. It is not particularly eugenic, but about alleviating the suffering of the child and the parents. But there is slippage," she said. "The more you can test for and screen out, the more people do. And the example this person gave was the high number of people who will abort a fetus that is found to have an extra digit."

A mere 11 years after the completion of the Human Genome Project, it is technically possible to scan an embryo's entire genome during the IVF process. If parents are already aborting pregnancies to avoid extra fingers, how many will resist the temptation to implant only the embryo with the "best" genome?

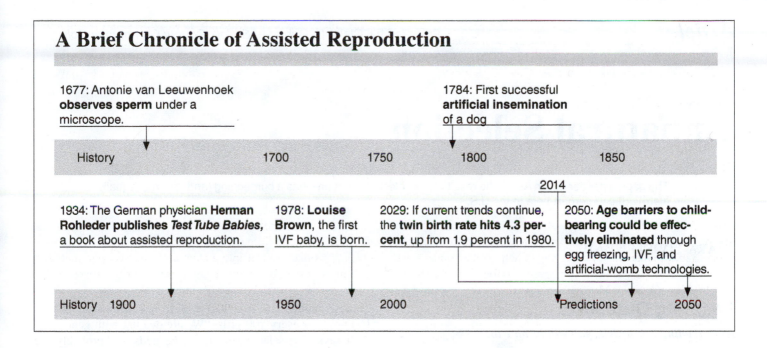

A Brief Chronicle of Assisted Reproduction

1677: Antonie van Leeuwenhoek **observes sperm** under a microscope.

1784: First successful **artificial insemination** of a dog

| History | 1700 | 1750 | 1800 | 1850 |

2014

1934: The German physician **Herman Rohleder** publishes *Test Tube Babies,* a book about assisted reproduction.

1978: **Louise Brown**, the first IVF baby, is born.

2029: If current trends continue, the **twin birth rate hits 4.3 percent,** up from 1.9 percent in 1980.

2050: **Age barriers to childbearing could be effectively eliminated** through egg freezing, IVF, and artificial-womb technologies.

| History | 1900 | 1950 | 2000 | Predictions | 2050 |

Which is to say, the future of reproduction might be increasingly diverse families making increasingly similar babies.

Critical Thinking

1. Why does Madrigal suggest that babies created using these new technological advances may be "increasingly similar"?

2. What are some of the potential legal issues with these new reproductive technologies?

3. What safeguards can be put in place to keep each of these innovations ethical and in the best interests of each potential child?

Create Central

www.mhhe.com/createcentral

Internet References

NCBI "Emotions and Ethical Considerations of Women Undergoing IVF"

http://www.ncbi.nlm.nih.gov/pmc/articles/PMC3258403/

RH Reality Check "Nine Women Receive Uterus Transplants in Sweden Raising Ethical Questions"

http://rhrealitycheck.org/article/2014/01/23/nine-women-receive-uterus-transplants-sweden-raising-ethical-questions/

The New York Times "Ethics Questions Arise as Genetic Testing of Embryos Increases"

http://www.nytimes.com/2014/02/04/health/ethics-questions-arise-as-genetic-testing-of-embryos-increases.html

The Telegraphy "Stem Cells Used to Make Artificial Sperm"

http://www.telegraph.co.uk/science/science-news/8682142/Stem-cells-used-to-make-artificial-sperm.html

Madrigal, Alexis. "Making Babies." *The Atlantic* 313. 5 (June 2014): 32–34.

Article Prepared by: Claire N. Rubman, *Suffolk County Community College*

Unnatural Selection

The gaping gender gap in Asia—the result of sex-selective abortion—has a burgeoning (and to some, equally alarming) counterpart here in the U.S.

MARA HVISTENDAHL

Learning Outcomes

After reading this article, you will be able to:

- Identify developmental disabilities more common in children born prematurely.

- Evaluate a future with one-third more males than females.

New Delhi, India

For Dr. Puneet Bedi, the intensive care unit in Apollo Hospital's maternity ward is a source of both pride and shame. The unit's technology is among the best in Delhi—among the best, for that matter, in all of India. But as a specialist in high-risk births, he works hard so that babies can be born. The fact that the unit's technology also contributes to India's skewed sex ratio at birth gnaws at him. Seven out of 10 babies born in the maternity ward, Bedi says, are male. He delivers those boys knowing that many of them are replacements for aborted girls.

A tall, broad-shouldered man with a disarmingly gentle voice, Bedi stands in the unit's control room, gazing into a sealed, temperature-controlled room lined with rows of cribs. He performs abortions himself. For sex-selective abortions, however, he reserves a contempt bordering on fury. To have his work negated by something as trifling as sex preference feels like a targeted insult. "You can choose whether to be a parent," he says. "But once you choose to be a parent, you cannot choose whether it's a boy or girl, black or white, tall or short."

A broad interpretation of parental choice, indeed, is spreading throughout India—along with China, Taiwan, Vietnam, Georgia, Azerbaijan, and Albania. Preliminary results from India's 2011 census show a sex ratio of only 914 girls for every 1,000 boys ages 6 and under, a decline from 2001. In some

Chinese counties the sex ratio at birth has reached more than 150 boys for every 100 girls. "We are dealing with genocide," Bedi says. Sex-selective abortion, he adds, is "probably the single most important issue in the next 50 years that India and China are going to face. If you're going to wipe out 20 percent of your population, nature is not going to sit by and watch."

> **If you're going to wipe out 20 percent of your population, nature will not sit by and watch.**

Bedi speaks with an immaculate British accent that hints at years spent studying at King's College London. The accent helps in this part of Delhi, where breeding can trump all else. His patients are the sort who live in spacious homes tended by gardeners, belong to bucolic country clubs, and send their children to study in the United States. India's wealthy are among the most frequent practitioners of sex selection, and in their quest to have a son Bedi is often an obstacle. His refusal to identify sex during ultrasound examinations disappoints many women, he says: "They think it's just a waste of time and money if you don't even know whether it's a boy or a girl."

India outlawed fetal sex identification and sex-selective abortion in 1994, but so many physicians and technicians break the law that women have little trouble finding one willing to scan fetal sex. Bedi says sex-selective abortion has caught on in Delhi because it bears the imprint of a scientific advance. "It's sanitized," he says. The fact that sex selection is a medical act, he adds, neatly divides the moral burden between two parties: Parents tell themselves their doctor knows best, while doctors point to overwhelming patient demand for the procedure.

Hospital administrators, for their part, have little incentive to do anything about the problem because maternity wards bring in substantial business. (At Apollo, a deluxe delivery suite outfitted with a bathtub, track lighting, a flat screen television, and a large window looking out onto landscaped grounds runs to $200 a night.) "When you confront the medical profession, there is a cowardly refusal to accept blame," Bedi says. "They say, 'We are doctors; it's a noble profession.' This is bullshit. When it comes to issues like ethics and morality, you can have an opinion, but there is a line which you do not cross. Everybody who [aborts for reasons of sex selection] knows it's unethical. It's a mass medical crime."

For as long as they have counted births, demographers have found an average of 105 boys born for every 100 girls. This is our natural sex ratio at birth. (The small gap neatly makes up for the fact that males are more likely to die early in life.) If Asia had maintained that ratio over the past few decades, the continent would today have an additional 163 million women and girls.

For Westerners, such a gender gap may be difficult to fathom: 163 million is more than the entire female population of the United States. Walk around Delhi's posh neighborhoods, or visit an elementary school in eastern China, and you can see the disparity: Boys far outnumber girls.

At first glance, the imbalance might seem to be the result of entrenched gender discrimination and local practices. Scholars and journalists typically look to the Indian convention of dowry, which makes daughters expensive, and to China's one-child policy, which makes sons precious, to explain sex selection in Asia. (Sons have long been favored in China, as in many other parts of the world.) But this logic doesn't account for why South Koreans also aborted female fetuses in large numbers until recently, or why a sex ratio imbalance has lately spread to the Caucasus countries—Azerbaijan, Georgia, and Armenia—and the Balkans, or why sex-selective abortion occurs among some immigrant communities in the United States.

What impact will hundreds of million of "surplus" men have on everything from health care to crime?

The world's missing females are an apparent paradox: Sex selection is occurring at a time when women are better off than ever before. "More and more girls are going to school and getting educated," says T.V. Sekher, a demographer at the International Institute for Population Studies in Mumbai. And in India, educated women are more likely to have a son than those with no degree. The women who select for sex include lawyers and doctors and businesspeople. Economic development has accompanied a drop in fertility rates, which decreases the chances of a couple getting the son they want without resorting to technology.

We might have seen this coming. Decades ago, Western hysteria over what many saw as an impending "population explosion" led American scholars and policymakers to scour the world for solutions to reducing the global birth rate. Studies from India and East Asia showed the major barrier to acceptance of contraception was that couples wanted at least one son. The advocates of population control saw that the barrier might be turned into an opportunity, however. If parents could be guaranteed a son the first time around, they might happily limit themselves to one or two children.

Beginning in the late 1960s, influential U.S. experts sounded their approval for sex selection everywhere from the pages of major scientific journals to the podiums at government sponsored seminars. "[I]f a simple method could be found to guarantee that first-born children were males," Paul Ehrlich wrote in *The Population Bomb* in 1968, "then population control problems in many areas would be somewhat eased."

Meanwhile, another group of scientists was figuring out how to determine fetal sex. These scientists' efforts focused on amniocentesis, which entails inserting a needle through a pregnant women's abdomen into the amniotic sac surrounding the fetus and removing a small amount of protective amniotic fluid, a substance rich with fetal cells that reveal its sex. They saw sex determination as a way to help women carrying sex-linked diseases like hemophilia have healthy children. But when amniocentesis, and later ultrasound, found their way to Asia decades later, it was their use as a population-control tool that stuck.

Sex selection's proponents argued that discrimination against women and girls wouldn't endure. As women became scarce, several prominent Western theorists proposed, they would also become more valuable, prompting couples to have daughters again. But in fact the opposite has happened. In their scarcity, women are being turned into commodities to be sold to and exploited by what demographers call "surplus men": the ones left over in an imagined world in which everyone who can marry does so. Scholars have begun to calculate the impact hundreds of millions of such men will have on everything from health care to crime.

Suining County, China

In a village in eastern China's agricultural belt, I meet Zhang Mei, a 37-year-old woman clad in men's pants and a black-and-white polka-dot shirt that billows around her thin frame. Zhang is from distant Yunnan province, a poor mountain region near the border with Tibet. Her neighbors say she arrived 20 years ago, after a long journey in which a trafficker took her east to deliver her into marriage. She had no idea where she was headed beyond the vague promise that she would find work there, and yet she had some faith in the trafficker, for she hadn't been kidnapped. Her parents had sold her.

The man who became her husband was gentle, but 15 years her senior, undeniably ugly, and one of the poorest residents of the village. Zhang learned that she had to work hard to make ends meet, and that she could not leave, even for a short trip home. Soon after she married, she found herself under pressure to have a son. One came on the third try, after two girls. But as the children grew, her husband complained it cost too much to educate their daughters, and since it is sons that matter in Suining, he sent one of the girls back to Yunnan to be raised by Zhang's parents: a return, one generation later, of a lost girl.

Today Zhang copes with lifelong detention by gambling at raucous *majiang* games, burying herself in soap operas, and praying. (She is Christian.) "I carry some burdens," she tells me, as we sit on the couch in her one-room home. "If I didn't pray, I would keep them all in my heart."

Zhang's story is perhaps the most obvious way in which the gender imbalance is altering societies in Asia. The U.S. Department of State lists the dearth of women in Asia as one of the principal causes of sex trafficking in the region. Some of those women, like Zhang, are sold into marriage. Others become prostitutes. But what happens to the men who can't find partners is significant as well.

Nothing can fully predict the effect of gathering tens of millions of young bachelors in one place for years on end. But preliminary conclusions can be drawn from places where the first generation touched by sex selection has reached adulthood. One line of speculation centers on testosterone, which occurs in high levels among young unmarried men. While testosterone does not directly cause violence in a young man, it can elevate existing aggressive tendencies, serving as a "facilitative effect" that predicts whether he will resort to violence. Gauging whether millions of high-testosterone men together spark more violence is complicated, particularly in China and India, which have experienced great social change in the past few decades. But some answers can be found through breaking down crime rates by region and time period.

In a 2007 study, Columbia University economist Lena Edlund and colleagues at Chinese University of Hong Kong used the fact that China's sex ratio at birth spiked in some provinces earlier than others to explore a link between crime rates and a surplus of men. The researchers found a clear link, concluding a mere 1 percent increase in sex ratio at birth resulted in a 5- to 6-point increase in an area's crime rate.

Other scholars speculate the gender imbalance is yielding depression and hopelessness among young men—which may explain why China has lately been hit with the sort of senseless violence that was once America's domain. In 2004 and 2010 the country saw separate waves of attacks on elementary schools and child care centers in which murderers went on rampages and bludgeoned and stabbed children to death.

Eight out of the 10 killers (all male) lived in eastern Chinese provinces with high sex ratios at birth; several were unemployed. One man told neighbors, before he was arrested and summarily executed, that he was frustrated with his life and wanted revenge on the rich and powerful. Another apparently told police he was upset because his girlfriend had left him.

Los Angeles, U.S.

"Be certain your next child will be the gender you're hoping for," promises the Web site of L.A.'s Fertility Institutes. Dr. Jeffrey Steinberg founded the clinic in 1986, just as in-vitro fertilization was taking off.

Today 70 percent of his patients come to select the sex of their baby. Steinberg's favored method is preimplantation genetic diagnosis, PGD, an add-on to in-vitro fertilization that allows parents to screen embryos before implanting them in the mother. Like amniocentesis and ultrasound before it, PGD was developed to test for defects or a propensity toward certain diseases.

But lab technicians working with eight-celled embryos can also separate XY embryos from XX ones, thus screening for sex—the first nonmedical condition to be turned into a choice. PGD thus attracts Americans who are perfectly capable of having babies the old-fashioned way but are hell-bent on having a child of a certain sex. So determined are they that they're willing to submit to the diet of hormones necessary to stimulate ovulation, pay a price ranging from $12,000 to $18,000, and live with IVF's low success rate. Decades after America's elite introduced sex selection to the developing world, they have taken it up themselves.

High-tech sex selection has its critics. They point to a litany of ethical issues: that the technology is available only to the rich, that it gives parents a degree of control over their offspring they shouldn't have, that it marks the advent of designer babies. But in surveys of prospective American parents over the past 10 years, 25 to 35 percent say they would use sex selection techniques if they were readily available; presumably that means more affordable and less invasive.

A squat, balding man who exudes a jovial confidence, Dr. Steinberg talks as if he has all the time in the world, peppering his stories with Hollywood gossip. (To wit: The producers of the show *CSI* once stopped by the clinic to evaluate a sperm cryopreservation tank's potential as a weapon.) The patient response to his clinic offering sex selection, Steinberg tells me after ushering me into a spacious corner office, has been "crazy."

The fertility doctors who perform preimplantation sex selection take care to distinguish it from sex-selective abortion. In America, they point out, patriarchy is dead, at least when it comes to choosing the sex of our children. As late as the 1970s, psychologists and sociologists found that Americans were far more likely to prefer sons to daughters. Not anymore.

National figures are not available, but two of America's leading clinics—HRC Fertility in Los Angeles and Genetics and IVF Institute in Fairfax, Virginia—independently report that between 75 and 80 percent of their patients want girls. The demand for daughters may explain why at Steinberg's clinic everything from the entrance wall to the scrubs worn by the laboratory workers are pink.

For the most part, however, Americans don't talk about gender preference. We say "family balancing," a term that implies couples have an inherent right to an equal number of boys and girls. (Many patients seeking sex selection via PGD already have a child of the opposite sex.) We talk about "gender disappointment," a deep grief arising from not getting what we want. The author of the reproductive technology guide *Guarantee the Sex of Your Baby* explains: "The pain that these mothers feel when they fail to bear a child of the 'right' sex is more than just emotional angst. The longing that they hold in their hearts can translate into real physical pain."

Rhetorical differences aside, "family balancing" is not in fact all that different from what is happening in China and India. In Asia, too, most parents who select for sex do so for the second or third birth. And examining why American parents are set on girls suggests another similarity: Americans who want girls, like Asians who opt for boys, have preconceived notions of how a child of a certain gender will turn out.

Bioethicist Dena S. Davis writes that people who take pains to get a child of a certain sex "don't want just the right chromosomes and the attendant anatomical characteristics, they want a set of characteristics that go with 'girlness' or 'boyness.' If parents want a girl badly enough to go to all the trouble of sperm sorting and artificial insemination, they are likely to make it more difficult for the actual child to resist their expectations and follow her own bent."

When Dr. Sunita Puri surveyed Bay Area couples undergoing PGD for sex selection, most of them white, older, and affluent, 10 out of 12 wanted girls for reasons like "barrettes and pink dresses."

Some mention that girls do better in school, and on this point the research backs them up: Girls are more likely to perform and less likely to misbehave, while boys have lately become the source of a good deal of cultural anxiety. Others mention more noble goals. They talk about raising strong daughters; women

mention having the close relationship they had—or didn't have—with their own mother.

But regardless of the reason, bioethicists point out, sex selection prioritizes the needs of one generation over another, making having children more about bringing parents satisfaction than about responsibly creating an independent human being.

At stake with preimplantation sex selection is much more than the global balance of males and females, as if that weren't enough. If you believe in the slippery slope, then sex-selective embryo implantation definitely pushes us a little further down it.

In 2009 Jeffrey Steinberg announced that the clinic would soon offer selection for eye color, hair color, and skin color. The science behind trait selection is still developing, and some later doubted whether he in fact was capable of executing it. Still, Steinberg might have eventually gone through with the service had his advertisement not set off an uproar. The press descended, the Vatican issued a statement criticizing the "obsessive search for the perfect child," and couples who had used PGD for medical reasons balked, fearing frivolous use of reproductive technology would turn public sentiment against cases like theirs. For the moment, at least, Americans had problems with selecting for physical traits, and Steinberg retreated.

Having children has become more about bringing parents satisfaction than creating independent human beings.

"The timing was off is all," he tells me. "It was just premature. We were ahead of our time. So we said, 'OK, fine. We'll put it on the back burner.'" In the meantime, he says, couples obsessed with blue or green eyes continue to call the office. He keeps their names on a mailing list.

Critical Thinking

1. Differentiate between sex-selective abortion and preimplantation sex selection.

2. What are some negative consequences in a society where males far outnumber females?

3. Why would selection for offspring traits (e.g., skin color, eye color, hair color) create ethical issues in a society?

4. If you could afford it, would you choose to preselect traits for your own offspring using preimplantation genetic diagnosis (PGD)?

Create Central

www.mhhe.com/createcentral

Internet References

American Academy of Pediatrics
www.aap.org

Medicine Plus Health Information/Prenatal Care
www.nim.nih.gov/medicineplus/prenatalcare.html
National Children's Study
www.nationalchildrensstudy.gov

MARA HVISTENDAHL is a China-based correspondent with *Science* magazine. She's also written for *Harper's, Scientific American,* and *Popular Science*. This piece is adapted from her new book, *Unnatural Selection: Choosing Boys Over Girls, and the Consequences of a World Full of Men* (PublicAffairs, 2011).

Article

Prepared by: Claire N. Rubman, *Suffolk County Community College*

The Islamic Republic of Baby-Making

How the supreme leader's revolutionary acceptance of cutting-edge fertility treatments is changing lives in Iran—and unsettling the deeply conservative Sunni Middle East

AZADEH MOAVENI

Learning Outcomes

After reading this article, you will be able to:

- Detail the consequences of infertility before the Ayatollah's fatwa in 1999.

- Explain the outcome of "consanguineous" marriages in Iran.

- Describe how the "hidden story" of the Middle East has impacted the Shiite and Sunni communities.

On a sultry evening last fall, a private fertility clinic in the southern Iranian city of Shiraz was so busy that the harried receptionist struggled to accommodate all the women seeking its services. On a mantelpiece rested a framed fatwa from Ayatollah Ali Khamenei providing religious sanction for **sperm** and **egg** donations—placed there, perhaps, to reassure these women that they had the supreme leader's approval for what they were about to do. Many had traveled long distances from smaller towns to reach the clinic, and the packed waiting area was abuzz with conversation, as women swapped stories about treatment, drugs, and their shared struggles to conceive a child.

"I couldn't afford this five years ago, but I've saved up now and am ready to try," said one 30-year-old woman seated in the waiting room.

While the world's attention has been focused on Iran's nuclear program, the country has been quietly working on a different sort of breakout capacity. The Islamic Republic—governed by its strict mullahs, who've managed to botch progress in fields ranging from domestic manufacturing to airport construction—has unexpectedly transformed itself into the fertility treatment capital of the Muslim Middle East. Iran now boasts more than 70 clinics nationwide, which attract childless couples, Sunni and Shiite alike, from throughout the region. This initiative has raised challenges to traditional views on parenthood and marriage and has helped chip away at taboos about sexual health—even as it has left some of Iran's conservative Sunni neighbors aghast.

"Doctors in the Gulf are horrified by the way the Iranians have allowed this," says Soraya Tremayne, an Oxford University professor and an expert on fertility in Iran. "They say, 'We would never allow this among us.'" For generations of Iranians, infertility was once a marriage-unraveling, soul-decaying trauma. It was memorialized in films like Dariush Mehrjui's *Leila,* in which a conniving mother bullies her son into taking a second wife when his first fails to conceive. The first wife, ashamed of her infertility and still in love with her husband, goes along with the plan, but the emotional strain destroys their marriage and the husband is ultimately left with a child, but bitterly alone. The film screened just a few years before Khamenei's 1999 fatwa and was a major hit, resonating with the multitude of Iranian women and men facing the prospect of a childless marriage and the intolerable alternative of polygamy.

Iran, like other Middle Eastern countries, has an extremely high infertility rate. More than 20 percent of Iranian couples cannot conceive, according to a study conducted by one of the country's leading fertility clinics, compared with the global rate of between 8 and 12 percent. Experts believe this is due to the prevalence of consanguineous marriages, or those between cousins. Male infertility is "the hidden story of the Middle East," says Marcia Inhorn, a Yale University medical anthropologist and a specialist on assisted reproduction in the region. Couple that with a shocking, multidecade decline in the average number of children born per woman, and it means that fertility treatment is needed in Iran more than ever.

Still, the pressure on a married couple—and particularly the woman—to produce children remains intense.

"We live in an Eastern society, and having children remains a very significant thing in our culture," says Sara Fallahi, a physician who practices in one of Shiraz's three fertility clinics. "Even for this generation that's getting married later and wanting smaller families, most still definitely want one child."

Iran's first in vitro fertilization (IVF) clinic opened up in Yazd, a desert city in central Iran, more than 20 years ago. It immediately found itself inundated with clients. By the mid-2000s, it was so popular that lines stretched out the door. Couples who had traveled from rural areas would camp outside in hopes of getting an appointment. More clinics soon opened in Tehran and across the country.

IVF quickly gained acceptance in other parts of the Middle East, but physicians ran into religious restrictions prohibiting more advanced forms of fertility treatment. Standard IVF involves fertilizing an **egg** with **sperm** in a laboratory and then returning the embryo into the womb, a process requiring that both the **egg** and **sperm** of the respective partners be viable, which is not always the case. The next step in treating infertility requires a third party—that is, an **egg** or **sperm** donor from outside the couple. In Islam, the ethics of such treatment are murky: Patients initially worried they might be committing adultery or that children born of such unions would be illegitimate.

But childless couples continued to demand a way to conceive. In Iran, medical specialists set about finding a religious solution, seeking the support of sympathetic mujtahids (clerics qualified to read and interpret the Quran).

The Shiite tradition of reinterpreting Islamic law was central to the clerics' willingness to go along—in stark contrast to Sunni jurisprudence's focus on scholarly consensus and literal readings of the Quran, which has meant few fresh legal rulings on modern matters.

Although, to Westerners, Iran's Shiite clerics might appear reactionary, they are downright revolutionary when it comes to bioethics. In recent years, they have handed down fatwas allowing everything from stem-cell research to cloning.

Their edicts did necessitate some Quranic contortions, however. The religiously acceptable solutions offered at first, like temporary marriage between an **egg** donor and the fertile male partner, proved too complicated, requiring a married donor to endure a flurry of divorces and remarriages. And some clerics who disagree with Khamenei's fatwa still advocate temporary marriage as a way of avoiding the adulterous implications of third-party donations. But this approach is easier for husbands, who can contract a temporary marriage with a female **egg** donor without needing to divorce the infertile wife; for a fertile wife to be able to receive **sperm** from a donor, she must divorce her husband, wait a religiously mandated 3 months before marrying the **sperm** donor, then divorce him, and finally remarry her original husband.

Iranian clerics' willingness to issue innovative religious rulings coincided with a changing political and demographic climate that also spurred fertility treatments. In the wake of the 1979 revolution, the country embarked on a quest to boost population, but by the late 1980s and early 1990s, as Iran struggled to rebuild in the aftermath of its devastating war with Iraq and with the baby boom in full effect, many questioned whether the country's economy, schools, and cities could handle the population growth. So the authorities reversed course, implementing a set of policies that gently persuaded traditional Iranians to have fewer children.

According to Oxford's Tremayne, authorities carefully avoided words like "reduction" and "control" and instead proposed "regulation of the family," emphasizing that the policy was intended not only to reduce family size but also to enable infertile couples to have families. The bargain worked, as traditionalists embraced the government's antinatal policies and Iran's fertility treatment centers multiplied. By promoting contraception and vasectomies, among other strategies, and withdrawing state subsidies after the second child, Iran managed to reduce its population growth rate from 3.8 percent in 1986 to 1.5 percent in 1996. But it may have worked too well: today, Iran finds itself below the replacement rate of 2.1 children per woman.

In 1999, Khamenei issued his landmark fatwa making third-party **sperm** and **egg** donation permissible. "Both the **egg** donor and the infertile mother must abide by the religious codes regarding parenting," the ayatollah decreed, setting out the various conditions that made the act permissible before God. Through Khamenei's edict, the Islamic Republic had made clear at the highest level that the state was ready to sanction Iranians' efforts to make babies—whatever it took.

Today, the era when infertility was discussed in hushed tones is giving way to a lively culture of intervention and openness. Women chat openly about IVF on state television, couples recommend specialists and trade stories on Internet message boards, and practitioners have begun pushing insurance companies to cover treatment. And the state runs subsidized clinics, so the cost for treatment is lower than almost anywhere else in the world: a full course of IVF, including drugs, runs the equivalent of just $1,500, according to Fallahi.

Khamenei's fatwa was revolutionary for Shiite Muslims everywhere, and it cleared the way for many clinics in Lebanon, which has a significant Shiite population, to follow suit. But according to Yale's Inhorn, Sunnis are also responding to the ruling, with some infertile couples from the Arab world heading to Tehran clinics that employ Arabic interpreters. Sunni countries like Egypt, Turkey, and the United Arab Emirates practice classic IVF widely, but offer no treatment options for men and women who require third-party reproductive assistance to conceive.

"Some Sunni couples have been able to wrap their minds around **egg** donation," says Inhorn. "They can tell themselves, 'Well, at least there's one fatwa that says it's OK. Some branch of Islam says so.' This makes them more at ease."

Still, Fallahi, the physician, says that anxious clients at her clinic in Shiraz often raise the question of religious approval. "They want to be sure what they're doing is not haram," or forbidden by Islamic law, she says. Parliament legalized embryo donation in 2003, providing some legal backing to the supreme leader's religious ruling. Fallahi stresses, however, that Khamenei's edict is the opinion of one marja, or source of emulation, and that not all ayatollahs agree. "We tell people that parliament has approved this, but that they need to check with the marja they follow to see if he gives permission." In some ways, fertility treatment may be the rare area where the Iranian regime has moved forward before society is ready. Although legislators approved embryo donation, they overruled Khamenei on **sperm** donation, banning the procedure in 2003. As a result, the practice was pushed underground, and those clinics that quietly offer the treatment are vulnerable to prosecution. Sara Bamdad, a researcher in Shiraz who conducted a survey on public attitudes about assisted reproduction, found that only 34 percent of respondents approved of **egg** donation. "Lawmakers should be thinking about the future and what is going to happen to these children when they're older," says Bamdad. "If a society can't accept a child that's born of assisted reproduction, then there'll be so many problems in the future."

Iran's legal system has yet to catch up with the implications of third-party fertility treatments. Under Iran's Islamic family law, babies born of **sperm** or **egg** donation fall into the legal category of adopted children and stepchildren, who are not permitted to inherit property from non biological parents. Couples thus must find alternative ways to put aside assets to provide for these kids, and the rights and responsibilities of biological parents (the **egg** or **sperm** donors, who are meant to remain confidential but whose identities are sometimes disclosed in practice) remain unclear. But if religious rulings are still murky, the baby-making revolution may be gently removing cultural taboos around other areas of sexual health. The Avicenna Infertility Clinic in Tehran, the country's most prominent fertility treatment center, has recently opened a health clinic that treats sexual dysfunction and sexually transmitted diseases.

Tremayne recounts visiting a fertility clinic where a large room full of men and women sat watching a video transmission of a surgery to fertilize a woman's **egg** on a giant television screen. "Our intention is to create a new culture so that people understand how babies are conceived and how infertility can be treated," a doctor told Tremayne. Scenes like this are part of a broader effort to educate the public, and while it may take years for infertility to lose its stigma in Iranian culture, the discussion of bodies and their biological functions and failings may be gradually helping Iranian men and women share responsibility for what has for centuries been the profound nang, or dishonor, laid at the feet of women.

The pursuit of cutting-edge baby-making has launched a process that could ultimately change what it means to be married and infertile, what it means to be a parent, even what it means to be kin in the Islamic Republic. As Iran struggles with the collision between its people's evolving values and the tenets of Islamic law, its success with fertility treatment suggests that it just may be possible to reconcile these competing pressures. But whether it will catch on in the Sunni Middle East is an open question.

"Iran is surging ahead using [these technologies] in all their forms," Tremayne says, "going places where the Sunni countries in the region cannot follow."

Critical Thinking

1. How do infertility rates in Iran compare with other countries such as the United States?

2. How do marriage laws in Iran conflict with fertility treatments that are currently available and future treatments such as artificial sperm or uterus transplants?

Create Central

www.mhhe.com/createcentral

Internet References

Central Intelligence Agency The World Fact Book Total Fertility Rates

https://www.cia.gov/library/publications/the-world-factbook/field

faculty.washington.edu Modernization and Consanguineous Marriage in Iran

http://faculty.washington.edu/charles/pubs/1994-ModernizationConsanguineousMarriageIran.pdf

Islamweb.net Infertility: the Struggle to Conceive

http://www.islamweb.net/womane/nindex.php?page=readart&id=149490s/2127.html

IVF.net IVF Clinics Middle East

http://www.ivf.net/ivf/royan-institute-o3899.html

The National Center for Biotechnology Information Making Muslim babies: IVF and gamete donation in Sunni versus Shi'a Islam

http://www.ncbi.nlm.nih.gov/pmc/articles/PMC1705533

UN.org Recent Changes and the Future of Fertility in Iran

http://www.un.org/esa/population/publications/completingfertility/2RevisedABBASIpaper.PDF

Moaveni, Azadeh. "The Islamic Republic of Baby-Making." *Foreign Policy.* 204 (January, 2014): 1–8.

Article   Prepared by: Claire N. Rubman, *Suffolk County Community College*

Beyond the Baby Weight

Most expectant mothers know that how they take care of their body during pregnancy will affect the health of their newborn child. Now, new research suggests that some aspects of prenatal care, specifically maternal weight gain, may impact a child's health well into adolescence.

ERIC REITHER

Learning Outcomes

After reading this article, you will be able to:

- Articulate why children born to obese women are more likely to be obese as adolescents.

- Discuss the "troubling intergenerational cycle" among native Hawaiian and Pacific women.

- Explain the term *epigenetics* and its effect on a developing fetus' body weight in later life.

Using the Utah Population Database, Utah State University Associate Professor Eric Reither and his colleagues have been able to tease out links between timing of prenatal care and obesity rates among different ethnic groups in the state of Utah. The Utah Population Database is one of the most comprehensive population records in the nation, tracking information including timing of initial prenatal care, mother's and child's weights at time of birth, weight of a child upon receiving their driver's license, and ethnicity.

Reither's research divided information from the population database along ethnic lines for three groups: Native Hawaiian and other Pacific Islanders (NHOPI), Asians, and non-Hispanic Whites. The researchers decided to focus on these groups because their lifestyles, access to health care, and rates of disease vary greatly.

"Their socioeconomic characteristics tend to be different," said Reither. "So, for example, levels of education, levels of income tend to be different across those groups. Also, groups from mainland Asia in the U.S. have some of the lowest levels of obesity observed among any ethnic group. Conversely, Native

Hawaiians and Pacific Islanders tend to have quite high levels of obesity and diabetes. A lot of research examines these groups as a single entity, obscuring their considerable differences."

Having such a large and diverse population sample allowed researchers to compare many variables. "We were interested in the effects that prenatal care could have in narrowing some pretty stark ethnic differences in obesity," said Reither. Among other important influences like mother's education and family structure, two major factors appear to influence a child's rate of obesity during their adolescent years: a mother's weight during pregnancy and her access to prenatal care.

"We suspect that timely prenatal care encourages mothers to adopt healthy behaviors early," said Reither. "Overweight women are more likely to have larger babies and are more likely to gain weight in excess of doctors' recommendations during pregnancy." In their article, "Prenatal Care, Childhood Obesity, and Ethnic Health Disparities: Analyses from a Unique Population Database" published in the *Journal of Heath Care for the Poor and Underserved,* the researchers suggested that the best way for overweight women to achieve optimal health outcomes for their babies was to gain a limited but healthy amount of weight during pregnancy.

As upward trends in obesity continue, teaching women about the risks of being obese during pregnancy may be more important than ever. According to the Utah Population Database, rates of obesity in expectant mothers were 4 percent among Asians, 9 percent among non-Hispanic Whites, and 14 percent among NHOPIs. Of course, an overweight mother does not guarantee that a child will become obese, leading the researchers to believe that something else about prenatal care plays a role in children's lives.

Results from analyses of the population database suggest that children of obese women are far more likely to be obese during adolescence—especially if their mother did not receive prenatal care until after the first trimester. "Women who initiated prenatal care at an early stage of pregnancy were much less likely to have offspring who struggled with obesity in adolescence," Reither pointed out.

Timing appears to be key for pregnant women seeking prenatal care. Reduced adolescent obesity was only seen in mothers who visited doctors during their first trimester. Even women who received the same quality of care and visited the doctor the same number of times, but who waited to begin visits until later in their pregnancies were more likely to have children who were overweight during adolescence than women who initiated prenatal care early on.

> **"If expectant mothers can prevent obesity and other health complications during pregnancy, their offspring will have better chances for healthy lives down the road."**
>
> —Eric Reither

What occurs in a mother's body during the first trimester is known to have a significant effect on the developing fetus. "If expectant mothers can prevent obesity and other health complications during pregnancy, their offspring will have better chances for healthy lives down the road," Reither said.

Although the genes that a child receives from their parents are fixed, the structure of the genes is not. Changes in structure can be caused by environmental factors which can turn individual genes on or off. These small changes in the genome—known as epigenetics—can have large effects throughout a person's lifetime. A woman's weight during her first trimester of pregnancy may change which genes are activated in her child, possibly increasing the child's risk for obesity later in life.

Reither suggests that changes in gene expression happen early in pregnancy, which is why healthy changes to a mother's diet have a bigger effect if they are implemented in the first trimester. "Doctors now will recommend early in pregnancy—and in fact, even before considering pregnancy—that women do certain things to improve their health," Reither said. "Actually, that both partners do certain things for a period of time to maximize potential health outcomes."

Although it doesn't appear that these epigenetic changes can be reversed with healthy lifestyle changes in later months of pregnancy, Reither does not want to dissuade mothers from making changes if they miss the first trimester window. "I think that if halfway through a pregnancy a woman realized that she

could do a little better in terms of diet and exercise that, of course, is preferable to no changes in behavior," he said.

Rates of obesity can vary widely between ethnic groups. In Utah, NHOPI women were more likely than women of other ethnicities to be obese and were about 20 percent less likely to initiate prenatal care in their first trimester of pregnancy. This relationship between maternal obesity, high birth weight, and adolescent obesity is what Reither referred to as a "troubling intergenerational cycle" in his article.

"The idea is that after a few generations, both from an epigenetic standpoint and from a sociological standpoint, these things can become fairly entrenched," Reither said. For researchers trying to determine how to best break this intergenerational cycle, determining where changes need to be made can be difficult, as both social and genetic factors influence a person's weight. "You start looking for interventions—ways that you can break through cycles and you know there's no simple answer to that, no magic bullet, but it seems that early adoption of prenatal care could be one useful tool to help break these cycles of obesity among certain ethnic groups."

Reither and his colleagues hope that this study will encourage insurance companies and public health agencies to adopt programs that encourage all pregnant women to visit with their doctors as early as possible. "The evidence suggests that early initiation of prenatal care really does help. Doctors are well positioned to encourage good nutrition, reasonable levels of physical activity, and appropriate weight gain to help women and their offspring avoid obesity and related health complications."—ET

Critical Thinking

1. How does the use of the longitudinal research paradigm in this study enhance our understanding of pregnancy and weight gain?

2. How can this important information about weight gain during pregnancy be disseminated to all ethic groups?

Create Central

www.mhhe.com/createcentral

Internet References

How a Pregnant Woman's Choices Could Shape a Child's Health
http://www.npr.org/blogs/health/2013/09/23/224387744/how-a-pregnant-womans-choices-could-shape-a-childs-health

Pregnancy weight gain: What's healthy?—Mayo Clinic
http://www.mayoclinic.org/healthy-living/pregnancy-week-by-week/in-depth/pregnancy-weight-gain/art-20044360

Reither, Eric. "Beyond the Baby Weight." *Utah Science* 67. 1 (Spring/Summer 2013): 16–19.

Article

Prepared by: Claire N. Rubman,
Suffolk County Community College, Selden, NY

Maternal Obesity and the Development of Child Obesity

Lee Stadtlander

Learning Outcomes

After reading this article, you will be able to:

- Discuss ideal weight gain during pregnancy and the distribution of that weight in terms of blood volume, tissue growth, and fat deposits.

- Clearly define obesity and the rates for adults and children in America.

- Articulate the effects of obesity during pregnancy for both the mother and the developing fetus.

Marie is pregnant with her first child: At a weight of 200 pounds and a height of 5'6", her body mass index (BMI) is 32, which is considered obese according to the Centers for Disease Control (2011). How could her obesity affect her health during pregnancy? How could her weight affect her baby, and are there long-term implications for her child? This article will explore these issues.

Obesity in adults is defined as having a BMI greater than or equal to 30; BMI is calculated from a person's weight and height. As an example, a 5'6" woman weighing 185 lbs. would have a BMI of 30 and be considered obese. The most recent national data on obesity prevalence among U.S. adults, adolescents, and children show that more than one-third of adults and almost 17 percent of children and adolescents were obese in 2009–2010 (Ogden, Carroll, Kit, & Flegal, 2012).

Maternal Obesity and the Effect on the Mother

For obese women, the Mayo Clinic (2011) suggests a weight gain of 11–25 pounds during pregnancy. During pregnancy, fat deposits, blood volume expansion, and increases in breast and uterine tissue contribute to 55 percent of the weight gained, and an additional 15–20 percent is due to the placenta and amniotic fluid, with the remaining 25–30 percent due to the weight of the fetus (Fraser & Lawlor, 2012; Institute of Medicine and National Research Council, 2009). It is normal for women to gain between 4.4–13.2 lbs. (2–6 kg) of fat during pregnancy (Nelson, Matthews, & Poston, 2010); this weight is important for providing the fetus with essential nutrients for normal growth and development.

There is evidence that greater gestational weight gain is associated with a higher risk of gestational diabetes (Hedderson, Gunderson, & Ferrara, 2010) and pre-eclampsia (Steegers, von Dadelszen, Duvekot, & Pijnenborg, 2010). Diabetes in the mother also increases the risk of diabetes in the child, while pre-eclampsia is consistently associated with higher blood pressure in the child (Ferreira, Peeters, & Stehouwer, 2009). It has been estimated that up to half of the cases of gestational diabetes can be attributed to prepregnancy obesity (Kim et al., 2010). Torloni et al. (2009) provided the metric that for every unit increase in BMI pre-pregnancy, the risk of gestational diabetes increases by 0.92 percent.

Maternal obesity has been implicated in leading to maternal death. In a study conducted in the United Kingdom by the Centre for Maternal and Child Enquiries (2011), 27 percent of the 261 pregnancy-related deaths reported between 2006 and 2008 were in obese women. Similarly, the California Department of Public Health (2011) reported that 30 percent of the 386 women who died in pregnancy between 2002 and 2003 were obese. These findings reflect that the leading causes of mortality in pregnant women, thrombo-embolism, pre-eclampsia, and cardiovascular diseases, have a higher prevalence in the obese compared to the non-obese (Oteng-Ntim & Doyle, 2012). In the Centre for Maternal and Child Enquiries study, 75 percent of the mothers dying from thrombo-embolism were overweight or obese, as were 61 percent of mothers dying from heart disease.

Summary and Implications for Child Birth Professionals

The research suggests that obese pregnant women are at greater risk for diabetes, pre-eclampsia, and maternal death. Such evidence suggests that obesity should be considered as a high risk in pregnancy, requiring frequent monitoring of weight gain, blood pressure, and blood glucose levels.

Effects on the Fetus and Newborn with Maternal Obesity

Elevated maternal BMI has been shown to increase the risk of miscarriage, fetal death, preterm birth, congenital defects, and other neonatal complications, which are elevated further with maternal diabetes (Ojha, Budge, & Symonds, 2012).

Fetal Death

Nohr et al. (2005) explored the relationship between fetal death and gestational age by maternal BMI. Nohr et al. reported the risk associated with maternal obesity and fetal death increased with increasing gestational age, being greatest at term (over 37 weeks). The current data suggests that obesity increases the risk of fetal death from the second trimester onward, with a greater chance of stillbirth at or beyond term. The underlying mechanism between obesity and fetal death appears to be related to metabolic risk factors in the mother, such as reduced insulin sensitivity, lipid disorders, and increased levels of inflammatory indicators (Bell, Tennant, & Rankin, 2012). These are thought to directly contribute to the development of gestational hypertension, pre-eclampsia, and other disturbances of prenatal function, and to impair glucose tolerance and gestational diabetes (Sattar, Ramsey, Crawford, Cheyne, & Greer, 2003; Wolf et al., 2001).

Obesity leads to other issues. It is difficult to assess fetal size both clinically and by ultrasound in women with high BMI (Phatak & Ramsay, 2010). Therefore, some of the risk of stillbirth in obese pregnant women may be due to lower rates of recognition of poor fetal growth and fetal compromise. More speculative explanations of the mechanisms leading to fetal death with obesity include the presence of sleep apnea and resulting decrease in oxygen to the fetus (Franklin et al., 2000), the reduced ability to detect fetal movement (Fretts, 2005), and lower rates of diagnosis of congenital abnormality (Phatak & Ramsay, 2010).

Congenital Abnormalities

Congenital abnormality is a term used to describe a range of disorders in fetal development that result in structural or other abnormalities present at birth. Congenital abnormalities are one of the major causes of stillbirths and infant deaths, accounting for 20 percent of infant deaths in the United States (Heron et al., 2009). Evidence suggests that there may be a link between maternal obesity, neural tube defects (e.g., spinal bifida), and cardiovascular anomalies (Rasmussen, Chu, Kim, Schmid, & Lau, 2008; Stothard, Tennant, Bell, & Rankin, 2009).

One likely mechanism for such abnormalities is maternal diabetes and early pregnancy hyperglycemia (elevated blood glucose). Pre-existing diabetes is a well-established risk factor for congenital abnormalities, particularly cardiovascular and neural tube defects (Balsells, Garcia-Patterson, Gich, & Corcoy, 2009). Zabihi and Loeken (2010) speculate that hyperglycemia results in oxidative stress, which disrupts critical genes controlling embryonic development.

Another cause of congenital defects with obesity that has been proposed is a folate deficiency (Mojtabai, 2004). Folate is a water-soluble B vitamin that is naturally present in some foods and is available as a dietary supplement. Folate is the generic term for both naturally occurring food folate and folic acid, the form of the vitamin that is used in dietary supplements and fortified foods (National Institutes of Health, 2012). Folate is known to be a protective factor against neural tube defects and possibly other defects, such as cardiovascular abnormalities (Czeizel, 2009). Women with high BMI have been shown to have lower serum folate levels (Mojtabai, 2004); therefore, their children are at risk for such defects.

Summary and Implications for Childbirth Professionals

Obesity has been shown to increase the risk of fetal death, preterm birth, and congenital abnormalities such as neural tube and cardiovascular defects. These risks are increased with maternal diabetes, thus requiring careful monitoring throughout pregnancy. Folate deficiencies have also been implicated, which suggest that folic acid supplements starting pre-pregnancy continues to be considered beneficial.

Long-Term Effects on the Child

There is conflicting evidence from studies as to whether high maternal BMI results in obesity in offspring. In one compelling study, Rooney, Mathiason, and Schauberger (2011) followed 777 obese mothers and children from prenatal through adulthood. Rooney et al. found that pre-pregnancy maternal obesity was a strong predictor of childhood, adolescence, and early adulthood obesity: Among mothers who were obese at pre-pregnancy, 52 percent of their offspring were obese at childhood, 62 percent at adolescence, and 44 percent at early adulthood.

A second persuasive study, conducted by Smith et al. (2009), examined siblings of mothers with extreme obesity (BMI>40) who had undergone bariatric (stomach reduction) surgery. Smith et al. found that siblings born after the surgery had lower rates of obesity than those siblings born before the surgery. Smith et al. reported that children born after the bariatric surgery had improved metabolic profiles as compared to their siblings.

Other studies have found a small relationship between maternal obesity and subsequent obesity in the children (for example, see Whitaker, Jarvis, Beeken, Boniface, & Wardle, 2010). In contrast, several large studies (Lake, Power, & Cole, 1997; Patel et al., 2011; Subramanian, Ackerson, & Smith, 2010) have found the relationship of maternal BMI with offspring obesity is similar to those of paternal BMI and the siblings' BMI. This suggests that both the mother's and the father's genetics and family lifestyle characteristics also influence such relationships.

Implications for Childbirth Professionals

The relationship between maternal obesity and long-term effects on the child remains conflicted. Some studies have reported that children of obese mothers are more likely to be obese, while others have found only a small relationship. It does appear that extreme maternal obesity and metabolic disturbances such as diabetes result in long-term effects in the child.

Childbirth educators have the opportunity to affect this cycle in a number of ways. Prospective obese mothers should be encouraged to work towards a healthier BMI, control diabetes, and to begin folic acid supplements before pregnancy. Obese women's gestational weight gain should be carefully monitored, along with their blood pressure and blood glucose. Extremely obese women (>40 BMI) who have potentially high risk pregnancies may be referred to an obstetrician. Providing education and literature on healthy eating habits during pregnancy may be a way to offer motivation for lifelong change for not just the mother but for the entire family.

References

Balsells, M., Garcia-Patterson, A., Gich, I., & Corcoy, R. (2009). Maternal and fetal outcome in women with type 2 vs. type 1 diabetes mellitus: A systematic review and metaanalysis, *The Journal of Clinical Endocrinology and Metabolism, 94*, 4284–4291.

Bell, R., Tennant, P. W. G., & Rankin, J. (2012). Fetal and infant outcomes in obese pregnant women. In M. W. Gillman & L. Poston (Eds.), *Maternal obesity* (pp. 56–69). Cambridge, United Kingdom: Cambridge University Press.

California Department of Public Health. (2011). The California pregnancy associated mortality review: Report from 2002 and 2003 maternal death reviews. Retrieved from http://www.cdph.ca.gov/data/statistics/Pages/CaliforniaPregnancy-AssociatedMortalityReview.aspx

Centers for Disease Control. (2011). Healthy Weight—It's not a diet, it's a lifestyle! Retrieved March 14, 2014, from http://www.cdc.gov/healthyweight/assessing/bmi/adult_bmi/index.html

Centre for Maternal and Child Enquiries. (2011). Saving mothers' lives: Reviewing maternal deaths to make motherhood safer: 2006–2008. *BJOG: An International Journal of Obstetrics and Gynaecology, 118*(Suppl. 1), 1–203. doi:10.1111/j.1471-0528.2010.02847.x

Czeizel, A. (2009). Periconceptual folic acid and multivitamin supplementation for the prevention of neural tube defects and other congenital abnormalities. *Birth Defects Research. Part A, Clinical and Molecular Teratology, 85*, 260–268.

Ferreira, I., Peeters, L. L., & Stehouwer, C. D. (2009). Preeclampsia and increased blood pressure in the offspring: Meta-analysis and critical review of the evidence. *Journal of Hypertension, 27*(10), 1955–1959.

Franklin, K., Holmgen, P., Jönsson, F., Poromaa, N., Stenlund, H., & Svanborg, E. (2000). Snoring, pregnancy-induced hypertension, and growth retardation of the fetus. Chest, 117, 137–141.

Fraser, A., & Lawlor, D. A. (2012). Long-term consequences of maternal obesity and gestational weight gain for offspring obesity and cardiovascular risk: Intrauterine or shared familial mechanisms? In M. W. Gillman & L. Poston (Eds.), *Maternal obesity* (pp. 87–99). Cambridge, United Kingdom: Cambridge University Press.

Fretts, R. C. (2005). Etiology and prevention of stillbirth. *American Journal of Obstetrics & Gynecology, 193*, 1923–1935.

Hedderson M. M., Gunderson E. P., & Ferrara, A. (2010). Gestational weight gain and risk of gestational diabetes. *Obstetrics & Gynecology, 115*(3), 597–604.

Heron, M., Hoyert, D., Murphy, S., Xu, J., Kochanek, K.D., & Tejada-Vera, B. (2009). Deaths: Final data for 2006. *National Vital Statistics Reports, 57*(14), 1–134.

Institute of Medicine and National Research Council. (2009). *Weight gain during pregnancy: Reexamining the guidelines.* Washington, DC: National Academies Press.

Kim, S. Y., England, L., Wilson, H. G., Bish, C., Satten, G. A., & Dietz, P. (2010). Percentage of gestational diabetes mellitus attributable to overweight and obesity. *American Journal of Public Health, 100*(6), 1047–1052.

Lake, J. K., Power, C., & Cole, T. J. (1997). Child to adult body mass index in the 1958 British birth cohort: Associations with parental obesity. *Archives of Diseases in Childhood, 77*(5), 376–381.

Mayo Clinic. (2011). Pregnancy weight gain: What's healthy? Retrieved from http://www.mayoclinic.com/health/pregnancy-weight-gain/PR00111

Mojtabai, R. (2004). Body mass index and serum folate in childbearing age women. *European Journal of Epidemiology, 19*(11), 1029–1036.

Nelson, S. M., Matthews, P., & Poston, L. (2010). Maternal metabolism and obesity: Modifiable determinants of pregnancy outcome. *Human Reproduction Update, 16*(3), 255–275.

National Institutes of Health. (2012). Dietary supplement fact sheet: Folate. Retrieved from http://ods.od.nih.gov/factsheets/Folate-HealthProfessional/

Nohr, E. A., Nech, B. H., Davies, M. J., Frydenberg, M., Henriksen, T. B., & Olsen, J. (2005). Prepregnancy obesity and fetal death: A study within the Danish National Birth Cohort. *Obstetrics & Gynecology, 106*, 250–259.

Ogden, C. L., Carroll, M. D., Kit, B. K., & Flegal, K. M. (2012). *Prevalence of obesity in the United States, 2009–2010* [NCHS Data Brief No. 82]. Retrieved from http://www.cdc.gov/nchs/data/databriefs/db82.pdf

Ojha, S., Budge, H., & Symonds, M.E. (2012). Adipose tissue development and its potential contribution to later obesity. In M. W. Gillman & L. Poston (Eds.), *Maternal obesity* (pp.124–134). Cambridge, United Kingdom: Cambridge University Press.

Oteng-Ntim, E., & Doyle, P. (2012). Maternal outcomes in obese pregnancies. In M. W. Gillman & L. Poston (Eds.), *Maternal obesity* (pp. 35–44). Cambridge, United Kingdom: Cambridge University Press.

Patel, R., Martin, R. M., Kramer, M. S., Oken, E., Bogdanovich, N., Matush, L., . . . Lawlor, D. A. (2011). Familial associations of adiposity: Findings from a cross-sectional study of 12,181 parental-offspring trios from Belarus. *PLOS One 6*(l), e14607.

Phatak, M., & Ramsay, J. (2010). Impact of maternal obesity on procedure of mid-trimester anomaly exam. *Journal of Obstetrics & Gynecology, 30*, 447–450.

Rasmussen, S. A., Chu, S. Y., Kim, S. Y., Schmid, C. H., & Lau, J. (2008). Maternal obesity and risk of neural tube defects: A metaanalysis. *American Journal of Obstetrics & Gynecology, 198*, 611–619.

Rooney, B. L., Mathiason, M . A., & Schauberger, C. W. (2011). Predictors of obesity in childhood, adolescence, and adulthood in a birth cohort. *Maternal and Child Health Journal, 15*, 1166–1175.

Sattar, N., Ramsey, J., Crawford, L., Cheyne, H., & Greer, I. (2003). Classic and novel risk factor parameters in women with a history of preeclampsia. *Hypertension, 42*, 39–42.

Smith, J., Cianflone, K., Biron, S., Hould, F. S., Lebel, S., Marceau, S.,... Marceau, P. (2009). Effects of maternal surgical weight loss in mothers on intergenerational transmission of obesity. *The Journal of Clinical Endocrinology and Metabolism, 94*(11), 4275–4283.

Steegers, E. A., von Dadelszen, P., Duvekot, J. J., & Pijnenborg, R. (2010). Pre-eclampsia. *Lancet*, 376(9741), 631–644.

Stothard, K. J., Tennant, P. W. G., Bell, R., & Rankin, J. (2009). Maternal overweight and obesity and the risk of congenital anomalies. *Journal of the American Medical Association, 301*, 636–650.

Subramanian, S. V., Ackerson, L. K. & Smith, G. D. (2010). Parental BMI and childhood undernutrition in India: An assessment of intrauterine influence. *Pediatrics, 126*(3), e663-e671.

Torloni, M. R., Betnin, A. P., Horta, B. L., Nakamura, M. U., Atallah, A. N., Moron, A. F., & Valente, O. (2009). Pre-pregnancy BMI and the risk of gestational diabetes: A systematic review of the literature with meta-analysis. *Obesity Review, 10*(2),194–203.

Whitaker, K. L., Jarvis, M. J., Beeken, R. J., Boniface, D., & Wardle, J. (2010). Comparing maternal and paternal intergenerational transmission of obesity risk in a large population-based sample. *The American Journal of Clinical Nutrition, 91*(6), 1560–1567.

Wolf, M., Kettyle, E., Sandler, L., Ecker, J. L., Roberts, J., & Thadhani R. (2001). Obesity and preeclampsia: The potential role of inflammation. *Obstetrics & Gynecology, 98*, 757–762.

Zabihi, S., & Loeken, M. R. (2010). Understanding diabetic teratogenesis: Where are we now and where are we going? *Birth Defects Research. Part A, Clinical and Molecular Teratology, 88*, 779–790.

Critical Thinking

1. How does our society convey weight-related issues during pregnancy to women before they become pregnant?

2. Why is the research conflicted about the relationship ·between high maternal BMI and obesity in offspring?

3. How can we affect change in our society with regard to maternal obesity?

Internet References

Father's Obesity May be a Risk Factor in Autism, Study Says
http://www.mindbodygreen.com/0-13262/fathers-obesity-may-be-a-risk-factor-for-autism-study-says.html

Obese Parents Increase Kids' Risk of Being Overweight
http://news.stanford.edu/news/2004/july21/med-obesity-721.html

Obesity in Pregnancy ACOG
http://www.acog.org/Resources-And-Publications/Committee-Opinions/Committee-on-Obstetric-Practice/Obesity-in-Pregnancy

Pregnancy and Obesity: Know the Risks
http://www.mayoclinic.org/healthy-lifestyle/pregnancy-week-by-week/in-depth/pregnancy-and-obesity/art-20044409

Prenatal and Early Life Influences
http://www.hsph.harvard.edu/obesity-prevention-source/obesity-causes/prenatal-postnatal-obesity

---

LEE STADTLANDER is a researcher, professor, and the coordinator of the Health Psychology program at Walden University. As a clinical health psychologist, she brings together pregnancy and health care issues.

Unit 2

UNIT

Prepared by: Claire N. Rubman,
Suffolk County Community College, Selden, NY

Development during Infancy and Early Childhood

When you look at a newborn baby, what is he or she capable of? How long will it be until this little bundle of joy steals, plays video games, or feels sorry for a friend? Whether this is our child or a child we are taking care of, what can we do to enhance development? What are the best decisions in terms of vaccinations at the doctor's office or toys in the toy box?

One of the first decisions that a mother must make for her neonate is whether to breastfeed or whether to rely on formula. "Breastfeeding Through the Dog Days of Summer" by Angeletti focuses on some of the difficulties associated with nursing, especially during the vacation months of summer. She offers many helpful suggestions and tips that might encourage a new mother to continue to breastfeed.

Another major decision that parents must make in infancy concerns their child's medical wellbeing: To provide our infants with the best possible start in life, the potential exists to vaccinate them against such childhood diseases as polio, measles, mumps, and rubella. Is it possible, however, that the very vaccines that were developed to protect our infants from disease could, instead, be harming our children? Sparrow's article, "The Truth about Measles" explores the relationship between the resurgence of such diseases as polio, measles, and whooping cough and the reluctance of some parents to vaccinate their children. Sparrow reviews the debate which reaches back to 1998 that was fueled in part by a researcher in England, Dr. Andrew Wakefield. Wakefield claimed that the vaccine itself caused intestinal damage and a release of toxins which affected the brain. Similarly, it was widely believed that the neurotoxin, Thimerosal, caused autism in children but since its removal from children's vaccinations, the rates of autism have not decreased accordingly lending credence to the notion that it was not the root cause of autism. Sparrow addresses the potential risk to young children who are not vaccinated as a result of this "vaccination scare."

There are other times when parents have less control over the decision making process. Curry's article on bullying and harassment in the sports arena highlight the role that parents can play, quite literally, from the sidelines. As a coach, Curry discusses the importance of a parent's positive attitude.

When our children are not on the soccer field or baseball diamond, they love to be entertained. In our technologically savvy world, children's toys have become increasingly more advanced. Stephen Gass compares blocks and dolls with iPads and computers. Children born in the technological era, known as "digital natives," are anticipated to take initiative, respond to their own natural curiosity and persist longer in difficult tasks. Despite this initial allure of technology, it may not be an ideal educational tool according to recent research. Gass recommends playing, exploration, and experimentation as ideal learning tools for optimal cognitive development. He concludes that simplicity is the best tool for children's learning reminding the reader that the focus should not be on what the adult brings to the child—digital versus traditional toys per se, but rather what the child takes away from the experience.

Hanna Rosin's article, "The Touch-Screen Generation" continues this discussion in more detail. She discusses technology from a cognitive and social perspective citing such issues as the "video deficit," that is, children can remember significantly more information if it is presented by a real person rather than a video screen. To explain this phenomenon, she cites Troseth's research which concludes that children seek out "socially relevant information" but they learn from an early age that the television screen does not provide any actual interaction as it lacks this "two way exchange of information." Rosin alludes to the American Academy of Pediatrics guidelines in 2011 that children under the age of 2 should not watch any television but she doesn't seem convinced! She challenges this notion by presenting possible educational gains from educational television or iPad apps. She questions what Maria Montessori, the founder of the Montessori approach, would have thought of this technology. Rosin, a mother herself, decides to allow her (almost) 2 year old son to follow the "Prensky Rules"—basically, technology without time limits. She claimed that for 10 days her son played with an iPad for two hour stretches several times per day then he lost interest in it altogether. What can we conclude about technology and the role of research in child psychology?

Rosin experimented, albeit informally, on her youngest child. Would she have been as cavalier with her first or second child? Rosin discusses that younger brothers may be more likely to be homosexuals and younger children in general were more likely to end up in the emergency room with asthma. Are these statistical anomalies or does birth order really matter?

Article

Prepared by: Claire N. Rubman,
Suffolk County Community College, Selden, NY

Breastfeeding through the "Dog Days" of Summer

Editor's Note: "Dog days" refers to a 40-day period in a Northern Hemisphere summer coinciding with the rising of Sirius, the Dog Star. In popular terms, "dog days" means hot summer days.

MICHELLE ANGELETTI

Learning Outcomes

After reading this article, you will be able to:

- Discuss why pacifiers are not ideal for infants when the mother is breastfeeding.
- Articulate the benefits of breastfeeding when a mother and infant are traveling.
- List ideal ways for a mother to work on boosting her milk supply.

The summer months are a special time of year often filled with travel and visits with family and friends. Many of us find ourselves busy planning vacations, making reservations, shopping and packing for trips, traveling out of town, or preparing our homes to welcome guests. While generally exciting, these activities can consume large amounts of time, cause an already busy breastfeeding mother to feel stressed, and interfere with the breastfeeding relationship. As La Leche League Leaders, we can offer useful suggestions to help protect, promote, and support breastfeeding.

Overcoming Breastfeeding Challenges

While the summertime increase in activity is very exciting, it can also be quite overwhelming to a breastfeeding mother. With all the extra activities, the mother and child's regular routines may be disturbed. Additionally, extra activities may lead to feedings that are postponed or inadvertently skipped, leading to breastfeeding problems such as engorgement, nursing strikes, mastitis or unexpected weaning, which can be caused by delayed or missed feedings. Breastfeeding breaks can also benefit a breastfeeding mother by providing a time to relax and reconnect with her child.

If a mother finds that she has been missing feedings, Leaders can offer several suggestions to help boost her milk supply. Because the increased suckling will help stimulate her milk production, a mother can increase the number of breastfeeding sessions each day and sleep in close proximity to her child at night to encourage night feedings. To keep all suckling at the breast, encourage the mother to avoid using soothers and pacifiers. Also, gentle breast compression can help empty the breast and maintain the baby's interest in feeding.

Sometimes a mother might be shy about breastfeeding while traveling. As Leaders, we can explain various methods of breastfeeding discreetly in public places. For example, mothers can wear loose-fitting shirts and blouses that unbutton from the bottom. Underneath, she may wear a tank T-shirt with slits for breastfeeding access and still cover her midriff while feeding. Leaders and more experienced mothers can also demonstrate discreet nursing in a sling. In addition to the travel itself, a mother may experience stress caused by visits with unsupportive relatives. She may hear negative or hurtful comments and criticism from strangers or even staff at hotels and airports. Leaders can share ways that a mother can deal with this criticism. At meetings, Leaders can encourage mothers in the Group to share their experiences of combining breastfeeding and traveling.

Breastfeeding has numerous benefits for children, but there are specific benefits while traveling. Breastfeeding strengthens a child's immune system, which will help fend off diseases present in crowded places, such as airports and amusement parks. If a child does become sick while traveling, reassure the mother to breastfeed more often. Additionally, during the hot summer months, breastfeeding provides all the hydration that an exclusively breastfeeding infant needs. There is generally no need to provide supplemental juice or water to children who are less than six months of age (2003 *Breastfeeding Answer Book,* page 38). For children traveling on planes, the suckling action of breastfeeding helps to reduce ear tube pain and children can be encouraged to breastfeed during ascent and descent. Another important point that should not be overlooked is the comfort that breastfeeding provides to children. Being in a mother's arms helps to calm a child who might be stressed and anxious from being around strangers or in unfamiliar places.

Guidelines for Traveling with Breast Milk

Some mothers may be traveling with expressed milk or a breast pump. These mothers need to be aware of the relevant local, country, or international guidelines on traveling with formula, breast milk, and juice. According to the US Transportation Security Administration (TSA) policy, breast milk has been placed in the same category as liquid medication and is not subject to the three-ounce liquid limitation. Mothers are allowed to take breast milk and pumps on board airplanes, but they must declare these items when passing through TSA security checkpoints. While security officers may ask mothers to open a pump for inspection, mothers should not be asked to taste breast milk. It is recommended that mothers print and carry the relevant local, country, or international guidelines with them while traveling. The US TSA guidelines can be found online at: http://www.tsa.gov/traveling-formula-breast-milk-and-juice.

While a mother is allowed to bring breast milk and baby food in her carry-on baggage, it is recommended that she carry small quantities in her carry-on luggage and pack the remainder in her checked luggage. Leaders can remind a mother to take additional batteries, needed electrical current adapters or converters, and a manual pump in case of emergencies. Leaders can also share information about milk storage and handling with a mother before she travels.

Minimize Stress

While summertime activities can be wonderful, they can also be quite stressful to a breastfeeding mother. Stress can be caused by the anticipation of critical house guests or dysfunctional family dynamics that play out at family gatherings. There could also be the fear of criticism from family or friends who do not share her parenting philosophy. As Leaders, we can help a mother identify her stressors and prepare for them. Sometimes having a plan of action and support from her local LLL Group can reduce stress. At meetings, we can encourage mothers to share how they cope with or respond to criticism about breastfeeding or parenting choices. While there are lots of ways to respond to criticism, Leaders can help a mother find the methods that are most comfortable to her.

There are often traditions that families participate in, such as an annual barbecue or family reunion at the beach, and expectations that these traditions are going to be maintained. While spending much of her time caring for her child, a breastfeeding mother may be concerned about having enough time to do all of the things she did before the baby arrived. This is a wonderful opportunity for Leaders to offer some anticipatory suggestions to help a mother prepare and successfully maneuver through some of the common challenges that the summer holidays may pose.

While some mothers believe that stress can dry up their milk, this is not accurate. Stress does not affect a mother's milk production, but it does inhibit the hormone oxytocin that is responsible for her let-down or milk-ejection reflex. Basically, a mother who is experiencing a lot of stress may have a delayed let-down, which she may easily confuse with a supply issue. If a mother is experiencing a high level of stress that appears to be interfering with her ability to breastfeed, we can share simple stress reduction techniques, such as removing herself and baby from the stressful environment, finding a calm place where she can relax, deep-breathing exercises, and focusing on her baby.

Delete, Delay, Delegate

As Leaders, we can talk about developing realistic expectations for a breastfeeding mother. We can encourage her to think about those activities that are really important to her and those that make her busy, but have less meaning or value. It may be helpful to her to consider balancing expectations for holiday festivities with her own needs and those of her child. She can consider if there are activities that she could delete, delay or delegate. Are there activities that don't really have any value, but that she has done traditionally without much thought? If so, then she may want to consider deleting them from her list. For example, instead of serving a large variety of different foods at a family gathering, perhaps she could limit it to a few favorite items.

Are there things that are often done during the summer that could wait until later? For example, if visiting the dentist or getting routine maintenance for the car could wait until after the vacation time, then those might be good items to delay.

Are there things that other family members could do? If so, she may want to consider delegating them to family and friends. For example, if she is preparing a large meal, she may ask friends and family to prepare a special side dish or dessert. If she is responsible for cooking and feels overwhelmed, there is the option of purchasing items from her local grocer. In addition to food, other vacation tasks can also be delegated. Her husband and older children could be responsible for specific chores, such as their own packing.

Focus on Fun!

Finally, as Leaders, we can remind mothers to keep the focus on having fun. Here are some useful hints to help make traveling fun this summer:

- Pack a large resealable plastic bag of small, inexpensive toys like those found at the discount store. Mothers can look for a variety of items that will entertain, but won't create a crisis if lost while traveling.
- Pack miniature-sized coloring and activity books and a small resealable plastic bag of used crayons, washable markers or colored pencils that can be easily taken in the car, on planes, and into restaurants.
- Pack snacks and an extra change of clothes for emergencies.
- As an alternative to strollers, children can be carried in slings or attached to a parent with a safety harness/leash.

With a little planning ahead and an understanding that changes may need to be made to previous events in order to accommodate a breastfeeding child's needs, mothers can successfully balance breastfeeding during the long and often busy hot and sultry days of summer.

Critical Thinking

1. What are the benefits of the La Leche League?
2. Why is breastfeeding potentially different in summer or winter?

Internet References

Breastfeeding and Summer Travel
    http://msue.anr.msu.edu/news/breastfeeding_and_summer_travel
Exclusive Breastfeeding
    http://www.who.int/nutrition/topics/exclusive_breastfeeding/en/
La Leche League International
    http://www.llli.org

MICHELLE ANGELETTI is a La Leche League Leader, the Area Professional Liaison for LLL of Florida and Caribbean Islands, USA, and the Associate Professional Liaison Department Administrator (APLDA) for the LLL Alliance for Breastfeeding Education Area Network, USA. She has a master's degree and PhD in social work, and is Associate Professor of Health Services Administration at Florida Gulf Coast University. Michelle lives in Fort Meyers, Florida, USA, with her husband, three daughters, and toy poodle puppy.

Article

Prepared by: Claire N. Rubman,
Suffolk County Community College, Selden, NY

The Truth about The Measles

The return of the world's most contagious disease

ANNIE SPARROW

Learning Outcomes

After reading this article, you will be able to:

- Discuss Andrew Wakefield's role in the vaccination debate.

- Explain the term "global herd immunity."

- Explain the relationship between polio, smallpox, measles, and vaccines.

No cough, no measles. That was one of the many mantras and memory aids I learned in medical school. Most were designed to reduce tomes like *Gray's Anatomy* to a few rules. Much of the time, it was easy to miss the point, especially when the subject seemed to be an obscure disease.

Five years into a typical Western medical education, none of us had ever seen measles. Nor were we bothered. Apart from HIV, microbes like measles seemed prehistoric. Still, I remembered this particular rule, offered by a revered professor, even as I wondered why he was so focused on a cough instead of "Koplik spots," the little white dots in the mouth that are specific to measles.

Then I spent 10 weeks in a pediatric infectious-disease ward in Cape Town. I thought I would see "African diseases" like hemorrhagic fever and HIV, which I did. But I also saw measles, rubella, scarlet fever, syphilis, rheumatic fever, typhoid, tuberculosis and many other causes of rash and fever. Suddenly, I could see the point of my professor's rule. The very first signs of measles are a fever and cough, followed by a runny nose and red eyes. The appearance of a rash three or four days later is usually what prompts parents to bring their child to the emergency room. The problem is that, at any given time, half the preschool children in the ER have a fever, rash or both. The

differential diagnosis—which can range from mild roseola to devastating meningococcal sepsis—is hard enough in immunized children. In an unimmunized child, the ailment might also be rubella—harmless for the child, but catastrophic for unimmunized pregnant patients—or chicken pox.

Or it might be measles, in which case you need to know—fast—because measles is the most contagious disease on earth. Among unimmunized people exposed to the virus, 90 percent will contract the disease. And each of these people will spread it to 12 to 18 others in an unvaccinated community. Complications like pneumonia and meningitis can be permanent, deadly or both, especially for immune-compromised patients such as those with cancer. And, in the ER, one of these kids might be in the next bed.

Older Americans remember measles as a common childhood disease that just had to be suffered through, but it is still frequently deadly in low- and middle-income countries. In 2014, an average of 400 kids died each day of measles, most under the age of 5. In the current US outbreak, 20 percent of patients were hospitalized in California during the first six weeks of the year. And one in fifteen kids will develop more serious complications, such as severe pneumonia, otitis media with the possibility of permanent deafness, and acute encephalitis. The cruel, late complication of subacute sclerosing panencephalitis (SSPE), a progressive brain disease, is inevitably fatal. In Germany, which has seen an explosion of measles for reasons similar to those in the United States, 27 children died of SSPE between 2005 and 2010. One teenager died of SSPE just last year.

So a doctor needs to be able to diagnose measles at "hello," not wait for the results of two blood tests taken two weeks apart while the child spreads measles, as happened at Disneyland. And, as I rapidly realized, using Koplik spots as a diagnostic aid is better suited to passing exams than clinical practice. Toddlers with measles tend to be extremely irritable and not wildly eager to open their mouths on request for viewing. Nor would you want to get that close if you were uncertain whether you had been immunized.

The crucial question thus becomes: Cough, or no cough? If there's no cough, it's not measles. Period. Which is good, as excluding measles early averts both parental and departmental panic. But if an unimmunized child or adult is coughing, take it very seriously. Ensure that the child is kept away from places where he or she could spread the disease. Educate parents on how to treat the symptoms. And get the child out of the ER as quickly as possible before he or she infects other patients and staff.

These steps have become particularly vital now that measles, long forgotten, is back in the United States. After disappearing in 2000, it has re-emerged alongside nasty allegations about the danger of the vaccine by anti-vaccination ideologues and unscrupulous politicians, even though the vaccine is safe, and mass measles vaccination is the single best public-health intervention we have.

As doctors, we know a few things that are fundamental to our well-being. Most of these are public-health measures that enable us to live much longer and better lives than people did 200 years ago. These measures of mass salvation include water purification, toilets and sanitation, garbage collection and disposal, nutrition and vaccination to protect children from infectious diseases like smallpox, polio and measles.

Smallpox was a truly nasty disease, with a fatality rate of 30 percent. Its eradication was the result of achieving global herd immunity, a feat of international cooperation and cost-effective investment in a global good. Herd immunity comes from mass vaccination and eliminates the virus. It protects the entire community, particularly children and adults who can't safely be immunized, as well as babies too young to be vaccinated. When the global campaign began in 1967, there were 10 million to 15 million cases of smallpox a year. Places that had attained herd immunity, such as Europe and North America, had to maintain it to prevent imported cases from India and Africa from triggering an epidemic while mass vaccination campaigns created global herd immunity. Ten years later, the virus died out. Smallpox eradication is the public-health success story of the twentieth century, and because of it we are now determined to try to eradicate other infectious diseases, such as polio and measles.

Polio, perhaps the most frightening disease of the twentieth century, because of its invisible spread and devastating effect, crippled tens of thousands of children each year before the discovery of a vaccine 60 years ago. Americans can be rightly proud of the March of Dimes, an enormous effort driven by American mothers, which raised tens of millions of dollars to find a vaccine. The global campaign to eradicate polio required massive international cooperation, overcoming Cold War divisions, to bring the number of global polio cases today down to a few hundreds a year.

Measles, like polio and smallpox, is a horrible disease. Second only to smallpox in the total number of deaths it has caused over the past two millennia, it's still a major killer of young children in the developing world. The creation of a vaccine was widely welcomed. It is usually delivered jointly with vaccines for mumps and rubella, known in combination as MMR. Two shots provide 99 percent protection and lifelong immunity.

But because of vaccination lapses, measles is now on the rise. There were 23 separate outbreaks in the United States in 2014, involving 644 individual cases—a record number since measles was eliminated from the United States 15 years ago. So far in 2015, there have been 170 cases in 17 states and the District of Columbia, 74 percent of which are linked to Disneyland. Blaming it on Mexico and porous borders, as some opportunistic politicians have done, has no basis in reality; there were only two cases in Mexico in January, both imported from the US. Globally, the number of deaths rose from 122,000 in 2012 to 146,000 in 2013, reversing a 12-year downward trend. In November 2014, the World Health Organization gave up on meeting its target for measles control.

And it gets worse. Measles is so contagious that it is used as the indicator disease to show deficits in immunization coverage of all vaccine-preventable diseases—which means the problem goes well beyond measles. We are now seeing outbreaks of whooping cough in the US, mumps in Britain and tuberculosis more widely. Just last year, the WHO announced a public-health emergency of international concern for polio.

Why is this happening? In syria, the government's effort to withhold childhood vaccinations in areas considered politically unsympathetic to the dictatorship was one reason for the popular uprising. Small wonder that polio returned to that country, and that, according to available data, there were over 10,000 cases of measles there in 2014. Parents are desperate for vaccines, and last year medical workers braved Bashar Assad's barrel bombs to vaccinate 1.4 million children in northern Syria for polio, achieving 92 percent coverage. Similarly, in West Africa, people are begging for Ebola vaccines. Yet in the United States, the anti-vaccination movement has seen increasing numbers of parents refuse measles and other vaccines "on behalf" of their unprotected children.

That misguided movement began with the unconscionable malpractice of Andrew Wakefield. A doctor who has since lost his license, he and his co-authors of a 1998 article in *The Lancet* made up a syndrome consisting of diarrhea and developmental disorder ("re-gressive autism") that he tried to link to the MMR vaccine for the purpose of financial gain. He was not at the time a practicing doctor, and had no expertise with autism, but he manipulated parental fears and an editor's penchant for controversial papers to secure publication in a respected journal. Extraordinarily, despite a financial conflict of interest, despite the fact that he'd fabricated the syndrome and falsified data to fit his criteria, his paper passed peer review.

That paper was then used to support litigation against three companies that produced the MMR vaccine, and to lobby for use of Wakefield's own measles-only vaccine. Wakefield went on to make over $600,000 in fees alone from the lawyer who brought the lawsuit.

In his 1998 paper, Wakefield alleged that eight children developed autism six days after receiving the MMR vaccine. I remember the paper well, because I was a pediatric fellow in London at the time. I and every other pediatrician were immediately besieged by parents demanding measles-only vaccines. We were staggered by Wakefield's ridiculously small, uncontrolled and clearly biased study about a syndrome that none of us had heard of, even though the MMR vaccine had been widely used since 1968. But it was also hard to imagine that *The Lancet* would publish something with such obvious global ramifications unless there was irrefutable scientific evidence uncontaminated by financial interest.

It took six years for *The Lancet* to admit Wakefield's financial conflict of interest, but it did not retract the paper until 2010. Meanwhile, the rise of measles in the United States, the United Kingdom and other parts of Europe reflects the damage done; in February, a toddler died in Berlin amid the biggest outbreak in years. And the consequences extend well beyond the West. In Nigeria, Ebola was successfully stopped in 2014, and polio is close to being eliminated, yet this country has the second-highest number of kids not vaccinated for measles, after India. Among the reasons Nigerian parents have been known to refuse to vaccinate their children is that they are familiar with the anti-vaccine movement incited by Wakefield. If American parents aren't vaccinating their children, why should they?

Vaccination rates of 94 percent are needed to prevent measles transmission in high-risk areas like childcare centers and schools. Yet in Orange County, California, and West Hollywood, many schools have childhood immunization rates of less than 92 percent, with some schools having rates as low as 38 percent—levels seen in developing countries. *The Lancet* could help now by publishing an unequivocal editorial discarding the myth once and for all.

Using vaccination as a political tool is contrary to the public good. Yet some politicians seem unable to assert collective responsibility over individualism: Chris Christie dithers about balancing parental choice and public health, while Rand Paul offers uninformed opinions. A White House spokesman said that "people should evaluate this for themselves," though he urged a bias toward "good science." Seriously? Should we also start debating the value of safe drinking water and sanitation?

In medical school, I couldn't see myself in a career in public health, which seemed like a "done deal" whose value was obvious. But I returned to it a convert after 10 years as a critical-care pediatrician. Kids are the most vulnerable, with their poorly developed immune systems. They are also the most vulnerable to the politicization of the public good, the only ones without a direct say in the debates about their welfare.

Parents are understandably confused, but rising polarization isn't helping. Amid the controversy, it's easy to miss the point: A very serious disease is getting on with its job of invading, infecting and re-colonizing the country, and we are losing control of it. The "herd" can afford an occasional, unvaccinated free-rider, but when large numbers of people place their own ideologies and idiosyncrasies above public health, it is children who suffer the consequences.

It is particularly because of these children that we need to take infectious disease more seriously. And in an increasingly crowded and connected world, we need to think of public health not simply locally but globally. Air travel means it is impossible to stop viruses from spreading around the planet, and building the homeland walls higher won't help; the only reliable antidote is global public health. We have to pay attention to the neglect of infrastructure in West Africa, where Ebola erupted, and the Syrian military's deliberate destruction of public-health systems in opposition-held areas, where polio emerged. Middle East respiratory syndrome now threatens from the Persian Gulf. All of these diseases can easily spread to the West, with profound implications. Just look at the effect of a few cases of Ebola in the United States.

If the threat of measles isn't enough for you to reject anti-vaccination folklore, here's a little-known fact about the benefit of vaccination. The measles vaccine doesn't only protect against measles. Because it contains a small amount of a live virus, the immune system must rev up to fight it, which in turn reduces mortality from other infectious diseases—including pneumonia and sepsis—by 50 percent. This protective effect lasts until a vaccine is administered with a killed rather than a live virus, such as the one for diphtheria and tetanus. So do you want to protect your kids? Give them the measles vaccine.

And all of us should get educated. Education is a social vaccine against the sustained ignorance that blocks effective responses to public-health threats. But education alone is not sufficient to overcome self-interest. We all need to act for the public good. Individuals and institutions that are allowed to prioritize personal preference or financial and political gain ahead of children's health are irresponsible and unethical, and they should not call the shots. In the short term, children's health and lives are at risk; in the long term, we jeopardize the local and global control of these previously conquered diseases. Prevention is not only better than cure—which isn't an option for most of these diseases—it's also more cost-effective.

Our common desire to protect children's health was always the best reason to eliminate these diseases, and it remains our best hope for bringing us all back to common ground. Let's not allow spin doctors and myths to prevail over our shared aim of shielding the world's children from the world's oldest and deadliest diseases.

Critical Thinking

1. How can we prevent countries such as Syria from using vaccines as a political tool?

2. How can we best educate parents about the truth surrounding vaccines?

Internet References

Children's Vaccines: Research on the Risks for Children and Possible Neurological Consequences
> http://www.healing-arts.org/children/vaccines

Immunization Schedules
> http://www.cdc.gov/vaccines/schedules/index.html

The Crash and Burn of an Autism Guru
> http://www.nytimes.com/2011/04/24/magazine/mag-24Autism-t.html?_r=0

Vaccines ProCon.org
> http://www.procon.org

ANNIE SPARROW, a pediatrician and public-health expert, is assistant professor and deputy director of the Human Rights Program at the Arnhold Global Health Institute at Mount Sinai in New York.

Article   Prepared by: Claire N. Rubman,
                           Suffolk County Community College, Selden, NY

Good News, Bad News

Despite efforts to curb harassment, intimidation and bullying, these issues still make their way to our head-lines each season. What can you do to protect your child from such incidents?

TOM CURRY

Learning Outcomes

After reading this article, you will be able to:

- Describe eight possible measures for parents to identify and combat poor conduct in sports.

- Explain the power of positive thinking in relation to bully-ing, harassment and intimidation in sports.

I have been in the coaching profession since I was 18 years old. Starting as a volunteer at our local church coaching the 8th grade basketball team, I also coached the Babe Ruth league baseball in our town, along with numerous other sports at various times. That covers 44 years of coaching vari-ous sports at many levels. I have been the athletic director at three schools since 1990. I have seen so many positive things happen in and around athletics and have been privileged to work with some of the finest people I have known in and out of the business. Good people, good coaches and administrators, along with concerned parents and adults, all trying their best to help kids make good decisions and be productive citizens.

It has become alarming that, despite efforts to curb harass-ment, intimidation and bullying (HIB), these issues still make their way to our headlines each season. Schools and organiza-tions go the extra mile to discuss with teachers, coaches and students the problems and laws concerning HIB and the poten-tial for serious harm to all concerned. Yet, recent stories indi-cate that there is still a lot more to do. What can you, as a parent do to protect your child from such incidents as they grow up in these times?

Pay attention to what is going on in the sports programs your child is involved in. Are there traditions or rituals that are mak-ing your child uncomfortable or not want to attend practices or

games? Do the coaches reinforce positive behaviors, good team ideals and embrace good leadership ideas and skills? Are you uncomfortable with a particular tradition or policy that seems to be "a business as usual" policy?

Create a dialogue with your child, other kids and parents about things other than wins and losses! What do you want your child to take with him or her from this sports program? Continue this dialogue with coaches, supervisors, principals and community leaders. Let good character development be the focal point of your programs and developing responsible citi-zens be the goal of sports programs everywhere.

Promote leadership and sportsmanship in youth and school sports and activities. Be the role model for positive parent behavior at games, events and practices. Many times as parents, we must fight the urge to be a negative part of the experience our children face in athletics. If we fail to set a good, positive example for our children, we may actually do more harm than good to their future. Ask yourself some questions . . . Am I try-ing to re-live my life through my child? Am I affecting his or her experience in a positive way or is the outcome negative? Many parents think they are helping their child by "sticking up" for him or her. I heard of a story recently where a mother went to a lower level baseball game to watch her son pitch. The young man struggled through the first two innings and the coach decided after 10 runs that maybe he should switch positions with another player. The mother took exception and it took the local police department to get her off the field from the pitcher's mound where she had sat on the beach chair she brought, refusing to move. The young man quit the team the next day, suffering from a good case of embarrassment.

Know your child. Watch for signs of disinterest or not want-ing to attend practices or games. Are any of their habits chang-ing? Sleep? Diet? School? Friends? Talk about things other than playing time and winning games. Point out positive behaviors you see athletes exhibiting at the professional and college levels. Cite examples of some of our leaders in all walks of life and what they did in athletics to help them along the way. Frequently discuss situations in sports that are not what sports are really about. Tell your child why you think something is wrong and how they should be behaving while on the field or in the gym

Speak up if you think something is amiss, but do it in the right way. Going after a coach or anyone in public is not a good way to make a point. Ask to speak to the coach privately about your concern. If you think there is a case of HIB, give the coach a chance to correct the situation. It could just be inappropriate behavior by a kid or kids which can be addressed by the coach or leadership. Zero tolerance is the only answer for harassment, intimidation and bullying, but it is also important to recognize that not every incident is an HIB incident. A discussion with the coach or leadership may resolve the problem and would go a long way to make everyone more accountable and make everyone more on the lookout for potential problems. Sometimes it is best to think "evolution, not revolution." Today our kids are bombarded with examples of poor behavior on some of the reality television shows on the networks and on cable. Behaviors which may seem funny on television may actually be quite wrong and hurtful in real life.

Reward good behavior. Society looks to punish poor behavior and people who may be the aggressor and in some cases the victims. I suggest that we really recognize those teams, schools and organizations that do things the right way. See a good example of sportsmanship and write that school or organization a note telling them you noticed. It amazes me that, each day our students do some extraordinary things and some things that are really above and beyond the norm. Let's all start to recognize those efforts instead of always dwelling on the negative things that can and do come up.

Bad news is everywhere. The media descends on stories with "the latest on the 'whatever' scandal" is on that day. The details about the situation, the people involved bring correspondents, news teams and reporters in droves to the scene for immediate updates on the crisis.

Good news travels slower. The media sometimes runs "feel good stories" but the day-to-day things our kids, coaches and teachers may do often go unnoticed. Maybe we, as parents, coaches, educators and community members should and could pay more attention to those things that really make us who we are. By doing so, we just might change the tide of the poor behavior and actions that can make us hang our heads and say, "How could this happen?" There are three types of people in the world . . . those that make things happen . . . those that watch things happen . . . and those who wonder, what happened? I think we know what group is best to be in! Let's make that good news travel faster and be the force of change. The time has come to act against harassment. intimidation and bullying and the action against HIB starts inside each of us.

Critical Thinking

1. How can children be empowered to speak up if they see injustice?

2. How does television contribute to the climate of intimidation, harassment and bullying in sports?

Internet References

Coach Bullying: More Frequent than You Might Think
    http://www.cnn.com/2014/01/13/health/coaches-bullying/index.html
Help us Fight Bullying in Sports
    http://www.youthsportspsychology.com/youth_sports_psychology_blog/?p=621
Stomp Out Bullying: Bullying and Sports
    http://www.stompoutbullying.org/index.php/information-and-resources/about-bullying-and-cyberbullying/bullying-and-sports
The Real Damage Bullying Coaches Can Inflict on Kids
    http://time.com/5382/the-real-damage-bullying-coaches-can-inflict-on-kids

TOM CURRY has been an Athletic Director in Bergen County, New Jersey, as well as an adjunct professor in the Wellness and Exercise Science Department at Bergen Community College for 24 years. He has coached high school basketball and golf and was voted Bergen County Basketball Coach of the Year in 2002. He has spoken at the New Jersey Medical Society Sports Symposium and to parent groups on various issues pertaining to youth sports. He was inducted into the NJ Coaches Hall of Fame in 2012.

Article Prepared by: Claire N. Rubman, *Suffolk County Community College*

How to Choose the Right Apps for Early Learning

STEPHEN GASS

Learning Outcomes

After reading this article, you will be able to:

- Explain the term *digital native*.
- Articulate the educational outcome of technological "bells and whistles" on student learning.
- Define the acronym P.L.A.Y.

Expert Perspective
Young Children Learn Best from Carefully Vetted Content

"Make no mistake about why these babies are here—they are here to replace us."
—Jerry Seinfeld

Good news: Babies are born wired to learn. Instinctively, our youngest "digital natives" (those who have only ever lived in a technocentric, screen-centric world) will:

- Take initiative
- Act on their natural curiosity
- Make clear choices
- Try different approaches
- Stick to a task to persist at a goal
- Share their discoveries and seek social interaction

At minimum, it sounds as if babies are ready to take on the four C's of the 21st century curriculum (creativity, critical thinking, communication, collaboration). Good news, again.

While these nascent skills will form the foundations for all future learning, they require scaffolding and exercise to insure the viability of the foundation. With the inextricable link between technology and 21st century success, an ever-growing library of baby/toddler/preschool apps and e-books, and the ubiquity of tots holding tablets and phones, the inevitable question becomes this: How might we use these digital tools to best build those foundations?

What the Research Tells Us

Currently, much of the data about young **children** and digital devices is device-oriented. As this literature review shows, several studies report on kids' average hours of screen time per day (2.2 to 4.6 hours for 2- to 5-year-olds); others reflect a strong and positive attitude about the educational value of digital devices among a majority of parents; still others confirm toddlers' and preschoolers' ability to demonstrate the requisite motor and cognitive skills for clicking, tapping, swiping (at the older ages), and navigating through experiences of interest.

Unfortunately, we know less about the efficacy of the content or experience to deliver on the software's educational promises. While a few studies in the literature review above show students improving in certain skill areas after using particular pieces of software, a set of generalizable rules, hallmarks, and features that might guide early educators' choices is scant.

One study that does examine user experience looks at the design of the clickable hot spots found in most **children's** interactive experiences. The findings suggest that when hot spots support, reinforce, or extend the e-story **children** are reading, the **children** are better able to retell the story. Extraneous or incidental "bells and whistles" had the opposite effect. While the former approach is quite common, more than likely as an educator, you are not surprised to learn that extraneous information, regardless of its entertainment value, can sabotage a well-constructed lesson.

In the context of the paucity of interactive content research, the point of this example is to illustrate that as educators, armed only with your instincts and knowledge of best practices, you are able to identify the resource best suited to any given learning goal and learner.

With that in mind, and with reinforcement from the vast archive of early childhood research literature that suggests that playing, exploring, and experimenting with open-ended materials (as well as building concepts through direct experience with people and objects) are essential for healthy growth and development, here are some guidelines for navigating the landscape of 21st century digital early learning.

Playground vs. Playpen

In order to be in the best possible position to effectively "replace" us, today's **children** must be active learners who can readily go beyond producing the right short answer to knowing where, when, why, and how to apply information. Yet, the majority of today's digital experiences stop short, simply offering countless opportunities to identify, catch, and capture letters, shapes, numbers, and colors. Many, perhaps in an effort to prepare early learners for life in an agrarian society, also focus on naming favorite barnyard animals and noises.

Since the foundations of and attitudes toward learning are forged during the early years, it's essential that a **child's** digital learning play is built on more than naming things and receiving "good job" rewards, no matter how charmingly animated. When considering skill-building products in math or language, for example, look for digital equivalents of math manipulatives, such as Tangrams HD by Visual Learning Aids, that allow the **child** to play with math concepts; or seek out storytelling props that invite language play, such as Sock Puppets.

Toy vs. Tool

Classic toys such as dolls, blocks, balls, and role-playing sets (play kitchen, work bench, garage/roadway—all gender stereotypes aside) are familiar learning tools in many preschool and pre-preschool environments. In addition to providing opportunities for **children** to exercise certain motor skills, these types of materials are dependable standards for nurturing social, language, and a range of problem solving skills.

Many of the digital counterparts for these activities, however, are right-answer oriented, rather than allowing for truly open-ended play and exploration. Look for play experiences that avoid rigid rules, allow for exploration, and offer more than sound effects and easy cleanup, such as the Balls app by Iotic.

Real vs. Virtual

While hands-on interactions with objects and people in the real world are generally considered the preferred way for young **children** to learn, it's hard to resist the allure of a **child** at peace with a tablet.

A myriad of electronic "paint" and music-making products promise countless hours of creative play. Look for those that, like a master arts teacher, can provoke a little exploration that may lead to a deeper understanding of how to build a piece of music or create an image to express an idea. A good example is Singing Fingers, an iPad app developed at MIT that lets the users finger-paint sounds (including their voice) on the screen, then play and explore the graphic musically.

Try to determine how readily these virtual explorations come off the screen and onto the floor, into the room, or on the walls through conversation, display, or live performance. And keep in mind that even the most profound curriculum or magical material is best served when there's a teacher, parent, or mentor to guide, interpret, narrate, scaffold, or extend the experience.

Today and Tomorrow

Despite the complexities of an increasingly digital world, it's often best to keep it simple. Regardless of the **child's** real world experience—from ducks to fire trucks—or the specific curricular goal, teachers can always just gather their group around the glow of the screen, do an image search, and compare, contrast, describe, and imagine away.

As early educators evaluate and wend their way through the mountain of apps, games, and digital "solutions," just remember that it's not about what technology can deliver, but what the **child** takes away.

P.L.A.Y. WORKS

When choosing apps or any other educational tool for young kids, early childhood expert Stephen Gass suggests keeping in mind the acronym P.L.A.Y.:

P is for position: Make sure the **child** is in a position where he or she can see what's happening.

L is for language: Whatever you do with a **child,** describe what's happening.

A is for action: Whether it's swiping or tapping, bring the **child** into the action as much as possible.

Y is for yuks: Have a good time, be silly, use silly voices. And if things go wrong, laugh about it!

Critical Thinking

1. What is the essence of play in early childhood and can technology capture it successfully?
2. Why is technology so appealing to parents as a learning tool?
3. What are the shortcomings of technology in early childhood education?

Create Central

www.mhhe.com/createcentral

Internet References

Hands-on Learning for Young Children
http://msue.anr.msu.edu/news/hands-on_learning_for_young_children

Pinterest
http://www.pinterest.com/margaretapowers/ece-tech/

Technology and Interactive Media as Tools in Early Childhood Programs Serving Children from Birth through Age 8
http://www.naeyc.org/files/naeyc/file/positions/PS_technology_WEB2.pdf

To iPad or not to iPad
http://www.academia.edu/4117396/To_iPad_or_not_to_iPad_iPads_in_Early_Childhood_Education

Using Technology in the Early Childhood Classroom
http://teacher.scholastic.com/professional/bruceperry/using_technology.htm

STEPHEN GASS has more than 20 years of experience in the design, development, and distribution of learning products, including **computer** software, online applications, toys, games, books, and video. He is president of Every Baby Company, an organization he founded for the development of early learning products, the first of which is Eebee's Adventures.

Gass, Stephen. "How to Choose The Right Apps for Early Learning." *T.H.E. Journal* 40. 9 (September, 2013): 20–22.

Article   Prepared by: Claire N. Rubman, *Suffolk County Community College*

The Touch-Screen Generation

Hanna Rosin

Learning Outcomes

After reading this article, you will be able to:

- Evaluate what tablets, iPads, and smartphones are doing to young children's brains.
- Distinguish between digital natives and digital immigrants and give characteristics of each.

On a chilly day last spring, a few dozen developers of children's apps for phones and tablets gathered at an old beach resort in Monterey, California, to show off their games. One developer, a self-described "visionary for puzzles" who looked like a skateboarder-recently-turned-dad, displayed a jacked-up, interactive game called Puzzingo, intended for toddlers and inspired by his own son's desire to build and smash. Two 30-something women were eagerly seeking feedback for an app called Knock Knock Family, aimed at 1-to-4-year-olds. "We want to make sure it's easy enough for babies to understand," one explained.

The gathering was organized by Warren Buckleitner, a longtime reviewer of interactive children's media who likes to bring together developers, researchers, and interest groups—and often plenty of kids, some still in diapers. It went by the Harry Potter-ish name Dust or Magic, and was held in a drafty old stone-and-wood hall barely a mile from the sea, the kind of place where Bathilda Bagshot might retire after packing up her wand. Buckleitner spent the breaks testing whether his own remote-control helicopter could reach the hall's second story, while various children who had come with their parents looked up in awe and delight. But mostly they looked down, at the iPads and other tablets displayed around the hall like so many open boxes of candy. I walked around and talked with developers, and several paraphrased a famous saying of Maria Montessori's, a quote imported to ennoble a touch-screen age when very young kids, who once could be counted on only to chew

on a square of aluminum, are now engaging with it in increasingly sophisticated ways: "The hands are the instruments of man's intelligence."

What, really, would Maria Montessori have made of this scene? The 30 or so children here were not down at the shore poking their fingers in the sand or running them along mossy stones or digging for hermit crabs. Instead they were all inside, alone or in groups of two or three, their faces a few inches from a screen, their hands doing things Montessori surely did not imagine. A couple of 3-year-old girls were leaning against a pair of French doors, reading an interactive story called *Ten Giggly Gorillas* and fighting over which ape to tickle next. A boy in a nearby corner had turned his fingertip into a red marker to draw an ugly picture of his older brother. On an old oak table at the front of the room, a giant stuffed Angry Bird beckoned the children to come and test out tablets loaded with dozens of new apps. Some of the chairs had pillows strapped to them, since an 18-month-old might not otherwise be able to reach the table, though she'd know how to swipe once she did.

Not that long ago, there was only the television, which theoretically could be kept in the parents' bedroom or locked behind a cabinet. Now there are smartphones and iPads, which wash up in the domestic clutter alongside keys and gum and stray hair ties. "Mom, everyone has technology but me!" my 4-year-old son sometimes wails. And why shouldn't he feel entitled? In the same span of time it took him to learn how to say that sentence, thousands of kids' apps have been developed—the majority aimed at preschoolers like him. To us (his parents, I mean), American childhood has undergone a somewhat alarming transformation in a very short time. But to him, it has always been possible to do so many things with the swipe of a finger, to have hundreds of games packed into a gadget the same size as *Goodnight Moon.*

In 2011, the American Academy of Pediatrics updated its policy on very young children and media. In 1999, the group had discouraged television viewing for children younger than 2, citing research on brain development that showed this age group's critical need for "direct interactions with parents and other significant care givers." The updated report began by acknowledging that things had changed significantly since then. In 2006, 90 percent of parents said that their children younger than 2 consumed some form of electronic media. Nonetheless, the group took largely the same approach it did in 1999, uniformly discouraging passive media use, on any type of screen, for these kids. (For older children, the academy noted, "high-quality programs" could have "educational benefits.") The 2011 report mentioned "smart cell phone" and "new screen" technologies, but did not address interactive apps. Nor did it broach the possibility that has likely occurred to those 90 percent of American parents, queasy though they might be: that some good might come from those little swiping fingers.

I had come to the developers' conference partly because I hoped that this particular set of parents, enthusiastic as they were about interactive media, might help me out of this conundrum, that they might offer some guiding principle for American parents who are clearly never going to meet the academy's ideals, and at some level do not want to. Perhaps this group would be able to articulate some benefits of the new technology that the more cautious pediatricians weren't ready to address. I nurtured this hope until about lunchtime, when the developers gathering in the dining hall ceased being visionaries and reverted to being ordinary parents, trying to settle their toddlers in high chairs and get them to eat something besides bread.

I fell into conversation with a woman who had helped develop Montessori Letter Sounds, an app that teaches pre-schoolers the Montessori methods of spelling.

She was a former Montessori teacher and a mother of four. I myself have three children who are all fans of the touch screen. What games did her kids like to play?, I asked, hoping for suggestions I could take home.

"They don't play all that much."

Really? Why not?

"Because I don't allow it. We have a rule of no screen time during the week," unless it's clearly educational.

No screen time? None at all? That seems at the outer edge of restrictive, even by the standards of my overcontrolling parenting set.

"On the weekends, they can play. I give them a limit of half an hour and then stop. Enough. It can be too addictive, too stimulating for the brain."

Her answer so surprised me that I decided to ask some of the other developers who were also parents what their domestic ground rules for screen time were. One said only on airplanes and long car rides. Another said Wednesdays and weekends, for half an hour. The most permissive said half an hour a day, which was about my rule at home. At one point I sat with one of the biggest developers of e-book apps for kids, and his family. The toddler was starting to fuss in her high chair, so the mom did what many of us have done at that moment—stuck an iPad in front of her and played a short movie so everyone else could enjoy their lunch. When she saw me watching, she gave me the universal tense look of mothers who feel they are being judged. "At home," she assured me, "I only let her watch movies in Spanish."

By their pinched reactions, these parents illuminated for me the neurosis of our age: as technology becomes ubiquitous in our lives, American parents are becoming more, not less, wary of what it might be doing to their children. Technological competence and sophistication have not, for parents, translated into comfort and ease. They have merely created yet another sphere that parents feel they have to navigate in exactly the right way. On the one hand, parents want their children to swim expertly in the digital stream that they will have to navigate all their lives; on the other hand, they fear that too much digital media, too early, will sink them. Parents end up treating tablets like precision surgical instruments, gadgets that might perform miracles for their child's IQ and help him win some nifty robotics competition—but only if they are used just so. Otherwise, their child could end up one of those sad, pale creatures who can't make eye contact and has an avatar for a girlfriend.

Norman Rockwell never painted *Boy Swiping Finger on Screen,* and our own vision of a perfect childhood has never adjusted to accommodate that now-common tableau. Add to that our modern fear that every parenting decision may have lasting consequences—that every minute of enrichment lost or mindless entertainment indulged will add up to some permanent handicap in the future—and you have deep guilt and confusion. To date, no body of research has definitively proved that the iPad will make your preschooler smarter or teach her to speak Chinese, or alternatively that it will rust her neural circuitry—the device has been out for only three years, not much more than the time it takes some academics to find funding and gather research subjects. So what's a parent to do?

In 2001, the education and technology writer Marc Prensky popularized the term *digital natives* to describe the first generations of children growing up fluent in the language of computers, video games, and other technologies. (The rest of us are *digital immigrants,* struggling to understand.) This term took on a whole new significance in April 2010, when the iPad was released. iPhones had already been tempting young children, but the screens were a little small for pudgy toddler hands to navigate with ease and accuracy. Plus, parents tended to be more possessive of their phones, hiding them in pockets or purses. The iPad was big and bright, and a case could be made that it belonged to the family. Researchers who study children's media immediately recognized it as a game changer.

Previously, young children had to be shown by their parents how to use a mouse or a remote, and the connection between what they were doing with their hand and what was happening on the screen took some time to grasp. But with the iPad, the connection is obvious, even to toddlers. Touch technology follows the same logic as shaking a rattle or knocking down a pile of blocks: the child swipes, and something immediately happens. A "rattle on steroids," is what Buckleitner calls it. "All of a sudden a finger could move a bus or smush an insect or turn into a big wet gloopy paintbrush." To a toddler, this is less magic than intuition. At a very young age, children become capable of what the psychologist Jerome Bruner called "enactive representation"; they classify objects in the world not by using words or symbols but by making gestures—say, holding an imaginary cup to their lips to signify that they want a drink. Their hands are a natural extension of their thoughts.

I have two older children who fit the early idea of a digital native—they learned how to use a mouse or a keyboard with some help from their parents and were well into school before they felt comfortable with a device in their lap. (Now, of course, at ages 9 and 12, they can create a Web site in the time it takes me to slice an onion.) My youngest child is a whole different story. He was not yet 2 when the iPad was released. As soon as he got his hands on it, he located the Talking Baby Hippo app that one of my older children had downloaded. The little purple hippo repeats whatever you say in his own squeaky voice, and responds to other cues. My son said his name ("Giddy!"); Baby Hippo repeated it back. Gideon poked Baby Hippo; Baby Hippo laughed. Over and over, it was funny every time. Pretty soon he discovered other apps. Old MacDonald, by Duck Duck Moose, was a favorite. At first he would get frustrated trying to zoom between screens, or not knowing what to do when a message popped up. But after about two weeks, he figured all that out. I must admit, it was eerie to see a child still in diapers so competent and intent, as if he were forecasting his own adulthood. Technically I was the owner of the iPad, but in some ontological way it felt much more his than mine.

Without seeming to think much about it or resolve how they felt, parents began giving their devices over to their children to mollify, pacify, or otherwise entertain them. By 2010, two-thirds of children ages 4 to 7 had used an iPhone, according to the Joan Ganz Cooney Center, which studies children's media. The vast majority of those phones had been lent by a family member; the center's researchers labeled this the "pass-back effect," a name that captures well the reluctant zone between denying and giving.

The market immediately picked up on the pass-back effect, and the opportunities it presented. In 2008, when Apple opened up its App Store, the games started arriving at the rate of dozens a day, thousands a year. For the first 23 years of his career, Buckleitner had tried to be comprehensive and cover every children's game in his publication, *Children's Technology Review*. Now, by Buckleitner's loose count, more than 40,000 kids' games are available on iTunes, plus thousands more on Google Play. In the iTunes "Education" category, the majority of the top-selling apps target preschool or elementary-age children. By age 3, Gideon would go to preschool and tune in to what was cool in toddler world, then come home, locate the iPad, drop it in my lap, and ask for certain games by their approximate description: "Tea? Spill?" (That's Toca Tea Party.)

As these delights and diversions for young children have proliferated, the pass-back has become more uncomfortable, even unsustainable, for many parents:

> He'd gone to this state where you'd call his name and he wouldn't respond to it, or you could snap your fingers in front of his face . . .

> But, you know, we ended up actually taking the iPad away for—from him largely because, you know, this example, this thing we were talking about, about zoning out. Now, he would do that, and my wife and I would stare at him and think, *Oh my God, his brain is going to turn to mush and come oozing out of his ears.* And it concerned us a bit.

This is Ben Worthen, a *Wall Street Journal* reporter, explaining recently to NPR's Diane Rehm why he took the iPad away from his son, even though it was the only thing that could hold the boy's attention for long periods, and it seemed to be sparking an interest in numbers and letters. Most parents can sympathize with the disturbing sight of a toddler, who five minutes earlier had been jumping off the couch, now subdued and staring at a screen, seemingly hypnotized. In the somewhat alarmist *Endangered Minds: Why Children Don't Think—and What We Can Do About It,* author Jane Healy even gives the phenomenon a name, the "'zombie' effect," and raises the possibility that television might "suppress mental activity by putting viewers in a trance."

Ever since viewing screens entered the home, many observers have worried that they put our brains into a stupor. An early strain of research claimed that when we watch television, our brains mostly exhibit slow alpha waves—indicating a low level of arousal, similar to when we are daydreaming. These findings have been largely discarded by the scientific community, but the myth persists that watching television is the mental equivalent of, as one Web site put it, "staring at a blank wall." These common metaphors are misleading, argues Heather Kirkorian, who studies media and attention at the University of Wisconsin at Madison. A more accurate point of comparison for a TV viewer's physiological state would be that of someone deep in a book, says Kirkorian, because during both activities we are still, undistracted, and mentally active.

Because interactive media are so new, most of the existing research looks at children and television. By now, "there is universal agreement that by at least age 2 and a half, children are very cognitively active when they are watching TV," says Dan Anderson, a children's-media expert at the University of Massachusetts at Amherst. In the 1980s, Anderson put the zombie theory to the test, by subjecting roughly 100 children to a form of TV hell. He showed a group of children ages 2 to 5 a scrambled version of *Sesame Street*: he pieced together scenes in random order, and had the characters speak backwards or in Greek. Then he spliced the doctored segments with unedited ones and noted how well the kids paid attention. The children looked away much more frequently during the scrambled parts of the show, and some complained that the TV was broken. Anderson later repeated the experiment with babies ages 6 months to 24 months, using *Teletubbies*. Once again he had the characters speak backwards and chopped the action sequences into a nonsensical order—showing, say, one of the Teletubbies catching a ball and then, after that, another one throwing it. The 6- and 12-month-olds seemed unable to tell the difference, but by 18 months the babies started looking away, and by 24 months they were turned off by programming that did not make sense.

Anderson's series of experiments provided the first clue that even very young children can be discriminating viewers—that they are not in fact brain-dead, but rather work hard to make sense of what they see and turn it into a coherent narrative that reflects what they already know of the world. Now, 30 years later, we understand that children "can make a lot of inferences and process the information," says Anderson. "And they can learn a lot, both positive and negative." Researchers never abandoned the idea that parental interaction is critical for the development of very young children. But they started to see TV watching in shades of gray. If a child never interacts with adults and always watches TV, well, that is a problem. But if a child is watching TV instead of, say, playing with toys, then that is a tougher comparison, because TV, in the right circumstances, has something to offer.

How do small children actually experience electronic media, and what does that experience do to their development? Since the '80s, researchers have spent more and more time consulting with television programmers to study and shape TV content. By tracking children's reactions, they have identified certain rules that promote engagement: stories have to be linear and easy to follow, cuts and time lapses have to be used very sparingly, and language has to be pared down and repeated. A perfect example of a well-engineered show is Nick Jr.'s *Blue's Clues,* which aired from 1996 to 2006. Each episode features Steve (or Joe, in later seasons) and Blue, a cartoon puppy, solving a mystery. Steve talks slowly and simply; he repeats words and then writes them down in his handy-dandy notebook. There are almost no cuts or unexplained gaps in time. The great innovation of *Blue's Clues* is something called the "pause." Steve asks a question and then pauses for about five seconds to let the viewer shout out an answer. Small children feel much more engaged and invested when they think they have a role to play, when they believe they are actually helping Steve and Blue piece together the clues. A longitudinal study of children older than 2 and a half showed that the ones who watched *Blue's Clues* made measurably larger gains in flexible thinking and problem solving over two years of watching the show.

For toddlers, however, the situation seems slightly different. Children younger than 2 and a half exhibit what researchers call a "video deficit." This means that they have a much easier time processing information delivered by a real person than by a person on videotape. In one series of studies, conducted by Georgene Troseth, a developmental psychologist at Vanderbilt University, children watched on a live video monitor as a person in the next room hid a stuffed dog. Others watched the exact same scene unfold directly, through a window between the rooms. The children were then unleashed into the room to find the toy. Almost all the kids who viewed the hiding through the window found the toy, but the ones who watched on the monitor had a much harder time.

A natural assumption is that toddlers are not yet cognitively equipped to handle symbolic representation. (I remember my older son, when he was 3, asking me if he could go into the TV and pet Blue.) But there is another way to interpret this particular phase of development. Toddlers are skilled at seeking out what researchers call "socially relevant information." They tune in to people and situations that help them make a coherent narrative of the world around them. In the real world, fresh grass smells and popcorn tumbles and grown-ups smile at you or say something back when you ask them a question. On TV, nothing like that happens. A TV is static and lacks one of the most important things to toddlers, which is a "two-way exchange of information," argues Troseth.

A few years after the original puppy-hiding experiment, in 2004, Troseth reran it, only she changed a few things. She turned the puppy into a stuffed Piglet (from the Winnie the Pooh stories). More important, she made the video demonstration explicitly interactive. Toddlers and their parents came into a room where they could see a person—the researcher—on a monitor. The researcher was in the room where Piglet would be hidden, and could in turn see the children on a monitor. Before hiding Piglet, the researcher effectively engaged the children in a form of media training. She asked them questions about their siblings, pets, and toys. She played Simon Says with them and invited them to sing popular songs with her. She told them to look for a sticker under a chair in their room. She gave them the distinct impression that she—this person on the screen—could interact with them, and that what she had to say was relevant to the world they lived in. Then the researcher told the children she was going to hide the toy and, after she did so, came back on the screen to instruct them where to find it. That exchange was enough to nearly erase the video deficit. The majority of the toddlers who participated in the live video demonstration found the toy.

Blue's Clues was on the right track. The pause could trick children into thinking that Steve was responsive to them. But the holy grail would be creating a scenario in which the guy on the screen did actually respond—in which the toddler did something and the character reliably jumped or laughed or started to dance or talk back.

Like, for example, when Gideon said "Giddy" and Talking Baby Hippo said "Giddy" back, without fail, every time. That kind of contingent interaction (I do something, you respond) is what captivates a toddler and can be a significant source of learning for even very young children—learning that researchers hope the children can carry into the real world. It's not exactly the ideal social partner the American Academy of Pediatrics craves. It's certainly not a parent or caregiver. But it's as good an approximation as we've ever come up with on a screen, and it's why children's-media researchers are so excited about the iPad's potential.

A couple researchers from the Children's Media Center at Georgetown University show up at my house, carrying an iPad wrapped in a bright-orange case, the better to tempt Gideon with. They are here at the behest of Sandra Calvert, the center's director, to conduct one of several ongoing studies on toddlers and iPads. Gideon is one of their research subjects. This study is designed to test whether a child is more likely to learn when the information he hears comes from a beloved and trusted source. The researchers put the iPad on a kitchen chair; Gideon immediately notices it, turns it on, and looks for his favorite app. They point him to the one they have invented for the experiment, and he dutifully opens it with his finger.

Onto the screen comes a floppy kangaroo-like puppet, introduced as "DoDo." He is a nobody in the child universe, the puppet equivalent of some random guy on late-night public-access TV. Gideon barely acknowledges him. Then the narrator introduces Elmo. "Hi," says Elmo, waving. Gideon says hi and waves back.

An image pops up on the screen, and the narrator asks, "What is this?" (It's a banana.)

"This is a banana," says DoDo.

"This is a grape," says Elmo.

I smile with the inner glow of a mother who knows her child is about to impress a couple strangers. My little darling knows what a banana is. Of course he does! Gideon presses on Elmo. (The narrator says, "No, not Elmo. Try again.") As far as I know, he's never watched *Sesame Street,* never loved an Elmo doll or even coveted one at the toy store. Nonetheless, he is tuned in to the signals of toddler world and, apparently, has somehow figured out that Elmo is a supreme moral authority. His relationship with Elmo is more important to him than what he knows to be the truth. On and on the game goes, and sometimes Gideon picks Elmo even when Elmo says an orange is a pear. Later, when the characters both give made-up names for exotic fruits that few children would know by their real name, Gideon keeps doubling down on Elmo, even though DoDo has been more reliable.

As it happens, Gideon was not in the majority. This summer, Calvert and her team will release the results of their study, which show that most of the time, children around age 32 months go with the character who is telling the truth, whether it's Elmo or DoDo—and quickly come to trust the one who's been more accurate when the children don't already know the answer. But Calvert says this merely suggests that toddlers have become even more savvy users of technology than we had imagined. She had been working off attachment theory, and thought toddlers might value an emotional bond over the correct answer. But her guess is that something about tapping the screen, about getting feedback and being corrected in real time, is itself instructive, and enables the toddlers to absorb information accurately, regardless of its source.

Calvert takes a balanced view of technology: she works in an office surrounded by hardcover books, and she sometimes edits her drafts with pen and paper. But she is very interested in how the iPad can reach children even before they're old enough to access these traditional media.

"People say we are experimenting with our children," she told me. "But from my perspective, it's already happened, and there's no way to turn it back. Children's lives are filled with media at younger and younger ages, and we need to take advantage of what these technologies have to offer. I'm not a Pollyanna. I'm pretty much a realist. I look at what kids are doing and try to figure out how to make the best of it."

Despite the participation of Elmo, Calvert's research is designed to answer a series of very responsible, high-minded questions: Can toddlers learn from iPads? Can they transfer what they learn to the real world? What effect does interactivity have on learning? What role do familiar characters play in children's learning from iPads? All worthy questions, and important, but also all considered entirely from an adult's point of view. The reason many kids' apps are grouped under "Education" in the iTunes store, I suspect, is to assuage parents' guilt (though I also suspect that in the long run, all those "educational" apps merely perpetuate our neurotic relationship with technology, by reinforcing the idea that they must be sorted vigilantly into "good" or "bad"). If small children had more input, many "Education" apps would logically fall under a category called "Kids" or "Kids' Games." And many more of the games would probably look something like the apps designed by a Swedish game studio named Toca Boca.

The founders, Emil Ovemar and Bjorn Jeffery, work for Bonnier, a Swedish media company. Ovemar, an interactive-design expert, describes himself as someone who never grew up. He is still interested in superheroes, Legos, and animated movies, and says he would rather play stuck-on-an-island with his two kids and their cousins than talk to almost any adult. Jeffery is the company's strategist and front man; I first met him at the conference in California, where he was handing out little temporary tattoos of the Toca Boca logo, a mouth open and grinning, showing off rainbow-colored teeth.

In late 2010, Ovemar and Jeffery began working on a new digital project for Bonnier, and they came up with the idea of entering the app market for kids. Ovemar began by looking into the apps available at the time. Most of them were disappointingly "instructive," he found—"drag the butterfly into the net, that sort of thing. They were missing creativity and imagination." Hunting for inspiration, he came upon Frank and Theresa Caplan's 1973 book *The Power of Play*, a quote from which he later e-mailed to me:

What is it that often puts the B student ahead of the A student in adult life, especially in business and creative professions? Certainly it is more than verbal skill. To create, one must have a sense of adventure and playfulness. One needs toughness to experiment and hazard the risk of failure. One has to be strong enough to start all over again if need be and alert enough to learn from whatever happens. One needs a strong ego to be propelled forward in one's drive toward an untried goal. Above all, one has to possess the ability to play!

Ovemar and Jeffery hunted down toy catalogs from as early as the 1950s, before the age of exploding brand tie-ins. They made a list of the blockbusters over the decades—the first Tonka trucks, the Frisbee, the Hula-Hoop, the Rubik's Cube. Then they made a list of what these toys had in common: None really involved winning or losing against an opponent. None were part of an effort to create a separate child world that adults were excluded from, and probably hostile toward; they were designed more for family fun. Also, they were not really meant to teach you something specific—they existed mostly in the service of having fun.

In 2011 the two developers launched Toca Tea Party. The game is not all that different from a real tea party. The iPad functions almost like a tea table without legs, and the kids have to invent the rest by, for example, seating their own plushies or dolls, one on each side, and then setting the theater in motion. First, choose one of three tablecloths. Then choose plates, cups, and treats. The treats are not what your mom would feed you. They are chocolate cakes, frosted doughnuts, cookies. It's very easy to spill the tea when you pour or take a sip, a feature added based on kids' suggestions during a test play (kids love spills, but spilling is something you can't do all that often at a real tea party, or you'll get yelled at). At the end, a sink filled with soapy suds appears, and you wash the dishes, which is also part of the fun, and then start again. That's it. The game is either very boring or terrifically exciting, depending on what you make of it. Ovemar and Jeffery knew that some parents wouldn't get it, but for kids, the game would be fun every time, because it's dependent entirely on imagination. Maybe today the stuffed bear will be naughty and do the spilling, while naked Barbie will pile her plate high with sweets. The child can take on the voice of a character or a scolding parent, or both. There's no winning, and there's no reward. Like a game of stuck-on-an-island, it can go on for five minutes or forever.

Soon after the release of Toca Tea Party, the pair introduced Toca Hair Salon, which is still to my mind the most fun game out there. The salon is no Fifth Avenue spa. It's a rundown-looking place with cracks in the wall. The aim is not beauty but subversion. Cutting off hair, like spilling, is on the list of things kids are not supposed to do. You choose one of the odd-looking people or creatures and have your way with its hair, trimming it or dyeing it or growing it out. The blow-dryer is genius; it achieves the same effect as Tadao Cern's Blow Job portraits, which depict people's faces getting wildly distorted by high winds. In August 2011, Toca Boca gave away Hair Salon for free for nearly two weeks. It was downloaded more than 1 million times in the first week, and the company took off. Today, many Toca Boca games show up on lists of the most popular education apps.

Are they educational? "That's the perspective of the parents," Jeffery told me at the back of the grand hall in Monterey. "Is running around on the lawn educational? Every part of a child's life can't be held up to that standard." As we talked, two girls were playing Toca Tea Party on the floor nearby. One had her stuffed dragon at a plate, and he was being especially naughty, grabbing all the chocolate cake and spilling everything. Her friend had taken a little Lego construction man and made him the good guy who ate neatly and helped do the dishes. Should they have been outside at the beach? Maybe, but the day would be long, and they could go outside later.

The more I talked with the developers, the more elusive and unhelpful the "Education" category seemed. (Is *Where the Wild*

Things Are educational? Would you make your child read a text-book at bedtime? Do you watch only educational television? And why don't children deserve high-quality fun?) Buckleitner calls his conference Dust or Magic to teach app developers a more subtle concept than pedagogy. By *magic,* Buckleitner has in mind an app that makes children's fingers move and their eyes light up. By *dust,* he means something that was obviously (and ploddingly) designed by an adult. Some educational apps, I wouldn't wish on the naughtiest toddler. Take, for example, Counting With the Very Hungry Caterpillar, which turns a per-fectly cute book into a tedious app that asks you to "please eat 1 piece of chocolate cake" so you can count to one.

Before the conference, Buckleitner had turned me on to Noodle Words, an app created by the California designer and children's-book writer Mark Schlichting. The app is explicitly educational. It teaches you about active verbs—*spin, sparkle, stretch.* It also happens to be fabulous. You tap a box, and a verb pops up and gets acted out by two insect friends who have the slapstick sensibility of the Three Stooges. If the word is *shake,* they shake until their eyeballs rattle. I tracked down Schlichting at the conference, and he turned out to be a little like Maurice Sendak—like many good children's writers, that is: ruled by id and not quite tamed into adulthood. The app, he told me, was inspired by a dream he'd had in which he saw the word *and* floating in the air and sticking to other words like a magnet. He woke up and thought, *What if words were toys?*

During the course of reporting this story, I downloaded doz-ens of apps and let my children test them out. They didn't much care whether the apps were marketed as educational or not, as long as they were fun. Without my prompting, Gideon fix-ated on a game called Letter School, which teaches you how to write letters more effectively and with more imagination than any penmanship textbooks I've ever encountered. He loves the Toca Boca games, the Duck Duck Moose games, and random games like Bugs and Buttons. My older kids love The Num-berlys, a dark fantasy creation of illustrators who have worked with Pixar that happens to teach the alphabet. And all my kids, including Gideon, play Cut the Rope a lot, which is not exclu-sively marketed as a kids' game. I could convince myself that the game is teaching them certain principles of physics—it's not easy to know the exact right place to slice the rope. But do I really need that extra convincing? I like playing the game; why shouldn't they?

Every new medium has, within a short time of its intro-duction, been condemned as a threat to young people. Pulp novels would destroy their morals, TV would wreck their eyesight, video games would make them violent. Each one has been accused of seducing kids into wasting time that would otherwise be spent learning about the presidents, playing with friends, or digging their toes into the sand. In our generation, the worries focus on kids' brainpower, about unused synapses withering as children stare at the screen. People fret about television and ADHD, although that concern is largely based on a single study that has been roundly criticized and doesn't jibe with anything we know about the disorder.

There are legitimate broader questions about how American children spend their time, but all you can do is keep them in mind as you decide what rules to set down for your own child. The statement from the American Academy of Pediatrics assumes a zero-sum game: an hour spent watching TV is an hour not spent with a parent. But parents know this is not how life works. There are enough hours in a day to go to school, play a game, and spend time with a parent, and generally these are different hours. Some people can get so drawn into screens that they want to do nothing else but play games. Experts say exces-sive video gaming is a real problem, but they debate whether it can be called an addiction and, if so, whether the term can be used for anything but a small portion of the population. If your child shows signs of having an addictive personality, you will probably know it. One of my kids is like that; I set stricter limits for him than for the others, and he seems to understand why.

In her excellent book *Screen Time,* the journalist Lisa Guernsey lays out a useful framework—what she calls the three C's— for thinking about media consumption: content, context, and your child. She poses a series of questions—Do you think the content is appropriate? Is screen time a "relatively small part of your child's interaction with you and the real world?"— and suggests tailoring your rules to the answers, child by child. One of the most interesting points Guernsey makes is about the importance of parents' attitudes toward media. If they treat screen time like junk food, or "like a magazine at the hair salon"—good for passing the time in a frivolous way but noth-ing more—then the child will fully absorb that attitude, and the neurosis will be passed to the next generation.

"The war is over. The natives won." So says Marc Prensky, the education and technology writer, who has the most extreme parenting philosophy of anyone I encountered in my report-ing. Prensky's 7-year-old son has access to books, TV, Legos, Wii—and Prensky treats them all the same. He does not limit access to any of them. Sometimes his son plays with a new app for hours, but then, Prensky told me, he gets tired of it. He lets his son watch TV even when he personally thinks it's a "stupid waste." *SpongeBob SquarePants,* for example, seems like an annoying, pointless show, but Prensky says he used the rela-tionship between SpongeBob and Patrick, his starfish sidekick, to teach his son a lesson about friendship. "We live in a screen age, and to say to a kid, 'I'd love for you to look at a book but I hate it when you look at the screen' is just bizarre. It reflects our own prejudices and comfort zone. It's nothing but fear of change, of being left out."

Prensky's worldview really stuck with me. Are books always, in every situation, inherently better than screens? My daughter, after all, often uses books as a way to avoid social interaction, while my son uses the Wii to bond with friends. I have to admit, I had the exact same experience with *Sponge-Bob*. For a long time I couldn't stand the show, until one day I got past the fact that the show was so loud and frenetic and paid more attention to the story line, and realized I too could use it to talk with my son about friendship. After I first interviewed Prensky, I decided to conduct an experiment. For six months, I would let my toddler live by the Prensky rules. I would put the iPad in the toy basket, along with the remote-control car and the Legos. Whenever he wanted to play with it, I would let him.

Gideon tested me the very first day. He saw the iPad in his space and asked if he could play. It was 8 A.M. and we had to get ready for school. I said yes. For 45 minutes he sat on a chair and played as I got him dressed, got his backpack ready, and failed to feed him breakfast. This was extremely annoying and obviously untenable. The week went on like this—Gideon grabbing the iPad for two-hour stretches, in the morning, after school, at bedtime. Then, after about 10 days, the iPad fell out of his rotation, just like every other toy does. He dropped it under the bed and never looked for it. It was completely forgotten for about six weeks.

Now he picks it up every once in a while, but not all that often. He has just started learning letters in school, so he's back to playing LetterSchool. A few weeks ago his older brother played with him, helping him get all the way through the uppercase and then lowercase letters. It did not seem beyond the range of possibility that if Norman Rockwell were alive, he would paint the two curly-haired boys bent over the screen, one small finger guiding a smaller one across, down, and across again to make, in their triumphant finale, the small *z*.

Critical Thinking

1. Why did the American Academy of Pediatrics (2011) discourage any passive media use for children younger than age 2?
2. What are the advantages of learning to navigate digital technology in early childhood?

Create Central

www.mhhe.com/createcentral

Internet References

Internet Safety Rules: The Constant Pursuit of Keeping Your Child Safe Online
www.articlesbase.com/parenting-articles/internet-safety-rules
Study: 40 Percent of Kids Use iPads Before They Can Speak
http://nymag.com/thecut/2013
Tech and Young Children
www.techandyoungchildren.org

HANNA ROSIN is a national correspondent for *The Atlantic*.

Unit 3

UNIT

Prepared by: Claire N. Rubman,
Suffolk County Community College, Selden, NY

Development during Childhood: Cognition and Schooling

What does it mean to "educate" a child? Is there one list of facts that all children should know at any given age or is quality education comprised of a less tangible type of knowledge or skill set? Are we demanding too much from our children and, when we perceive that they are underperforming, are we inadvertently overmedicating them to compensate? Depression, attentional issues and a lack of concentration seem to plague our educational paradigm. According to the Centers for Disease Control, 6.4 million American children were diagnosed with ADHD in 2013. Two-thirds of these children were prescribed medication.

To combat the problem of attention deficits, Sroufe evaluates the use of drugs such as Ritalin or Adderall instead of food solutions. He reports on a large study of 600 students that initially touted the benefits of medication for attention deficit disorders but later found that any perceived benefits dissipated over time. He suggests that the focus ought to be on brain functioning among children with attentional deficits rather than medicating the behaviors. He advocates a de-emphasis on drug use among this vulnerable population.

Several articles in this unit look at the role that food plays in our child's ability to focus and concentrate. Murray and Turner hypothesize that the food that our children eat can contribute to their overall mental health. In his article, "5 Safe Brain Boosters for Kids", Murray promotes natural alternatives to address good mental health and combat childhood issues such as depression. Turner focuses on attention and concentration suggesting that vitamin deficiencies may be the underlying cause of some attentional issues.

Finally, the issues surrounding assessment are addressed. Teachers often provide invaluable insight and Schneider and Christison are no exception. In the article, "Are Exams Bad for Children?" these two teachers debate the relative advantages and disadvantages of exams within the school curriculum. They discuss the racial and economic inequalities of our current educational system. They discuss the growing discontentment among parents, children, and educators in the current educational climate and they look for viable options and educational models.

Prepared by: Claire N. Rubman,
Suffolk County Community College, Selden, NY

Article

Food for Thought

Safe Brain Boosters for Kids

MICHAEL T. MURRAY

Learning Outcomes

After reading this article, you will be able to:

- Explain the term "super nutrition."
- Discuss the levels of EPA and DHA in children with ADHD.
- Define "PharmaGaba" and its impact on brain development in children.

Brain cells are the most complex, long-living, and nutritionally demanding cells in the body. Studies show that intelligence, memory, behavior, and concentration are all influenced by proper nutrition, and this is especially important to the developing brain.

The goal should be to help children bathe their brains in "super nutrition," because high nutritional status equals higher mental function. And that means that what kids *don't* eat can be as important as what they do. Foods to avoid include smoked or cured meats, fried foods, any source of trans-fatty acids, junk food, refined sugar, and high-fructose corn syrup.

In general, the same ideas associated with healthy eating in adults apply to kids—lots of fresh fruits and veggies. If kids turn their noses up at leafy greens, getting a juicer and mixing in apple and carrot juice can camouflage the taste. But kids generally do like a number of brain-supporting veggies such as carrots, yams, and squash. For fruit, focus on berries. In animal studies, researchers have found that blueberries especially can help protect the brain and promote improved memory.

Giving kids a daily dose (25–50 mg, though there's no problem with doses up to 100 mg) of grape seed or pine bark extracts is also a good idea. One study found that one month of daily supplementation with Pycnogenol (a proprietary pine bark extract) at a dose of 1 mg per kg of body weight improved attention and concentration in children with ADHD.

Thought-full Supplements

In addition to grape seed and pine bark extracts, there are some other key nutritional supplements to consider.

- **A high potency multi.** Studies have shown that vitamin and mineral supplementation can increase non-verbal intelligence in some children. In other words, taking a daily multi can make some kids smarter. These studies highlight the essential role of many vitamins and minerals in brain function, especially thiamin, niacin, vitamin B_6, vitamin B_{12}, copper, iodine, magnesium, potassium, and zinc. A deficiency of any of these nutrients can result in impaired brain function.
- **Iron.** Deficiency of this key mineral is associated with decreased attentiveness, narrower attention span, decreased persistence, and decreased voluntary activity. Fortunately, these symptoms can be alleviated with supplementation. (See "Iron Deficiency & ADD/ADHD")
- **Eicosapentaenoic acid (EPA) and docosahexaenoic acid (DHA).** The developing brain is especially dependent upon adequate levels of these critical building blocks. Numerous studies have now shown that children with ADHD have a measurable reduction in tissue levels of EPA and DHA. Omega-3 (EPA+DHA) supplementation in ADHD has been studied extensively and is considered a sensible intervention even by many mainstream physicians. But these nutrients are critical

for all children. In a 2013 Oxford University study, levels of EPA+DHA "significantly predicted" the ability of children between the ages of seven and nine to concentrate and learn. The recommended dosage for children is 600–1,000 mg of EPA+DHA daily.

A Specialty Brain Booster

Recently, studies have indicated that enhancing gamma-Aminobutyric acid (GABA) activity may help improve mental function in children, and a natural form known as Pharma-GABA could be the best approach.

One of the most interesting studies on PharmaGABA was conducted by scientists from Japan's Kyorin University Medical School. Researchers divided 60 6th graders into two groups that received either 100 mg of PharmaGABA or a placebo. The students then took a math test and were also evaluated for signs and feelings of stress. The results were quite dramatic. The average number of questions answered by the PharmaGABA group was 20 percent higher than the placebo group, and the number answered correctly also increased by 20 percent. Researchers also measured the amount of a stress-related hormone in participants' saliva as well as how much anxiety the children experienced, and found that the PharmaGABA group was more relaxed and focused compared to the placebo group.

PharmaGABA is safe and has recently achieved generally recognized as safe (GRAS) status in the United States. There are no known side effects or drug interactions at recommended levels.

Critical Thinking

1. To what extent are parents aware of the benefits of natural alternatives to enhance their children's brain development?
2. What could communities do to encourage higher nutritional status for all children?

Internet References

6 Brain Boosting Herbs To Improve Your Productivity
http://www.lifehack.org/articles/lifestyle/6-brain-boosting-herbs-to-improve-your-productivity.html

Better Brains for Babies
http://www.bbbgeorgia.org/physicalNutrition.php

Nutrition and Early Brain Development Urban Child Institute
http://www.urbanchildinstitute.org/articles/updates/nutrition-and-early-brain-development

Smart Kids - Food for the Brain
http://www.foodforthebrain.org/smart-kids.aspx

Iron Deficiency & ADD/ADHD

Conventional physicians tend to overlook the most common nutrient deficiency in the United States—iron deficiency. This simple, essential nutrient can lead to low energy levels, poor immune function, and even symptoms of attention deficit disorder and hyperactivity. In fact, a recent study found that 84 percent of kids with ADD/ADHD were iron-deficient.

How provocative is that finding? Think about all of the prescriptions for Ritalin, Concerta, and Adderall that are being dispensed to kids who may simply need proper nutrition and adequate iron stores.

While ferrous sulfate is the most popular iron supplement, it often causes constipation or other gastrointestinal (GI) disturbance. Although it is best absorbed when taken on an empty stomach, doing so often causes nausea or GI upset. So, it is most often taken with food, and that greatly reduces its absorption.

One of the best forms of iron for kids, especially younger kids who cannot take pills and rely on chewable forms, is micronized ferrous pyrophosphate. It has no flavor, is free from gastrointestinal side effects, and provides a sustained release form of iron (up to 12 hours) with a high relative bioavailability—especially if taken on an empty stomach. For general health purposes, the following chart provides a good supplementation guideline.

Recommended Dietary Intake for Iron

INFANTS	
0–0.5 year	6 mg
0.5–1 year	10 mg
CHILDREN	
1–10 years	10 mg
YOUNG ADULTS & ADULTS	
Males 11–18 years	12 mg
Males 19+ years	10 mg
Females 11–50 years	15 mg
Females 51+ years	10 mg
Pregnancy	30 mg
Lactating	15 mg

MICHAEL T. MURRAY, ND, is regarded as one of the world's leading authorities on natural medicine. He is a graduate, former faculty member, and serves on the Board of Regents of Bastyr University in Seattle.

The author of over 30 books on health and nutrition, Dr. Murray is also Director of Product Science and Innovation for Natural Factors Nutritional Products. For more information, go to DoctorMurray.com.

Article   Prepared by: Claire N. Rubman,
                                    Suffolk County Community College, Selden, NY

Happy, Healthy Kids

Six Ways to Boost Mood, Calm ADHD, and Ease Anxiety

LISA TURNER

Learning Outcomes

After reading this article, you will be able to:

- Articulate how many children and adolescents in the United States experience mental health issues.

- Describe the role of fats and additives in good mental health.

- Explain how vitamins, protein, and herbal alternatives can alleviate some mental health issues such as depression, anxiety, or sleep disorders.

Only 30 years ago, it was thought that children did not experience depression or other mental health issues. We now know that an estimated 4 million children and adolescents in the U.S. suffer from serious mental disorders, and that as many as 21 percent of kids ages 9–17 have a diagnosable addictive or mental disorder that causes impairment.

Mental disorders in children range from depression, anxiety, and attention deficit disorder (ADD), to psychosis and schizophrenia. These conditions may be mild enough to cause only occasional, temporary distress—or severe enough to disrupt and damage lives.

But treating kids for mental disorders is tricky, especially since the effects of medications can vary, and side effects can be severe. If you suspect that your child has a mental disorder, it's critical to get a good diagnosis from a doctor or health care provider who specializes in pediatric mental health. In severe cases, medication and/or psychotherapy may be required.

However, many mental health conditions in kids, including ADHD, anxiety, and mild depression, can be soothed with natural alternatives. Even if medication is required, supplements and herbs can often enhance the treatment. Be sure to check with your health care provider first, and then consider some of these natural alternatives:

1. **Subtract the additives.** Studies suggest that food additives—including colorings, preservatives, artificial flavors, sugars, and MSG—exacerbate hyperactivity and can worsen symptoms of attention deficit hyperactivity disorder (ADHD). Gluten, added to many sauces, soups, and other products, may also be a problem. In one study, undiagnosed celiac disease was found to cause a number of issues, including ADHD and behavior disorders. And the artificial sweetener aspartame is broken down in the brain into aspartic acid, which can lead to anxiety and depression and inhibit serotonin production.

2. **Focus on fat.** It's crucial to brain health, maintaining flexibility of cell membranes to ensure they can better send and receive information. But the type of fat is important. Saturated fat may impact brain plasticity, and has been linked with symptoms of anxiety in some people. Omega-3 fats, however, keep nerve cell membranes flexible, and several studies suggest they help alleviate ADHD-related symptoms and depression. Some studies have also suggested that a deficiency in DHA, a type of omega-3, hampers transmission of serotonin, norepinephrine, and dopamine, neurotransmitters involved in mood. Wild Alaskan salmon, sardines, walnuts, and flax seeds are good food sources of omega-3s. Or choose a high-quality omega-3 supplement.

3. **Try herbal cures.** Some herbs have been shown in clinical trials to be both safe and effective. In one study of more than 100 kids under the age of 12, St. John's wort alleviated symptoms of mild to moderate depression. (But because it can interact with other

medications, it's especially important to talk with a doctor before using St. John's wort.) Valerian has been shown to alleviate anxiety and improve sleep, and studies show that lemon balm combined with valerian can safely treat restlessness and sleep disorders in children. And in another study, passionflower combined with St. John's wort and valerian significantly lessened depression, anxiety, and sleeplessness.

4. **Push B vitamins.** They're critical for normal neurological functioning. One study of 6,517 boys and girls ages 12–15 found that higher intake of B vitamins, especially folate and vitamin B_6, was associated with a lower prevalence of depression in early adolescence. Vitamin B_6 (pyridoxine) is a major cofactor in the synthesis of serotonin; vitamin B_{12} may also form SAM-e (S-adenosylmethionine), a compound linked with mood. Folate is also a factor in forming serotonin, norepinephrine, and SAM-e, and deficiencies of folate have been found in people with depression and anxiety.

5. **Eat to beat the blues.** Protein is key—a shortage can exacerbate anxiety and/or depression. Best sources: turkey, cheese, chicken, fish, beans, and almonds. Magnesium, found in leafy greens, pumpkin seeds, and beans, can ease depression. Zinc helps the brain produce GABA, a compound that combats anxiety and irritability. It's abundant in oysters and can also be found in crab, turkey, lentils, and yogurt. Vitamin E keeps nerve cell membranes flexible, allowing information to be smoothly transmitted. You'll find it in sunflower seeds, almonds, and other nuts.

6. **Teach relaxation.** Show kids how to unwind: Lie down with your child on the floor and do a simple body scan, imagining each part of the body—from toes to head—melting like an ice cube on a warm sidewalk. Help your child learn to follow her inhales and exhales; this helps her focus on her breath and calms the central nervous system. Start small, with a 5-minute session, and make it a daily ritual—right after school is a perfect time for keyed-up kids who need to unwind.

Critical Thinking

1. Why are so many of our children lacking the essential vitamins, fats, and nutrients for optimal brain development?

2. How can we promote healthy fats such as saturated fats while encouraging families to avoid less healthy foods?

Internet References

5 Foods that Negatively Affect Your Child's Mood
http://childdevelopmentinfo.com/adhd-add/five-foods-negatively-affect-childs-mood

Anxiety and Mood Disorders Center
http://www.childmind.org/en/clinics/centers/anxiety-and-mood-disorders-center

Mood Disorders & ADHD
https://www.healthychildren.org/English/health-issues/conditions/adhd/Pages/Mood-Disorders-ADHD.aspx

Scientists learn how what you eat affects your brain—and those of your kids
http://newsroom.ucla.edu/releases/scientists-learn-how-food-affects-52668

LISA TURNER is a certified food psychology coach, nutritional healer, intuitive eating consultant, and author. She has written five books on food and nutrition and developed the Inspired Eats iPhone app.

Article   Prepared by: Claire N. Rubman, *Suffolk County Community College*

Are Exams Bad for Children?

STEPHANIE SCHNEIDER AND MATT CHRISTISON

Learning Outcomes

After reading this article, you will be able to:

- Describe the misunderstandings that surround standardized tests.

- Explain the benefits of "contextualized assessment."

> **The most powerful evidence that tests harm children is the emerging resistance of parents, teachers, and students who see the damage first hand.**
>
> —Stephanie

Stephanie

A fellow teacher once shared with me this analogy to standardized testing: it's like checking to make sure a plant is growing properly by repeatedly ripping it out of the ground and examining the roots. When that plant is placed back into the soil, it does not remain the same but rather is traumatized by the drastic act.

Just as we know of better ways to grow plants, we know of better ways to assess children. More reliable methods of assessment can provide meaningful information that assist student learning, rather than a test that often serves as a punitive device.

If we are interested in children succeeding in school then we need to provide an education rich in context and relevance, accomplished through quality instructional time. Unfortunately, as the use of standardized tests increases, more classroom time is being dedicated to exam preparation and administration, which only results in a narrowing of the curriculum.

If we are interested in success for ALL children then we need to be clear that the current testing regime does nothing to address racial and economic inequalities and instead reinforces them. Often, we find in the United States that the data of such tests is used to rationalize policy that is damaging to schools in low-income neighbourhoods and in communities of color.

Finally, the most powerful evidence that tests harm children is the emerging resistance of parents, teachers, and students who see the damage first hand and are growing louder in their collective refusal to comply.

Matt

As both a teacher and a gardener, I agree that uprooting plants—and students—serves no purpose. Yet examinations, especially standardized tests, in and of themselves are not bad—any more than examining in detail the growth of a plant is bad. What is bad is how we use examinations and the misunderstandings that surround standardized testing in particular.

For the purpose of simplicity, I will refer to examinations in this discussion as "standardized testing and tests". Well-constructed, thoughtful, standardized tests have integrity in their validity and reliability. They are reliable in that well-constructed tests provide similar performances by the students in the same grade or taking the same course, under the similar or the same parameters (time, format, etc). What standardized testing does well is provide descriptive information for thoughtful use by well-trained and well-prepared teachers.

Yet, as you point out, this does not happen with much of the descriptive information we derive from well-constructed tests. The descriptive information—which can be used in a focused, diagnostic manner to provide the next steps for student learning—is often superseded by the ills of education you have presented: time constraints, justification of rankings and placements, and the reinforcement of inequities.

What we need is the hybrid: standardized testing used for its descriptive and diagnostic purposes without the simplistic and inappropriate agendas of those who wish to sort, restrict, and punish; along with the contextualized, rich and robust ongoing assessment of learning. If we want success for ALL students, then we must use ALL forms of assessment for the purposes they are intended, and neither hijack them for our own agendas nor reject them because they do not fit our preferences and current understandings.

> **We must use all forms of assessment for the purposes they are intended, and neither hijack them for our own agendas nor reject them because they do not fit our preferences.**
>
> — Matt

Stephanie

One could say standardized tests don't kill education; it is only the use of these tests that does. But for me, separating the use and intention is a futile task. It is their current manifestation that I deal with as a classroom teacher and even if the tests were of better quality, I still see the way testing favours certain kinds of skills as problematic.

I am required to give my kindergarten students the MAP (Measures of Academic Progress) test three times a year. Each time I explain this test is very different from what we do in the classroom. It never fails that children will try to help each other and I find myself telling them: "You may not help your friend solve that problem." I am forced to administer this test that prioritizes individual achievement and disallows any collaborative learning.

These tests do not inform my instruction. Since I am not allowed to see the content of the test, any resulting information is worthless.

I disagree that it is idealistic to use contextualized assessments—if there is a lack of training and experience on the part of teachers, then the solution is to redirect resources currently used for standardized tests to implement meaningful professional development on classroom-based assessments.

Any kind of assessment beyond that would have to be low stakes and should be given to a random selection of students only in certain grades. This can still provide valid information and yet limit the amount of resources and instructional time a test can occupy.

Matt

All forms of assessment—standardized testing and teacher-based classroom assessments—are subjective. What is emphasized (creativity, arithmetic proficiency, reading abilities, neatness, cooperation, and risk taking) and what is not emphasized sends a clear and often damaging message to students, parents, and teachers.

I agree with and see your critiques of standardized testing as valid, no pun intended. The politics and inappropriate uses of standardized testing do interfere with the daily work of teachers and learning in schools.

However, to turn against standardized testing and reject it is, in my mind, no better than embracing it as a panacea, as the solution to educational ills and woes, and as a means to sorting, selecting, and valuing students. What we must have is a balance, the complete picture of student learning in school contexts, working with others, working alone, creating, trying and experimenting, assessing processes and products in as many robust, well-thought-out, and well-developed (and open to change and constructive criticisms) assessments as possible.

Standardized testing is unlikely to disappear: and as such, we all need to take from it the insights it can provide while fighting against the political and power-based misuses that overshadow and stifle what standardized testing has to offer: descriptive information to help inform practice and support learning.

Stephanie

Imagining school without standardized testing (or very minimal testing) isn't too difficult because examples already exist. In fact, in some of the most highly regarded private schools, standardized tests are few and far between. Additionally, in the much-lauded example of education innovation, Finland, the standardized test is used infrequently and with low stakes.

I know that both these examples have their own circumstances but I suggest them because I want to demonstrate the possibility. Places do exist where teachers are trusted to educate students without the reliance on a standardized test.

That said, I do appreciate your effort to mitigate the misuse of such tests and I could certainly find a test more palatable if it really did provide valuable information and did not serve to punish and reward. If such a test were to exist I would require a few additional criteria.

First of all, a standardized test should not provide a lucrative profit to some entity. I would trust a test a lot more if I knew that no-one was making money off something that was potentially damaging to my students or school. Second, the test should be clear in its intent and not be used to determine a school's funding, a teacher's livelihood or a student's future. And finally, a test should be thoroughly vetted for bias with continued reflection coinciding with its use.

Matt

Ideally, you and I, as well as other parties, would work collaboratively so that the forms of assessment used would present the most well-rounded, helpful, and bias-free information to support student learning. As such a situation is unlikely to occur in the immediate future, I would add the following to your criteria.

First, standardized testing would be done outside of schools and school settings. It could be done as it is conducted in Finland: students write those tests when they are ready, having completed the requisite courses, and the examinations are held in community sites, with the test questions and answers published the following day for all community members to see, discuss, and review. Thus the standardized testing would be open to all types of scrutiny and transparency in and of its format, structure, and presentation.

Second, standardized testing would be voluntary, with those who wish to utilize the results paying for the costs of administration, creation, and development. Thus those who wish to use it would be known, and their intentions would be clear and connected directly with the testing. Should the results be used for admissions to postsecondary institutions, or ranking schools or other purposes, then those who participate would do so knowing who was to use them and why.

Perhaps this is idealistic, yet I know that open discussion about assessment and standardized testing will lead to improvements for students, learning, teachers, and the community at large.

Critical Thinking

1. Ideally, how could teachers assess student success without the use of standardized tests?

2. Under what circumstances could standardized tests be used more productively?

3. How could parents, teachers, and school districts work together to improve the current climate of testing and assessment?

Create Central

www.mhhe.com/createcentral

Internet References

How Tests Make Us Smarter

http://www.nytimes.com/2014/07/20/opinion/sunday/how-tests-make-us-smarter.html

Opting Out-The National Center for Fair and Open Testing

http://www.fairtest.org/get-involved/opting-out

Pros and Cons of Standardized Testing

http://worklife.columbia.edu/files_worklife/public/Pros_and_Cons_of_Standardized_Testing_1.pdf

Standardized Tests Pros and Cons

http://standardizedtests.procon.org/

Too Much Stress? Parents, Experts Discuss High-Stakes Standardized Test Anxiety

http://news.wjct.org/post/too-much-test-stress-parents-experts-discuss-high-stakes-standardized-test-anxiety

STEPHANIE SCHNEIDER teaches three- to six-year-olds at a public Montessori School in Milwaukee, Wisconsin, USA. She is also an active member of the Educators Network for Social Justice, a teacher activist group, and serves on the Executive Board of her local trade union, the Milwaukee Teacher Education Association. **MATT CHRISTISON** is a high school principal, sessional instructor in graduate studies at the University of Calgary, Alberta, Canada, and a lifelong questioner of the status quo. He earned a Doctorate of Education in 1996 from the University of Calgary, undertaking an analysis of gender performance differences on standardized testing.

Schneider, Stephanie and Matt Christison. "Are Exams Bad for Children?" *New Internationalist.* 464 (July/August, 2013): 30–32.

Article   Prepared by: Claire N. Rubman, *Suffolk County Community College*

Ritalin Gone Wrong

L. ALAN SROUFE

Learning Outcomes

After reading this article, you will be able to:

- Describe the initial success for children with attention deficits.

- Explain how stimulants can calm a child down in relation to ADD and medication.

- Explain the term *inborn defects* in relation to neurotransmitters and other brain anomalies.

Three million children in this country take drugs for problems in focusing. Toward the end of last year, many of their parents were deeply alarmed because there was a shortage of drugs like Ritalin and Adderall that they considered absolutely essential to their children's functioning.

But are these drugs really helping children? Should we really keep expanding the number of prescriptions filled?

In 30 years, there has been a 20-fold increase in the consumption of drugs for attention-deficit disorder.

As a psychologist who has been studying the development of troubled children for more than 40 years, I believe we should be asking why we rely so heavily on these drugs.

Attention-deficit drugs increase concentration in the short term, which is why they work so well for college students cramming for exams. But when given to children over long periods of time, they neither improve school achievement nor reduce behavior problems. The drugs can also have serious side effects, including stunting growth.

Sadly, few physicians and parents seem to be aware of what we have been learning about the lack of effectiveness of these drugs.

What gets publicized are short-term results and studies on brain differences among children. Indeed, there are a number of incontrovertible facts that seem at first glance to support medication. It is because of this partial foundation in reality that the problem with the current approach to treating children has been so difficult to see.

Back in the 1960s I, like most psychologists, believed that children with difficulty concentrating were suffering from a brain problem of genetic or otherwise inborn origin. Just as Type I diabetics need insulin to correct problems with their inborn biochemistry, these children were believed to require attention-deficit drugs to correct theirs. It turns out, however, that there is little to no evidence to support this theory.

In 1973, I reviewed the literature on drug treatment of children for *The New England Journal of Medicine.* Dozens of well-controlled studies showed that these drugs immediately improved children's performance on repetitive tasks requiring concentration and diligence. I had conducted one of these studies myself. Teachers and parents also reported improved behavior in almost every short-term study. This spurred an increase in drug treatment and led many to conclude that the "brain deficit" hypothesis had been confirmed.

But questions continued to be raised, especially concerning the drugs' mechanism of action and the durability of effects. Ritalin and Adderall, a combination of dextroamphetamine and amphetamine, are stimulants. So why do they appear to calm children down? Some experts argued that because the brains of children with attention problems were different, the drugs had a mysterious paradoxical effect on them.

However, there really was no paradox. Versions of these drugs had been given to World War II radar operators to help them stay awake and focus on boring, repetitive tasks. And when we reviewed the literature on attention-deficit drugs again in 1990 we found that all children, whether they had attention problems or not, responded to stimulant drugs the same way. Moreover, while the drugs helped children settle down in class, they actually increased activity in the playground. Stimulants generally have the same effects for all children and adults. They enhance the ability to concentrate, especially on tasks that are not inherently interesting or when one is fatigued or bored, but they don't improve broader learning abilities.

And just as in the many dieters who have used and abandoned similar drugs to lose weight, the effects of stimulants on children with attention problems fade after prolonged use. Some experts have argued that children with A.D.D. wouldn't develop such tolerance because their brains were somehow different. But in fact, the loss of appetite and sleeplessness in children first prescribed attention-deficit drugs do fade, and, as we now know, so do the effects on behavior. They apparently develop a tolerance to the drug, and thus its efficacy disappears. Many parents who take their children off the drugs find that behavior worsens, which most likely confirms their belief that the drugs work. But the behavior worsens because the children's bodies have become adapted to the drug. Adults may have similar reactions if they suddenly cut back on coffee, or stop smoking.

To date, no study has found any long-term benefit of attention-deficit medication on academic performance, peer relationships, or behavior problems, the very things we would most want to improve. Until recently, most studies of these drugs had not been properly randomized, and some of them had other methodological flaws.

But in 2009, findings were published from a well-controlled study that had been going on for more than a decade, and the results were very clear. The study randomly assigned almost 600 children with attention problems to four treatment conditions. Some received medication alone, some cognitive-behavior therapy alone, some medication plus therapy, and some were in a community-care control group that received no systematic treatment. At first this study suggested that medication, or medication plus therapy, produced the best results. However, after 3 years, these effects had faded, and by 8 years there was no evidence that medication produced any academic or behavioral benefits.

Indeed, all of the treatment successes faded over time, although the study is continuing. Clearly, these children need a broader base of support than was offered in this medication study, support that begins earlier and lasts longer.

Nevertheless, findings in neuroscience are being used to prop up the argument for drugs to treat the hypothesized "inborn defect." These studies show that children who receive an A.D.D. diagnosis have different patterns of neurotransmitters in their brains and other anomalies. While the technological sophistication of these studies may impress parents and nonprofessionals, they can be misleading. Of course the brains of children with behavior problems will show anomalies on brain scans. It could not be otherwise. Behavior and the brain are intertwined. Depression also waxes and wanes in many people, and as it does so, parallel changes in brain functioning occur, regardless of medication.

Many of the brain studies of children with A.D.D. involve examining participants while they are engaged in an attention task. If these children are not paying attention because of lack of motivation or an underdeveloped capacity to regulate their behavior, their brain scans are certain to be anomalous.

However brain functioning is measured, these studies tell us nothing about whether the observed anomalies were present at birth or whether they resulted from trauma, chronic stress, or other early-childhood experiences. One of the most profound findings in behavioral neuroscience in recent years has been the clear evidence that the developing brain is shaped by experience.

It is certainly true that large numbers of children have problems with attention, self-regulation, and behavior. But are these problems because of some aspect present at birth? Or are they caused by experiences in early childhood? These questions can be answered only by studying children and their surroundings from before birth through childhood and adolescence, as my colleagues at the University of Minnesota and I have been doing for decades.

Since 1975, we have followed 200 children who were born into poverty and were therefore more vulnerable to behavior problems. We enrolled their mothers during pregnancy, and over the course of their lives, we studied their relationships with their caregivers, teachers, and peers. We followed their progress through school and their experiences in early adulthood. At regular intervals we measured their health, behavior, performance on intelligence tests, and other characteristics.

By late adolescence, 50 percent of our sample qualified for some psychiatric diagnosis. Almost half displayed behavior problems at school on at least one occasion, and 24 percent dropped out by 12th grade; 14 percent met criteria for A.D.D. in either first or sixth grade.

Other large-scale epidemiological studies confirm such trends in the general population of disadvantaged children. Among all children, including all socioeconomic groups, the incidence of A.D.D. is estimated at 8 percent. What we found was that the environment of the child predicted development of A.D.D. problems. In stark contrast, measures of neurological anomalies at birth, I.Q. and infant temperament—including infant activity level—did not predict A.D.D.

Plenty of affluent children are also diagnosed with A.D.D. Behavior problems in children have many possible sources. Among them are family stresses like domestic violence, lack of social support from friends or relatives, chaotic living situations, including frequent moves, and, especially, patterns of parental intrusiveness that involve stimulation for which the baby is not prepared. For example, a 6-month-old baby is playing, and the parent picks it up quickly from behind and plunges it in the bath. Or a 3-year-old is becoming frustrated in solving a problem, and a parent taunts or ridicules. Such practices excessively stimulate and also compromise the child's developing capacity for self-regulation.

Putting children on drugs does nothing to change the conditions that derail their development in the first place. Yet those conditions are receiving scant attention. Policy makers are so convinced that children with attention deficits have an organic disease that they have all but called off the search for a comprehensive understanding of the condition. The National Institute of Mental Health finances research aimed largely at physiological and brain components of A.D.D. While there is some research on other treatment approaches, very little is studied regarding the role of experience. Scientists, aware of this orientation, tend to submit only grants aimed at elucidating the biochemistry.

Thus, only one question is asked: are there aspects of brain functioning associated with childhood attention problems? The answer is always yes. Overlooked is the very real possibility that both the brain anomalies and the A.D.D. result from experience.

Our present course poses numerous risks. First, there will never be a single solution for all children with learning and behavior problems. While some smaller number may benefit from short-term drug treatment, large-scale, long-term treatment for millions of children is not the answer.

Second, the large-scale medication of children feeds into a societal view that all of life's problems can be solved with a pill and gives millions of children the impression that there is something inherently defective in them.

Finally, the illusion that children's behavior problems can be cured with drugs prevents us as a society from seeking the more complex solutions that will be necessary. Drugs get everyone—politicians, scientists, teachers, and parents—off the hook. Everyone except the children, that is.

If drugs, which studies show work for 4 to 8 weeks, are not the answer, what is? Many of these children have anxiety or depression; others are showing family stresses. We need to treat them as individuals.

As for shortages, they will continue to wax and wane. Because these drugs are habit forming, Congress decides how much can be produced. The number approved doesn't keep pace with the tidal wave of prescriptions. By the end of this year, there will in all likelihood be another shortage, as we continue to rely on drugs that are not doing what so many well-meaning parents, therapists, and teachers believe they are doing.

Critical Thinking

1. Are parents aware of the research on the long- and short-term effects of attention-deficit medication on their children?

2. Are the side effect of medication for attention deficits, such as sleeplessness and a loss of appetite, worth the benefits of the medication for children?

3. Discuss the relationship between socioeconomic status and behavior problems.

Create Central

www.mhhe.com/createcentral

Internet References

ADD/ADHD Medications-Help Guide
  http://www.helpguide.org/mental/adhd_medications.htm

Behavioral Treatments for Kids With ADHD-Helping kids get organized and control problem behaviors
  http://www.childmind.org/en/posts/articles/2014-1-21-behavioral-treatment-kids-adhd

How Do ADHD Medications Work?
  http://www.sciencedaily.com/releases/2013/10/131016100222.htm

NIMH · Attention Deficit Hyperactivity Disorder
  http://www.nimh.nih.gov/health/publications/attention-deficit-hyperactivity-disorder/index.shtml

L. ALAN SROUFE is a professor emeritus of psychology at the University of Minnesota's Institute of Child Development.

Sroufe, Alan L. "Ritalin Gone Wrong." *The New York Times.* (January, 28, 2012).

Article

Prepared by: Claire N. Rubman,
Suffolk County Community College, Selden, NY

Giving ADHD a Rest: with Diagnosis Rates Exploding Wildly, Is the Disorder a Mental Health Crisis—or a Cultural One?

KATE LUNAU

Learning Outcomes

After reading this article, you will be able to:

- Define and give examples of symptoms of ADHD as defined by the DSM.

- Explain the "accountability rates" in North Carolina schools and the authors' assumed relationship with rates of ADHD diagnosis.

- Explain the term "brain doping."

Any visitor to North Carolina and California will know that the two states have their differences. The former is a typically "red state"; California is staunchly "blue." Each has certain geographic, ethnic and cultural peculiarities, different demographic makeup, family income levels, and more. Yet perhaps the most surprising divide, one many wouldn't expect, is that North Carolina appears to be a hotbed for attention deficit hyperactivity disorder, or ADHD—especially when compared to California. A child who lived in North Carolina instead of California in 2007, according to U.S. academics Stephen Hinshaw and Richard Scheffler, was 2½ times more likely to be diagnosed.

In their forthcoming book *The ADHD Explosion*, Hinshaw and Scheffler—a psychologist and health economist, respectively, at the University of California at Berkeley—examine the causes behind the startling and rapid rise in diagnosis rates

of ADHD, a neurobehavioural disorder that has somehow become epidemic. In the U.S., more than one in ten kids has been diagnosed; more than 3.5 million are taking drugs to curb symptoms, from lack of focus to hyperactivity. While ADHD typically hits middle-class boys the hardest, rates among other groups are steadily rising, including girls, adults, and minorities. Kids are being tested and diagnosed as young as preschool. In North Carolina, as many as 30 percent of teenage boys are diagnosed. Scheffler says, "It's getting scary."

According to psychologist Enrico Gnaulati, who is based in Pasadena, California, ADHD is now "as prevalent as the common cold." Various factors seem to be driving up the numbers, factors that extend from home to school to the doctor's office and beyond. "So many kids have trouble these days," says longtime ADHD researcher L. Alan Sroufe, professor emeritus at the University of Wisconsin at Madison. "I doubt it's a change in our genetic pool. Something else is going on."

A closer look at the case of North Carolina and California may be instructive. According to Hinshaw and Scheffler, North Carolinian kids between the ages of four and seventeen had an ADHD diagnosis rate of 16 percent in 2007. In California, it was just over 6 percent. Kids with a diagnosis in North Carolina also faced a 50 percent higher probability they'd get medication. After exhaustively exploring demographics, health care policies, cultural values, and other possible factors, they landed on school policy as what Scheffler calls "the closest thing to a silver bullet."

Over the past few decades, incentives have been introduced for U.S. schools to turn out better graduation rates and test scores—and they've been pushed to compete for funding. North Carolina was one of the first states with school accountability laws, disciplining schools for missing targets, and rewarding them for exceeding them. "Such laws provide a real incentive to have children diagnosed and treated," Hinshaw and Scheffler write: Kids in special education classes ideally get the help they need to improve their test scores and (in some areas) aren't counted in the district's test score average.

The rate of ADHD diagnosis varies between countries; as Hinshaw and Scheffler have shown, it even varies significantly within countries. This raises an important question: Is the ADHD epidemic really a mental health crisis, or a cultural and societal one?

ADHD is a "chronic and debilitating mental disorder," Gnaulati says, one that can last a lifetime. It's believed to affect between 5 and 10 percent of the population, and boys still seem especially prone. (Nearly one in five high school boys have ADHD, compared to 1 in 11 girls, according to the U.S. Centers for Disease Control and Prevention.) Kids with ADHD can have a hard time making and keeping friends. In one study of boys at summer camp, Hinshaw found that after just a few hours, those with an ADHD diagnosis were far more likely to be rejected than those without one. The disorder can persist into adulthood, raising the risk of low self-esteem, divorce, unemployment, and driving accidents; even getting arrested and going to jail, according to a report from the Centre for ADHD Awareness, Canada.

In fact, the brains of people with ADHD are different. They're short on receptors for the neurotransmitter dopamine, and their brain volume looks to be slightly smaller. But no medical test or brain scan can yet give a definitive diagnosis. The gold standard comes from the *Diagnostic and Statistical Manual of Mental Disorders*, or *DSM*, from the American Psychiatric Association. The latest version of this "bible of psychiatry," released in May, lists nine symptoms of inattention (making careless mistakes on homework; distractibility; trouble staying organized), and nine of hyperactivity or impulsivity (interrupting others; climbing when it's inappropriate; and excessive talking, to give some examples). They'll sound familiar to anyone who's spent time with kids. "Every child is to some extent impulsive, distractible, disorganized, and has trouble following directions," says Gnaulati, author of *Back to Normal*, an investigation of why what he calls "ordinary childhood behaviour" is often mistaken for ADHD.

The *DSM* specifies that a child should be showing many symptoms consistently, in two or more settings (at home and at school, for example), a better indication that he isn't just acting out because of a bad teacher, or an annoying sibling. "Studies show that if you stick to the two-informant requirement, the number of cases falls by 40 percent," says Gnaulati. Surprisingly often, the diagnoses seem to be hastily given, and drugs dispensed.

It was once thought that stimulants affected people with ADHD differently—calming them down, revving up everyone else—but we now know that's not the case. Virtually everybody seems to react the same in the short term, Sroufe says. "They're attention-enhancers. We've known that since the Second World War," when they were given to radar operators to stay awake and focused. Those with true ADHD show bigger gains, partly because their brains may be "underaroused" to begin with, write Hinshaw and Scheffler. (About two-thirds of U.S. kids with a diagnosis get medication; in Canada, it's about 50 percent.) Stimulants have side effects, including suppressing appetite, speeding up the heart rate, and raising blood pressure. Kids who take them for a long time might end up an inch or so shorter, according to Hinshaw and Scheffler's book, because dopamine activity interferes with growth hormone. And those who don't need them will eventually develop a tolerance, needing a greater and greater quantity to get the effect they're after.

"Brain doping" is by now a well-known phenomenon among college and university students across North America. Many students don't see stimulant use as cheating: One 2012 study found that male college students believe it's far more unethical for an athlete to use steroids than for a student to abuse prescription stimulants to ace a test. "Some red-hot parents want to get their kid into Harvard, Berkeley or Princeton," Scheffler says. "They're going to need a perfect score, so they're going to push." With an ADHD diagnosis, students can seek special accommodations at school, like more time on tests including the SAT, a standardized college entrance exam. With parents, students, and even school boards recognizing the potential benefits that come with diagnosis, ADHD is occurring with increasing frequency among groups other than the white middle class, where rates have typically been highest: According to Hinshaw and Scheffler, African American youth are now just as likely, if not more, to be diagnosed and medicated.

Drug advertisements could also be driving rates of diagnosis upward. Hinshaw and Scheffler describe one ad from Johnson & Johnson, maker of the stimulant Concerta, which shows a happy mother and a son who's getting "better test scores at school" and doing "more chores at home," the text reads. "The message is clear: the right pill breeds family harmony," they write. Sometimes, another underlying health problem will be mistakenly diagnosed as ADHD. In his new book, *ADHD Does Not Exist*, Richard Saul documents 25 conditions that can look like ADHD; most common are vision and hearing issues. "Until you get glasses, it's very hard to understand what [the teacher] is speaking about if you can't see the board," he says.

"Same with hearing." Conditions ranging from bipolar disorder to Tourette's syndrome can also be mistaken for ADHD, Saul writes. Despite the strongly worded title of his book, he believes that 20 percent of those diagnosed are "neurochemical distractible impulsive" and have what we'd term ADHD. The rest are being misdiagnosed, and as a result, he says, "the right treatment is being delayed."

Sleep deprivation is another big cause of misdiagnosis. "It's paradoxical, but especially for kids, it does create hyperactivity and impulsivity," says Vatsal Thakkar of New York University's Langone Medical Center. Given mounting academic pressures, and the screens that populate virtually every room, many kids simply aren't getting enough downtime. A child's relative immaturity can factor in, too. In 2012, a study in the *Canadian Medical Association Journal* found that the youngest kids in a classroom were more likely to have an ADHD diagnosis, and to be prescribed medication. Those born in December are nearly a full year younger than some of their peers, a big difference, especially in kindergarten. (In the U.S., half of all kids with ADHD are diagnosed before age six.)

Gnaulati, who has a son, worries the deck's been stacked against boys, who are more prone to blurt out an answer, run around the classroom, or otherwise act out. "During the kindergarten years, boys are at least a year behind girls in basic self-regulation," he says. Gnaulati notes that school teachers, pediatricians, and school psychologists are all more likely be female—which he argues could be a contributing factor. "In a sense," he writes, "girl behaviour has become the standard by which we judge all kids."

In Canada, we don't track ADHD diagnosis rates as closely as in the U.S. But the rate of diagnosis does look to be picking up here, and elsewhere, too. A study by Hinshaw and Scheffler compared the use of ADHD drugs to countries' per capita gross domestic product. "Richer countries spend more [on ADHD medications]," Scheffler says. "But some countries still spend more than their income would predict." They found that Canada, the U.S., and Australia all had a greater use of these drugs than GDP suggests. A 2013 paper in the *British Journal of Medicine* notes that Australia saw a 73 percent increase in prescribing rates for ADHD medications between 2000 and 2011. The Netherlands had a similar spike—the prevalence of ADHD, and the rate at which ADHD drugs were prescribed to kids, doubled between 2003 and 2007.

Peter Conrad of Brandeis University, outside Boston, is studying how the *DSM* definition of ADHD (which we use in Canada) has been exported around the globe, leading to more kids diagnosed and treated. "Until the late '90s, most diagnosis in Europe was done under the World Health Organization's *International Classification of Diseases*," which is much more strict, he notes. (The *ICD*, for example, required symptoms of inattention, impulsivity, and hyperactivity, while an older version of the *DSM* required only two.)

European countries began to adopt the *DSM* definition, a response to the fact that so much research on ADHD comes out of the U.S.—and the *DSM* began to be seen as the standard. "France and Italy still have low rates," says Conrad, "partly because they don't use the *DSM*." A 2013 study from the University of Exeter found that U.K. kids were much less likely than those in the U.S. to be diagnosed with ADHD, which may be due to tougher criteria, or to parents' resistance to medicating their kids. Even so, other countries are catching up. According to Hinshaw and Scheffler, the use of ADHD medication is rising over five times faster around the world than in the U.S.

Many of the same pressures that motivate diagnosis in the U.S. are at play in Canada, although in different ways. Given the tight job market and increasing academic demands, students are under more pressure to succeed than ever. And while our school test results aren't tied to funding like in the U.S., "high-stakes testing" is increasingly important, says Elizabeth Dhuey, a University of Toronto economist who studies education.

For one thing, it's a point of pride for schools. Results from Ontario's EQAO standardized test are reported in the media and used to rank and compare institutions. ("EQAO: How did your school fare in Ontario's standardized tests?" reads one 2012 *Toronto Star* headline.) What constitutes an "exceptionality" and triggers special services also varies between provinces. In Newfoundland, ADHD has been an "exceptionality" for the past two decades; in Ontario, it isn't considered a special category, but ADHD students can access special education and other extra help on a case-by-case basis. And in B.C., school districts can get supplemental funding for students with ADHD, according to the ministry of education.

These pressures aren't abating—if anything, many are getting stronger—and so, it seems likely we haven't yet reached peak ADHD. Scheffler and Hinshaw raise the possibility that, within the decade, ADHD rates in the U.S. might reach 15 percent or higher; and that as many as four-fifths of those diagnosed could have a prescription.

The hope lies in finding better scientific markers—a definitive test that could confirm true cases of ADHD, and those who will benefit most from treatment, including medication. Otherwise, we're facing the prospect of a generation of kids living with a serious mental health diagnosis, and quite possibly taking powerful drugs long term into adulthood, with all the potential side effects they entail. Whatever is contributing to ADHD's startling rise, it's clear that this isn't a contagious disease kids are swapping on the playground. In many cases, we're giving it to them.

Critical Thinking

1. Explain the relationship between academic pressure and rates of ADHD diagnosis.
2. Why have countries such as Australia and the Netherlands seen a spike in their rates of ADHD diagnosis while other countries such as the UK or are much less likely to see such diagnoses?

Internet References

7 Facts You Need To Know About ADHD
    http://www.adhdawarenessmonth.org/adhd-facts

ADHD Not a Real Disease, Says Leading Neuroscientist
    http://themindunleashed.org/2014/10/adhd-real-disease-says-leading-neuroscientist.html

Attention-Deficit/Hyperactivity Disorder (ADHD) Symptoms and Diagnosis
    http://www.cdc.gov/ncbddd/adhd/diagnosis.html

DSM-5TM - ADHD Institute
    http://www.adhd-institute.com/assessment-diagnosis/diagnosis/dsm-5tm

Kate Lunau, "Giving ADHD a Rest: With Diagnosis Rates Exploding Wildly, Is the Disorder a Mental Health Crisis-or a Cultural One?" from *Maclean's* 127.8 (March 3, 2014).

Unit 4

Prepared by: Claire N. Rubman,
Suffolk County Community College, Selden, NY

UNIT

Development during Childhood: Family and Culture

In our fast paced, high pressure, technologically oriented society, parents shoulder an enormous burden. They are, after all, legally and morally responsible for their children's behavior. Parents have the unenviable task of protecting their children from the perils of bullying, underage drinking, inappropriate posts on Twitter, Facebook Instagram or other social media and the general dangers of children roaming on an unsupervised "information highway." As their children develop into adolescents, parents also have to contend with the changes associated with puberty and the neurological changes that define adolescent thought and behavior.

Some parents attempt to circumvent some of the social and emotional pitfalls of childhood and early adolescence by homeschooling their children. In her article, "Do-it-(All)–Yourself Parents," Perlstein discusses the 300,000 children and adolescents in the United States who have opted out of public education in favor of homeschooling as an educational option. She reviews benefits of this educational paradigm including less bullying, more individualized instruction and more family time. She also discusses the positive response to homeschooled students from colleges and universities.

The educational pressures that children face from the implementation of the "Common Core" standards and the push to send more children to prestigious colleges resonate in D'Agostino's article. Children's educational failures should not, he suggests, be medicated away. Indeed, he hypothesized that the very essence of childhood should not be seen as a medical condition. D'Agostino claims that we are "drugging" our children. In his article, "The Drugging of the American Boy," he claims that we, as a society are "pathologizing boyhood." D'Agostino suggests that the increased pressure on schools from government programs such as the "Race to the Top" have contributed to the increased rates of diagnosis with extra time or excluded exam scores as an incentive.

These stifled children need a release from the academic pressures of our current school culture. In her article, "Social Media: Students Behaving Badly," Meg Hazel explores a child's freedom of expression on the Internet. She addresses the role of the school and of the Supreme Court in censuring or punishing children for expressing themselves using social media.

Some of our children may act out using social media as a tool while others turn to the more tangible world to vent their frustrations or experience a cathartic release from social pressures. Some of these children resort to bullying while others are the victims of such hateful behaviors. While bullying is a pervasive problem in childhood, we need to refocus our attention on the root causes and our approach to the bully and the victim. According to the research, around 25% of our children have been bullied with many of the incidences never being reported. Susan Porter describes why our current approach to bullying is inadequate in the article "Why Our Approach to Bullying Is Bad for Kids." The prefrontal cortex of the brain is targeted as poorly developed. This means that impulse control, empathy, and judgment can be limited or impaired in children as they progress towards adolescence. The preadolescent brain also turns inward to focus on the self which creates egocentric individuals who have a tendency towards oversensitivity as they struggle with their developing sense of self. These developmental constraints, coupled with the zero tolerance policy in place in public schools can, according to Porter, impact a child's delicate self-esteem and developing resilience. Until the brain's executive function matures, how should we address bullying behaviors in our preadolescent population?

Focusing again on the developing teenage brain, Cary discusses the failure of current government policies to address the problems associated with underage drinking in her article "Time to Lower the Drinking Age." She hypothesizes that lowering the drinking age would make teens less likely to binge drink or turn to alternatives to alcohol such as illegal prescription use, especially on college campuses.

Article   Prepared by: Claire N. Rubman, *Suffolk County Community College*

Do-It-(All)-Yourself Parents

They raise chickens. They grow vegetables. They knit. Now a new generation of urban parents is even teaching their own kids.

LINDA PERLSTEIN

Learning Outcomes

After reading this article, you will be able to:

- Contrast reasons for homeschooling today with those in the past.
- Summarize what is meant by "differentiated instruction."

I n the beginning, your kids need you—a lot. They're attached to your hip, all the time. It might be a month. It might be five years. Then suddenly you are expected to send them off to school for seven hours a day, where they'll have to cope with life in ways they never had to before. You no longer control what they learn, or how, or with whom.

Unless you decide, like an emerging population of parents in cities across the country, to forgo that age-old rite of passage entirely.

When Tera and Eric Schreiber's oldest child was about to start kindergarten, the couple toured the high-achieving public elementary school a block away from their home in an affluent Seattle neighborhood near the University of Washington. It was "a great neighborhood school," Tera says. They also applied to a private school, and Daisy was accepted. But in the end they chose a third path: no school at all.

Eric, 38, is a manager at Microsoft. Tera, 39, had already traded a career as a lawyer for one as a nonprofit executive, which allowed her more time with her kids. But "more" turned into "all" when she decided that instead of working, she would homeschool her daughters: Daisy, now 9; Ginger, 7; and Violet, 4.

We think of homeschoolers as evangelicals or off-the-gridders who spend a lot of time at kitchen tables in the countryside. And it's true that most homeschooling parents do so for moral or religious reasons. But education observers believe

that is changing. You only have to go to a downtown Starbucks or art museum in the middle of a weekday to see that a once-unconventional choice "has become newly fashionable," says Mitchell Stevens, a Stanford professor who wrote *Kingdom of Children*, a history of homeschooling. There are an estimated 300,000 homeschooled children in America's cities, many of them children of secular, highly educated professionals who always figured they'd send their kids to school—until they came to think, *Hey, maybe we could do better.*

When Laurie Block Spigel, a homeschooling consultant, pulled her kids out of school in New York in the mid-1990s, "I had some of my closest friends and relatives telling me I was ruining my children's lives." Now, she says, "the parents that I meet aren't afraid to talk about it. They're doing this proudly."

Many of these parents feel that city schools—or any schools—don't provide the kind of education they want for their kids. Just as much, though, their choice to homeschool is a more extreme example of a larger modern parenting ethos: that children are individuals, each deserving a uniquely curated upbringing. That peer influence can be noxious. (Bullying is no longer seen as a harmless rite of passage.) That DIY—be it gardening, knitting, or raising chickens—is something educated urbanites should embrace. That we might create a sense of security in our kids by practicing "attachment parenting," an increasingly popular approach that involves round-the-clock physical contact with children and immediate responses to all their cues.

Even many attachment adherents, though, may have trouble envisioning spending almost all their time with their kids—for 18 years! For Tera Schreiber, it was a natural transition. When you have kept your kids so close, literally—she breast-fed her youngest till Violet was 4—it can be a shock to send them away.

Tera's kids didn't particularly enjoy day care or preschool. The Schreibers wanted a "gentler system" for Daisy; she was a perfectionist who they thought might worry too much about measuring up. They knew homeschooling families in their neighborhood and envied their easygoing pace and flexibility—late bedtimes, vacations when everyone else is at school or work. Above all, they wanted to preserve, for as long as possible, a certain approach to family.

Several homeschooling moms would first tell me, "I know this sounds selfish," and then say they feared that if their kids were in school, they'd just get the "exhausted leftovers" at the end of the day. Says Rebecca Wald, a Baltimore homeschooler, "Once we had a child and I realized how fun it was to see her discover stuff about the world, I thought, why would I want to let a teacher have all that fun?"

It's 12:30 P.M. on a Thursday, and Tera and her daughters have arrived home from a rehearsal of a homeschoolers' production of *Alice in Wonderland*. Their large green Craftsman is typical Seattle. There are kayaks in the garage, squash in the slow cooker, and the usual paraphernalia of girlhood: board games, dolls, craft kits. Next to the kitchen phone is a printout of the day's responsibilities. Daisy and Ginger spend about two hours daily in formal lessons, including English and math; today they've also got history, piano, and sewing.

Laws, and home-crafted curricula, vary widely. Homeschoolers in Philadelphia, for instance, must submit a plan of study and test scores, while parents in Detroit need not even let officials know they're homeschooling. Some families seek out a more classical curriculum, others a more unconventional one, and "unschoolers" eschew formal academics altogether. There are parents who take on every bit of teaching themselves, and those who outsource subjects to other parents, tutors, or online providers. Advances in digital learning have facilitated homeschooling—you can take an AP math class from a tutor in Israel—and there's a booming market in curriculum materials, the most scripted of which enable parents to teach subjects they haven't studied before.

So far, Tera says, these books have made the teaching itself easy—insofar as anything is easy about mothering three kids nonstop. The girls have started their lessons at the kitchen table, but there are also sandwiches to be assembled, cats who want treats, and girls who want drinks or ChapStick or napkins or, in the youngest's case, attention.

"Violet, Ginger is getting a lesson, so you have to be quiet," Tera says from across the open kitchen, while heating tea and coaching Ginger on sounding out Y words. "The first word: is it two syllables? What does Y say at the beginning of a word?"

"Yuh."

"At the end?"

"Eee? Yucky."

"Yucky is correct."

Tera sits down to eat a bowl of salmon salad while helping Ginger with her reading workbook. Daisy is reading a fantasy book about wild cats. Violet is playing with a big clock.

"Sam has a c-ane and a c-ape," Ginger says. "Sam has a c-ap and a c-an."

"If you use your finger, it will work better," Tera says.

Teaching Daisy to read was a breeze. With Ginger it's been more complicated, and Tera has had to research different approaches. She gives her lots of workbook activities, because Ginger retains information better when she's writing and not just listening. Since hearing about a neurological link between crawling and reading, Tera also has Ginger circle the house on hands and knees 10 times daily.

A school, Tera says, might not have teased out precisely how Ginger learns best. This is something I heard often from urban homeschoolers: the desire to craft an education just right for each child. They worry that formal schooling might dim their children's love of learning (yet there is a flip side: a reduced likelihood of being inspired along the way by the occasional magical teacher, full of passion and skill). They want their children to explore the subjects that interest them, as deeply as they care to go. For Daisy and Ginger, that has meant detours into herbalism, cat shows, musical theater, and deer.

Many parents are happy to sidestep environments that might be too intense, loading kids up with homework, making them feel an undue burden to perform. "The pressure from the reform movement today, from kindergarten on, has been all about 'Let's push, push, push for academic achievement,'" says Michael Petrilli, executive vice president of the Thomas B. Fordham Institute, an education think tank, and the author of a forthcoming book about urban parents' schooling decisions. Some urban homeschooled kids, particularly those with special needs, were previously enrolled in school but not served well there.

In truth, some conventional schools are making strides toward diagnosing and remedying each child's weaknesses. "Differentiated instruction"—the idea that teachers simultaneously address students' individual needs—is a catchphrase these days in public schools. And many elementary classrooms are no longer filled by rows of desks with children working in lockstep. But it is also true that you can never tailor instruction more acutely than when the student-teacher ratio is 1–1.

The Schreiber girls spend most of their time out and about, typically at activities arranged for homeschoolers. There are Girl Scouts and ceramics and book club and enrichment classes and park outings arranged by the Seattle Homeschool Group, a secular organization whose membership has grown from 30 families to 300 over the last decade. In a way, urban homeschooling can feel like an intensified version of the extracurricular madness that is the hallmark of any contemporary middle-class family, or it can feel like one big, awesome field trip.

Institutions throughout the country have discovered a reliable weekday customer in urban homeschoolers. "Everywhere you turn there's a co-op or a class or a special exhibit," says Brian Ray, founder of the National Home Education Research Institute in Oregon. Three years ago, the Museum of Science and Industry in Chicago began to court homeschoolers with free admission, their own newsletters, and courses designed specifically for them. Participation has doubled each year. "The more we offer, the more we sell out," says Andrea Ingram, vice president of education and guest services.

A mini-industry of homeschool consultants has cropped up, especially in New York City, whose homeschooling population has grown 36 percent in eight years, according to the school district. (While states usually require homeschoolers to register, many parents choose not to, so official estimates skew low.) In Seattle, even the public-school system runs a center that offers classes just to homeschoolers.

"My kids actually have to tell me to stop," says Erin McKinney Souster, a mother of three in Minneapolis, whose kids have learned to find an academic lesson in something as mundane as the construction of a roller-rink floor. "Everything is always sounding so cool and so fun."

Still, you can't help but wonder whether there's a cost to all this family togetherness. There are the moms, of course, who for two decades have their lives completely absorbed by their children's. But the mothers I got to know seem quite content with that, and clearly seem to be having fun getting together with each other during their kids' activities.

And the kids? There's concern that having parents at one's side throughout childhood can do more harm than good. Psychologist Wendy Mogel, the author of the bestselling book *The Blessing of a Skinned Knee*, admires the way homeschoolers manage to "give their children a childhood" in an ultracompetitive world. Yet she wonders how kids who spend so much time within a deliberately crafted community will learn to work with people from backgrounds nothing like theirs. She worries, too, about eventual teenage rebellion in families that are so enmeshed.

Typical urban homeschooled kids do tend to find the space they need by the time they reach those teenage years, participating independently in a wealth of activities. That's just as well for their parents, who by that time can often use a breather. And it has made them more appealing to colleges, which have grown more welcoming as they find that homeschoolers do fine academically. In some ways these students may arrive at college more prepared, as they've had practice charting their own intellectual directions, though parents say they sometimes bristle at having to suffer through courses and professors they don't like.

Tera figures that her daughters are out in the world enough to interact with all sorts of people. She feels certain they will be able to be good citizens precisely because of her and Eric's "forever style of parenting," as she calls it, not in spite of it. It's hard for Tera to get too worried when she's just spent the weekend, as the Schreibers often do, hanging out on a trip with homeschooled kids of all ages, including confident, competent teenagers who were happy playing cards with their parents all evening, with no electronics in sight.

Milo, my 3-year-old, never wants to go to preschool. So the more I hung out with homeschoolers, the more I found myself picking him up from school early, to squeeze in some of the fun these families were having. I began to think, why not homeschool? Really, there's something of the homeschooler in all of us: we stuff our kids with knowledge, we interact with them more than our parents did with us. I am resourceful enough to make pickles and playdough; why couldn't I create an interdisciplinary curriculum around Milo's obsession with London Bridge? I calculated what we'd have to give up if I cut back on work (though some homeschooling moms work full time or at least occasionally—like Tera, who writes parenting articles).

But my husband and I are loyal to what we call "detachment parenting": we figure we are doing a good job if Milo is just as confident and comfortable without us as he is with us. Family for us is more a condition—a joyous one, for sure—than a project, one of several throughlines of our lives.

For many of the homeschoolers I met, family is more: the very focus of their lives. And they wouldn't want it any other way. One comfort Tera and Eric Schreiber held on to when they started homeschooling was that if it wasn't working out, they could enroll the girls in school, literally the next day. That developed into an annual reassessment. By now their rhythms are deeply their own; they are embedded in a community they love. And at the college up the road there are plenty of calculus tutors, should they need them one day.

Critical Thinking

1. Why is homeschooling "newly fashionable"?
2. Identify some of the pros of homeschooling.
3. Identify some of the cons of homeschooling.
4. Defend the proposition that an educator should be able to address each student's individual needs.
5. Is there a happy medium between too much and not enough family togetherness? Should family togetherness increase or decrease as children age?

Create Central

www.mhhe.com/createcentral

Internet References

Homeschool Laws and Regulations
http://homeschooling.about.com/od/legal

How to Homeschool: Homeschooling Requirements and Information
www.motherearthnews.com/how-to-home-school.aspx

You Can Homeschool—Introduction
www.youcanhomeschool.org

LINDA PERLSTEIN, a freelance writer and editor based in Seattle, is the author of two books about schools and children, *Tested* and *Not Much Just Chillin'*.

Article

Prepared by: Claire N. Rubman,
Suffolk County Community College, Selden, NY

The Drugging of the American Boy

RYAN D'AGOSTINO

Learning Outcomes

After reading this article, you will be able to:

- Discuss the implications of 6.4 million children with an ADHD diagnosis.
- Explain what the author means when he says "we are pathologizing boyhood."
- Explain the effect of Methylphenidate on the brain.

By the time they reach high school, nearly 20 percent of all American boys will be diagnosed with ADHD. Millions of those boys will be prescribed a powerful stimulant to "normalize" them. A great many of those boys will suffer serious side effects from those drugs. The shocking truth is that many of those diagnoses are wrong, and that most of those boys are being drugged for no good reason—simply for being boys. It's time we recognize this as a crisis.

If you have a son, you have a one-in-seven chance that he has been diagnosed with ADHD. If you have a son who has been diagnosed, it's more than likely that he has been prescribed a stimulant—the most famous brand names are Ritalin and Adderall; newer ones include Vyvanse and Concerta—to deal with the symptoms of that psychiatric condition.

The Drug Enforcement Administration classifies stimulants as Schedule II drugs, defined as having a "high potential for abuse" and "with use potentially leading to severe psychological or physical dependence." (According to a University of Michigan study, Adderall is the most abused brand-name drug among high school seniors.) In addition to stimulants like Ritalin, Adderall, Vyvanse, and Concerta, Schedule II drugs include cocaine, methamphetamine, Demerol, and OxyContin.

According to manufacturers of ADHD stimulants, they are associated with sudden death in children who have heart problems, whether those heart problems have been previously detected or not. They can bring on a bipolar condition in a child who didn't exhibit any symptoms of such a disorder before taking stimulants. They are associated with "new or worse aggressive behavior or hostility." They can cause "new psychotic symptoms (such as hearing voices and believing things that are not true) or new manic symptoms." They commonly cause noticeable weight loss and trouble sleeping. In some children, some stimulants can cause the paranoid feeling that bugs are crawling on them. Facial tics. They can cause children's eyes to glaze over, their spirits to dampen. One study reported fears of being harmed by other children and thoughts of suicide.

Imagine you have a six-year-old son. A little boy for whom you are responsible. A little boy you would take a bullet for, a little boy in whom you search for glimpses of yourself, and hope every day that he will turn out just like you, only better. A little boy who would do anything to make you happy. Now imagine that little boy—your little boy—alone in his bed in the night, eyes wide with fear, afraid to move, a frightening and unfamiliar voice echoing in his head, afraid to call for you. Imagine him shivering because he hasn't eaten all day because he isn't hungry. His head is pounding. He doesn't know why any of this is happening.

Now imagine that he is suffering like this because of a mistake. Because a doctor examined him for twelve minutes, looked at a questionnaire on which you had checked some boxes, listened to your brief and vague report that he seemed to have trouble sitting still in kindergarten, made a diagnosis for a disorder the boy doesn't have, and wrote a prescription for a powerful drug he doesn't need.

If you have a son in America, there is an alarming probability that this has happened or will happen to you.

The Diagnosis

6.4 Million children between the ages of four and seventeen have been diagnosed with ADHD. By high school, nearly 20% of all boys will have been diagnosed with ADHD—a 37% increase since 2003.

On this everyone agrees: The numbers are big. The number of children who have been diagnosed with attention-deficit/hyperactivity disorder—overwhelmingly boys—in the United States has climbed at an astonishing rate over a relatively short period of time. The Centers for Disease Control first attempted to tally ADHD cases in 1997 and found that about 3 percent of American schoolchildren had received the diagnosis, a number that seemed roughly in line with past estimates. But after that year, the number of diagnosed cases began to increase by at least 3 percent every year. Then, between 2003 and 2007, cases increased at a rate of 5.5 percent each year. In 2013, the CDC released data revealing that 11 percent of American schoolchildren had been diagnosed with ADHD, which amounts to 6.4 million children between the ages of four and seventeen—a 16 percent increase since 2007 and a 42 percent increase since 2003. Boys are more than twice as likely to be diagnosed as girls—15.1 percent to 6.7 percent. By high school, even more boys are diagnosed—nearly one in five.

Almost 20 percent.

And overall, of the children in this country who are told they suffer from attention deficit/hyperactivity disorder, two-thirds are on prescription drugs.

And on this, too, everyone agrees: That among those millions of diagnoses, there are false ones. That there are high-energy kids-normal boys, most likely—who had the misfortune of seeing a doctor who had scant (if any) training in psychiatric disorders during his long-ago residency but had heard about all these new cases and determined that a hyper kid whose teacher said he has trouble sitting still in class must have ADHD. That among the 6.4 million are a significant percentage of boys who are swallowing pills every day for a disorder they don't have.

On this, too, everyone with standing in this fight seems to agree.

But on the subject of attention-deficit/hyperactivity disorder, that is where the agreement ends.

For example: Doctors, parents, and therapists give a lot of different explanations for the sharp rise. Increased awareness—that's a big one. *We know more now.* Other possibilities put forth: Too many video games. Too much refined sugar. Pharmaceutical companies pushing ADHD drugs. Lack of gym classes at schools. All of these factors are cited. And people have a lot of different ideas about what to do for the children who receive these diagnoses. Many believe that medicine should be the first treatment, either combined with behavioral therapy or not. Others feel that drugs should be a last resort after making every other alleviative effort you can find or think of, from hypnosis to herbal treatments to neurofeedback.

Given today's prevailing pharmaceutical culture, clinicians who believe that drugs should never be used to treat ADHD in children are very much in the minority. Marketing is powerful, and blockbuster drugs like Ritalin are big business. Business booms, market share grows when scripts are written, and countercultural doctors and therapists who advocate caution and who believe that diagnoses are made too easily—doctors and therapists who preach alternatives to drugs—are finding themselves the butt of jokes.

But more about them shortly.

The United States government first collected information on mental disorders in 1840, when the national census listed two generally accepted conditions: idiocy and insanity. A century later, psychiatrists knew more. They had options when making diagnoses, and by the 1940s difficult kids were classified as "hyperkinetic." Other terms would follow, like minimal brain dysfunction. In 1955, there came a pill doctors could prescribe for these children to temper their hyperactivity and make them behave more like "normal" children. It was a stimulant, so called because it heightened the brain's utilization of dopamine, which can improve attention and concentration. The active ingredient was a highly addictive compound called methylphenidate. The drug was called Ritalin.

By 1987, the American Psychiatric Association (APA) had settled on a more refined name for a disorder among children who exhibited the same set of symptoms, including trouble concentrating and impulsive behavior: attention-deficit/hyperactivity disorder. ADHD. At the time, in American schools, it was still considered unusual for a child to take Ritalin. It was, frankly, considered weird.

Today, it has simply become a default method for dealing with a "difficult" child.

"We are pathologizing boyhood," says Ned Hallowell, a psychiatrist who has been diagnosed with ADHD himself and has cowritten two books about it, *Driven to Distraction and Delivered from Distraction.* "God bless the women's movement—we needed it—but what's happened is, particularly in schools where most of the teachers are women, there's been a general girlification of elementary school, where any kind of disruptive behavior is sinful. What I call the 'moral diagnosis' gets made: *You're bad. Now go get a doctor and get on medication so you'll be good.* And that's a real perversion of what ought to happen. Most boys are naturally more restless than most girls, and I would say that's good. But schools want these little goody-goodies who sit still and do what they're told—these robots—and that's just not who boys are."

Especially when they're young. One of the most shocking studies of the rise in ADHD diagnoses was published in 2012 in the *Canadian Medical Association Journal.* It was called "Influence of Relative Age on Diagnosis and Treatment of Attention-Deficit/Hyperactivity Disorder in Children." Nearly one million children between the ages of six and twelve took part, making it the largest study of its kind ever. The researchers found that "boys who were born in December"—typically the youngest students in their class—"were 30 percent more likely to receive a diagnosis of ADHD than boys born in January," who were a full year older. And "boys were 41 percent more likely to be given a prescription for a medication to treat ADHD if they were born in December than if they were born in January." These findings suggest, of course, that an errant diagnosis can sometimes result from a developmental period that a boy can grow out of.

And there are other underlying reasons for the recent explosion in diagnoses. Stephen Hinshaw, a professor of psychology at the University of California, Berkeley, and the editor of *Psychological Bulletin,* the research publication of the American Psychological Association, presents evidence in a new book that ADHD diagnoses can vary widely according to demographics and even education policy, which could account for why some states see a rate of 4 percent of schoolchildren with ADHD while others see a rate of almost 15 percent. Most shocking is Hinshaw's examination of the implications of the No Child Left Behind Act of 2001, which gave incentives to states whose students scored well on standardized tests. The result: "Such laws provide real incentive to have children diagnosed and treated." Children with ADHD often get more time to take tests, and in some school districts, tests taken by ADHD kids do not even have to be included in the overall average. "That is, an ADHD diagnosis might exempt a low-achieving youth from lowering the district's overall achievement ranking"—thus ensuring that the district not incur federal sanctions for low scores.

In a study of the years between 2003 and 2007, the years in which the policy was rolled out, the authors looked at children between ages eight and thirteen. They found that among children in many low-income areas (the districts most "targeted" by the bill), ADHD diagnoses increased from 10 percent to 15.3 percent—"a huge rise of 53 percent" in just four years.

The Consequences

48% of subjects of one study who took ADHD medications experienced side effects like sleep problems and "mood disturbances." In another, 6% of children suffered psychotic symptoms, including thoughts of suicide.

Source: *Psychiatry,* April 2010; *The Canadian Journal of Psychiatry,* October 1999.

And yet among many of the people interviewed for this story, the most common explanation for the staggering increase in diagnoses is that doctors know more now. *Great strides have been made.* "I don't think there's an epidemic of new cases," says Mario Saltarelli, a neurologist and the senior vice-president of clinical development at Shire, which manufactures Adderall and Vyvanse. (Since our interview, he has left the company.) "It's always been there. It's now more appropriately understood and recognized." Instead of lumping together all the kids with high energy and bad behavior and calling them hyper, many experts say, doctors can identify the children who exhibit the symptoms specific to ADHD and treat them accordingly. "We were paying attention," says Jeffrey Lieberman, the president of the American Psychiatric Association and chairman of psychiatry at Columbia University Medical Center. "We [now] have reliable descriptions and the means of diagnosing."

Every 15 years or so, the APA publishes a book called the *Diagnostic and Statistical Manual of Mental Disorders,* which doctors around the world use as a guide for diagnosing mental disorders in their patients. Known as the DSM, it has been published seven times, first in 1952 and most recently in 2013. For each revision, a new task force of psychiatrists tweaks, refines, and often expands the descriptions, definitions, and symptoms of hundreds of psychiatric disorders. It's not uncommon for definitions to be written more broadly, thus broadening the universe of people who might be diagnosed with a given disorder.

In the *DSM-5,* the 916-page version that came out last year, there was one important change made to the section on ADHD. The age at which a child can be diagnosed with ADHD was raised from seven to twelve. In the previous edition of the *DSM,* in order to meet the criteria for diagnosis, several symptoms of ADHD had to be present by age seven. Citing "substantial research published since 1994," the authors increased the window for diagnosis by five years, meaning that 20 million more children are now eligible to be told they have ADHD.

And so if a child is deemed to meet the criteria for ADHD as defined in the *DSM*, even by a rushed pediatrician after a cursory twelve-minute examination, the clinical-practice guidelines strongly recommend medication as part of the first step in treating kids starting at age six. (Behavior therapy is recommended as a first step for four- and five-year-olds, followed by methylphenidate, or stimulants, if the behavior therapies "do not provide significant improvement and there is moderate-to-severe continuing disturbance in the child's function.")

A cynical person might wonder whether the task forces who write the *DSM* are influenced by pharmaceutical companies, seeing that with each new disorder they add and each new symptom they deem valid, more people can get expensive prescriptions. ADHD drugs alone were a $10.4 billion business in 2012, a 13 percent increase over the year before.

"I think it happens in an indirect but nonetheless powerful way," says Lisa Cosgrove, a clinical psychologist who is an associate professor at the University of Massachusetts, Boston, and a fellow at the Center for Ethics at Harvard. In a study of the *DSM-5*, she found that 69 percent of the task force acknowledged ties to the pharmaceutical industry. Many of these were likely indirect affiliations, but Cosgrove says that doesn't matter. "It's not that I think there's this quid pro quo kind of corruption going on. But when the individuals who are charged with the responsibility of developing criteria or with changing the symptom criteria—I don't think they are consciously aware of the way in which industry affiliations create pro-industry habits of thought." Cosgrove points to what she calls a "major gap" in the APA's disclosure policy for doctors who worked on the *DSM-5:* It allows unrestricted research grants from drug companies. "Now, unrestricted' means that the pharmaceutical company cannot in-house analyze the data . . . but there's a wealth of social-psych research that shows that when you are paid even small amounts—and there's the potential for future payment—it affects your behavior. If I get an unrestricted research grant from Pfizer for $500,000, and I'm hoping to get a $2 million grant, at some level I'm going to be aware of how I talk about the results."

The journal *Accountability in Research* chose Cosgrove's paper "Commentary: The Public Health Consequences of an Industry-Influenced Psychiatric Taxonomy" for publication in 2010, when a first draft of the *DSM-5* was made public. In the paper, Cosgrove and her coauthors lambasted the psychiatric community for supporting a manual that largely ignores side effects and promotes diagnosis by constantly adding symptoms and disorders. "A psychiatric taxonomy [i.e., the *DSM*] which touts indication for medications, but is effectively silent about their associated risks, is evidently unbalanced and raises questions about undue influence," they wrote. "The time has come

to seriously reconsider whether the heavily pharmaceutically funded APA should continue to be entrusted with the revision of the *DSM*."

Dr. Allen Frances, professor emeritus at Duke University School of Medicine, the former chairman of its psychiatry department, and the chairman of the *DSM-IV* (1994) task force, feels the problem is not corruption but the slow creep of misinformation. "I know the people. They're not doing it for the drug companies—they really believe what they're doing is right. They really believe ADHD is underdiagnosed, and they want to help people who should be getting medication. I just think they're dead wrong."

Frances points to the fact that in August 1997—the same year the CDC first started tallying ADHD cases in the United States—the Food and Drug Administration made it easier for pharmaceutical companies to advertise their drugs to consumers. Spending on direct-to-consumer drug advertising increased from $220 million in 1997 to more than $2.8 billion by 2002.

It's not that Frances believes ADHD is not a real and valid diagnosis; he just believes that these days it's made so frequently it has been rendered meaningless. "It's been watered down so much in the way it's applied that it now includes many kids who are just developmentally different or are immature," he says. "It's a disease called childhood."

Falsely diagnosing a psychiatric disorder in a boy's developing brain is a terrifying prospect. You don't have to be a parent to understand that. And yet it apparently happens all the time. "Kids who don't meet our criteria for our ADHD research studies have the diagnosis—and are being treated for it," says Dr. Steven Cuffe, chairman of the psychiatry department at the University of Florida College of Medicine, Jacksonville, and vice-chair of the child and adolescent psychiatry steering committee for the American Board of Psychiatry and Neurology.

The ADHD clinical-practice guidelines published by the American Academy of Pediatrics—the document doctors are supposed to follow when diagnosing a disorder—state only that doctors should determine whether a patient's symptoms are in line with the definition of ADHD in the *DSM*. To do this accurately requires days or even weeks of work, including multiple interviews with the child and his parents and reports from teachers, plus significant observation. And yet a 2011 study by the American Academy of Pediatrics found that one-third of pediatrician visits last less than 10 minutes. (Visits for the specific purpose of a psychosocial evaluation are around 20 minutes.) "A proper, well-done assessment cannot be done in ten or fifteen minutes," says Ruth Hughes, a psychologist who is the CEO of Children and Adults with ADHD (CHADD), an advocacy group.

Only one significant study has ever been done to try to determine how many kids have been misdiagnosed with ADHD, and it was done more than 20 years ago. It was led by Peter Jensen, now the vice-chair for psychiatry and psychology research at the Mayo Clinic, but at the time a researcher for the National Institute of Mental Health. After a study of 1,285 children, Jensen estimated that even way back then—before ADHD became a knee-jerk diagnosis in America, before one in seven boys had been given the diagnosis—between 20 and 25 percent were misdiagnosed. They had been told they had the disorder when in fact they did not.

Part of the problem is subjectivity, and the power of a culture that has settled on a drug-based solution. Decades of research have gone into trying to define the disorder in a clinical way, and yet the ultimate diagnosis—Your son has ADHD—is inherently subjective. And insurance companies don't reimburse or reward doctors for time spent doing the diligent work involved in giving a proper opinion. "You have to observe the behavior of the child over different environments. You have to talk to the parents. You have to talk to the teachers. I don't know an insurance company out there that pays for a pediatrician to call and talk to the teachers. They just don't," says Hughes.

Ned Hallowell does not accept insurance in his private psychiatry practice, which he says allows him to spend more time with patients. "But for the average person, it's the luck of the draw," he says. "Do they have a good, savvy pediatrician who can be careful about the diagnosis, or do they have somebody who just hears 'ADD' and writes a prescription?"

Lieberman, the APA president, says most doctors try to get it right. "Are there pressures that are packed on clinicians that make them less than optimally rigorous [in making a diagnosis]? Unfortunately, there are," he says. "But I mean, you have our healthcare financing system that's quite dysfunctional, and it's created a situation where doctors have to spend a certain amount of time with bureaucratic, administrative paperwork and regulatory-compliance stuff. . . . We also have a culture where there's pressure, both from schools as well as from parents, to do something—to alleviate the problem and enhance the performance of the child. That's no excuse, and doctors shouldn't succumb to that. But, you know, doctors are human. . . . We'd like everybody to be these heroic figures who fulfill the virtues of the Hippocratic oath. I think most doctors aspire to try to do that. But human limitations being what they are . . . *caveat emptor.*"

One man believes that drugging children's brains is too risky. That until we get a lot closer to achieving a foolproof diagnosis for ADHD, we need to think twice about giving a single pill to a single child. He believes that what is called attention-deficit/ hyperactivity disorder might in fact be a boy's greatest gift, the gift of energy. And that the best way to treat it is to first teach the boy to control the energy all by himself, because by learning to control it all by himself, a boy can channel that energy to help him succeed. That the responsible thing to do is first to see if there is some problem with the boy's heart—not with the way it pumps blood, but with its

ability to show and accept love. The man's name is Howard Glasser, and he is one of those countercultural clinicians who, as American society has become inured to giving psychotropic drugs to kids, has built a practice predicated on opposing the very idea.

If he were a child today, Glasser would be given a prescription for a stimulant in about five minutes. Little Howie was a wired kid. Obstreperous. But good. A good kid. And when he grew up and became a family therapist—he has applied to earn his doctorate in education from Harvard starting this fall—he created a way of dealing with wired, obstreperous, uncontrollable kids who are, beneath all that, good. And he believes all of them are good.

He calls the method the Nurtured Heart Approach, and it seems simple on the surface: You nurture the child's heart. If a child is hyperactive and defiant and has trouble listening and concentrating, Glasser feels it is our responsibility as a society—as grown-ups—to do everything we can for a child's heart before we start adding chemicals to his brain, because what if his brain is fine? What if the diagnosis isn't right? And even if it is, what if something else works?

Hyperactive, defiant—he was all those things. At home—the apartment his parents rented in Kew Gardens, a leafy, almost suburban corner of Queens—he was sometimes so defiant that his mother would shout into the air, asking what she had done to deserve this, her face brightening with incarnadine helplessness. His father was a salesman of electrical supplies, and he and Howie used to go at it pretty good. Sometimes, when it was his turn to teach Howie a lesson, his father would reach for the rubber machine belt. Howie took that punishment laughing. Heartbreaking laughter.

At school he would sit in the back of the class, cracking jokes until his teachers were overcome with that unique kind of exasperation that results from feeling outrage and disappointment at the same time. Outrage because you wouldn't believe the mouth on this kid. Disappointment because he was so smart. Because he had so much potential.

Man, was Howie Glasser smart. That was the problem nobody saw: He was a funny, clever kid who scored high in both English and math without much studying. School bored him. The teachers, though, had to teach to every student in the class, and Howie felt forgotten. He didn't need to listen, so he sat in the back of the room and goofed off, his gangly frame folded awkwardly into a too-small wooden chair. Kids would laugh, and he'd do it more. And every time the teachers got angry and pointed their fingers toward the principal's office, struggling to keep from screaming at Howie—to keep from smacking him, probably—they were only feeding his recalcitrance. Finally, someone was paying attention to him! Deep down Howie didn't like the negative attention, but it was better than no attention at all.

In junior high school, they wanted to hold him back. He couldn't handle the next grade, they said—he couldn't concentrate, he was hanging around with the wrong kids, he just wasn't ready. But then Howie took a test, and his score surprised even the teachers who knew he was smarter than he let on. He scored high enough to skip ahead and graduated high school at sixteen.

Glasser graduated from City College with a degree in psychology, then got a master's in counseling at New York University. He had started work on a PhD, also at NYU, but after a year or so he dropped out to do the thing he loved most, the thing that made all the noise go away, all the trouble, all the teachers who couldn't figure out how to harness and channel his energy, his hollering parents who didn't understand why he couldn't be more like his older brother: He worked with wood.

Howie's Woodworking opened on Third Avenue and East Twelfth Street in New York in 1980. He collected wood around the city—old floorboards from gutted townhouses, planks, pallets, scraps. He made planters and mosaics and odd pieces of furniture. People would see the sign and come in and ask if he could do bigger jobs—cabinetry, fine furniture, storefronts. Glasser would always tell them he could do it, even though he had no idea how. Then he'd hire people who could show him.

After a few years, Glasser moved out west, far from the overdrive of New York, to the Arizona desert. On his way out, in Boulder, Colorado, he got to know a man named Michael Davis, who, with his wife, Anita, was raising four sons, two of whom were adolescents at the time. The first time Glasser visited Davis's house, there was some kind of minor drama unfolding that day, the kind of argument that periodically bubbles up in a house where teenagers live.

And the way the Davises handled it made Glasser weep.

"Michael and Anita were talking to their kids in the most loving way. I had never until that day—ever—encountered anybody who talked to their kids that way. I had tears streaming down my face," he says. "In my world, in my circumscribed world, it was not the culture. It's kind of breathtaking to me now." Even as he tells this story almost 30 years later, Glasser has to pause, swallow hard, and clear his throat.

He eventually moved to Tucson with the woman who would be the mother of his only child, a daughter. Almost as soon as he arrived, he found a job at a family-therapy institute where he could use his psychology training. "It was like the sea parted," he says. He felt as if he was doing what he needed to be doing. He got a second job at a clinic that was known for helping kids with behavior problems. Many of them had been diagnosed with ADHD.

"I had been one of these kids," he says. "And here I am with twelve preadolescent kids who aren't on their meds on the weekends—I would meet with them on Saturday mornings. So you get to see: These are very interesting human beings. I got to experience the truth of these kids off medication."

Glasser would open up group discussions by asking what the rules should be. The children half-raised their hands and called out predictable answers: no hitting, no yelling, no bad words, no this, no that. The first time it happened, Glasser was seized with memories, a darkness moving over his brain like a shadow. "It was PTSD for me. I grew up with rules that start with *no*, and I hated rules that start with *no*. They always led to me getting in trouble, and ultimately getting hit," he says. "It got my attention that kids saw rules that way."

The clinic and the therapy institute both employed other bright young therapists, and they all called on their state-of-the-art psychology training to try to help the troubled families in their care. They used positive reinforcement. Instead of rules that started with no, they set rules like "Be respectful" and "Use nice words." This was all fine and hewed closely to the education and therapy trends of the day. Kids behaved better. Families improved. But they didn't change. Positive reinforcement is great, but there was only so far it could go with a difficult child. Glasser knew he hadn't truly scraped away the artifice of defiant behavior to get at whatever pain was festering inside these kids. He wasn't finding whatever it was that stirred them to yell and swear and make the grown-ups think they needed medication.

The problem with the positive rules was that there didn't seem to be a very good way to teach them. The old rules were mostly taught when children broke them. If the rule is "No hitting" and one kid hits another, you'd teach the child the rule in that moment. "What you just did was wrong." You'd tell him to go sit in the corner, or go to his room, or apologize. But in those moments, everyone's upset. The kid who got hit is crying, the hitter is angry and scared, and the grown-up is amping up the authority. The offending child gets all the attention. The rule doesn't stick.

Still, Glasser saw that kids seemed to like "no" rules because they're clear. The line of transgression was definite. He had an idea: What if he told the children how great they were when they didn't break a rule? It would be like a video game. When you do something great while playing a video game—when you simply do what the game expects—you get points and you get to keep going. When you go out of bounds or break one of the game's rules, no one yells at you or reminds you what rule you've broken. You simply miss a turn or lose points. And there is no grudge once you pay the fine. As Glasser wrote in his first book in 1999, *Transforming* the Difficult Child, "When the consequence is over, it's right back to scoring."

Kids love video games. "They don't need us to figure out a video game for them," he says. "They figure it out in three minutes, and then they become stars. The beauty of those games is the energy of success is so strong, consistent, reliable, available. If they break a rule in the next two seconds, the game unplugs momentarily. Grown-ups look at the consequences in these games and we don't always see the truth of what's going on. It looks to us like, Oh my God, huge consequence—blood spurting, heads rolling. But actually, the kid's out of the game for two seconds but it feels like an eternity to them because they've become such a devotee of being plugged in to success, and they vividly feel the energy of missing out. When the consequence is over, they don't just come back into the game, they come back ever more determined: I'm not gonna break another rule."

And so he thought, What if a child was sitting quietly, not bothering anyone, and you went out of your way to congratulate him on that, very specifically, by telling him how proud you are that he's not hitting anyone, not screaming, not throwing toys, but just sitting quietly? What if you gave a child the equivalent of points—what if you thanked him or hugged him—for not putting his feet on the couch? How would he respond to that?

He'll like it, it turns out.

"I started accusing kids of being successful for not breaking rules. Nobody ever in my professional career had done that," he says. "All of a sudden—and it was as weird as it could be—I knew I was speaking to some level of a kid's soul. I knew it was nourishing them in some way. It was like me weeping at Michael Davis's house. In my professional career, no kid had ever been told they were successful when it came to rules."

Many of the people I interviewed who have had direct experience with ADHD—parents of children who'd been diagnosed, psychiatrists, adult ADHD patients—assured me, within the first minute of our conversation, that ADHD is a real disorder, not some made-up condition.

"It's important to understand that ADHD is a very real, serious, neurobiological disorder," said Saltarelli, the neurologist who was formerly senior vice-president of clinical development at Shire, maker of Adderall and Vyvanse, which is now the most common brand of stimulant prescribed for ADHD. He repeated this point several times during our hour-long conversation.

"I don't think in the medical community or in the research community there is any question that this is a brain disorder. I really don't think that is in question," Ruth Hughes, the CHADD CEO, told me after I asked her about the validity of brain scans that purport to show ADHD, which have been disputed by other scientists.

"There is no doubt in my mind that I really believe this is a disorder, disease, condition, whatever you do—like, it is for real," said Tracie Giles, a parent of four children, two of whom have been diagnosed. She is the coordinator of the local CHADD chapter in Wayne County, Michigan.

The interesting thing is I never asked any of these people whether ADHD is real. But their defensiveness is understandable. ADHD isn't strep throat—there's no culture, no test. To find out if you have it, or if your son has it, or if your daughter has it, you just need a human being to say so—a physician or a psychiatrist—and that makes some people skeptical. Google "Does ADHD exist?" Up pop the detractors who call the very disorder into question.

ADHD has become the most controversial medical topic in America when it comes to children. In 2000, Bob Schaffer, then a Colorado congressman, called a hearing about ADHD medication before the House Committee on Education and the Workforce. "I had been in politics a long time even before I had this hearing," he says. "And you would think that with issues of national missile defense, the space program, the billions we spend on public education, the China trade bill I voted on—that something else would have resulted in more blowback, but I can't think of anything else that did. It inspired more personal hostility and defensiveness than anything else I'd ever been involved in."

The biggest reason: Managing ADHD, for most people who receive the diagnosis, includes taking medication. If the diagnosis is real, a prescription can turn around a child's life in an instant, improving his ability to concentrate and jacking up his self-esteem. Denying a child who needs the medicine is as cruel as forcing it on a kid who doesn't. Even Howard Glasser is not anti-medication—not entirely. He believes that in rare cases it can be effective as a temporary measure. But it's a terrifying choice to make for many parents.

Ned Hallowell once famously said that stimulants were "safer than aspirin," a statement he has since backed off of. ("That's almost a preposterous statement for anyone to say," says Saltarelli.) "I think that was misleading," Hallowell says now. "I was dealing with people who thought these medications were extremely dangerous, and if they're used properly, they are not. But now I don't say that anymore because I'm worried about high school students taking them without any medical evaluation." But Hallowell stands by his assertion—widely corroborated—that it's silly to try to treat ADHD without medicine. "I certainly am not gonna try to persuade you to use medication, but once you learn the facts, chances are you will want to. Because doing a year, say, of non-medication is sort of like saying, Why don't we do a year of squinting before we try eyeglasses."

The Epidemic

2003: The No Child Left Behind Act rewards schools for higher test scores. Kids with ADHD get more time to take tests, and sometimes their scores aren't counted in the overall average. As the law rolls out, ADHD diagnoses increase 53% in poor areas.

In 1999 the National Institute of Mental Health published its landmark study "Multimodal Treatment of ADHD," which was led by Peter Jensen; 579 children ages seven to nine took part. The study declared that the best treatment, across the board, is medication combined with behavioral therapy—but that the combination works only marginally better than medication on its own, with no behavioral component. This made a lot of parents feel better about accepting a prescription for their children, and the study is frequently cited by pharmaceutical companies, psychiatrists, and organizations like CHADD.

Research published since the multimodal study, however, suggests that treating kids who have ADHD with cognitive behavioral therapy can have the same positive effect as stimulants. A new study in the *Journal of Abnormal Child Psychology* shows that behavioral therapy, alone or in combination with stimulants, is far more effective than medication alone. The children in the study—forty-four boys, four girls, all diagnosed with ADHD—were given varying doses of medication and behavioral therapy, and researchers monitored their episodes of "noncompliance" each day. The worst-behaved children were the ones receiving only drugs and no behavioral therapy. Even kids given a placebo while also receiving some behavioral therapy behaved far better than kids being treated with drugs alone. The sweet spot was a low dose of medication plus behavioral therapy.

William Pelham of Florida International University, the lead author of the study and one of the original investigators on the multimodal study, says that these findings show that psychosocial treatments "are the key to long-term success. Medication alone is not the solution to the long term."

I wanted to talk to an actual person at a drug company about the difficult choice. I called Novartis, which manufactures Ritalin and Focalin XR. A media-relations specialist, Julie Masow, declined to make anyone from the company available to me for an interview, citing the fact that it was summer and people were traveling, and instead provided me with a vague written statement. But eventually Masow agreed to provide written answers to any questions I wished to send her via e-mail. It was a fairly fruitless exercise—a lot of anodyne corporatespeak about how "ultimately, the decision to prescribe an ADHD treatment for a child with ADHD is between the physician and the patient's parent/guardian" and "Patients and parents/guardians also receive a copy of the medication guide included in the drug package insert."

Novartis is right, to a point—pharmaceutical companies do not prescribe the drugs they manufacture. So do they care what happens once the drugs leave the factory? When I asked Saltarelli of Shire whether drug companies should do anything to make sure their products are used correctly, he said, "It is our responsibility to make sure that the drugs are being appropriately utilized. It's obviously impossible for us to be in any way involved in diagnosis, let alone in every doctor's office where diagnoses are being made. But we do feel an ethical obligation—and we've actually invested quite a bit to do whatever we possibly can through educational efforts to make sure that these drugs are being used appropriately." When I asked the same question of Novartis, the answer (via e-mail) was "Novartis supports only the appropriate use of ADHD medicines as indicated and prescribed by qualified, licensed health-care providers. Novartis does not participate in the diagnosis of patients with ADHD, as the diagnostic criteria. . ."

Karen Lowry, a nurse in Medford, New Jersey, helps run a local CHADD chapter. She has four children, the youngest of whom has ADHD. "When he was first diagnosed, we were adamantly against medication. *No, it might prevent his brain growth. We'll deal with behavioral programs. It's not happening,*" she says. "But as first grade progressed and we saw our child with an ADHD diagnosis experiencing hyperactivity, impulsivity, and inattentiveness in a classroom setting with a teacher who was really not very understanding, we saw a kid who was falling through the cracks. We saw a kid who was not developing friendships, peers who were always blaming him for everything that was going on around him. So my husband and I looked at each other again and said, Oh my gosh, we need to rethink this. Are we not being fair to him? What's worse? Not fully understanding the medication and what can happen in a positive way, or just standing our ground saying, We're unsure about this?"

Lowry and her husband ended up putting their youngest son on a stimulant. His behavior improved vastly, and the ADHD seemed to be under control. But toward the end of the school year, he developed severe facial tics, a side effect of some ADHD medications. They took him off the medication for the summer, a decision many parents make at some point. "He's adjusted pretty much," she says. "He's on a very low dose because he does get the headaches. It's sometimes hard to balance, you know, the side effect with the effects of the drug."

Overall, Lowry thinks they made the right call. It's a question she gets a lot from other parents of children with ADHD. "I would never tell anyone to put their kid on medication. All I will say is look at the results. And I always commend the parents who come to our classes, even if they're frantic: Your kid will be okay because you're here."

Ruth Hughes, CHADD's CEO, finds herself defending—or justifying—ADHD as a diagnosis regularly. More than 12,000 people are members of the organization. Its annual budget is about $3.5 million, of which up to 30 percent can come from the pharmaceutical companies that manufacture ADHD drugs, according to Hughes.

During our phone interview, I asked Hughes whether CHADD could be classified as pro-medication. "Well, I'm going to reframe this a little bit," she said. "We are pro-science, pro-research. Our issue is to make parents or adults who potentially have ADHD to be very well informed consumers of medical services."

I told her I was asking because while there are lots of books and articles out there about how to treat ADHD without medication, you hardly ever see anything about that on CHADD's website or in its bimonthly magazine, *Attention.*

"You don't," she said.

If we don't know what we're doing, maybe we shouldn't be doing it. Putting a child on highly addictive psychotropic drugs ought to be very difficult, not shockingly easy. And yet even if Peter Jensen's 20-year-old estimates about misdiagnosis are still correct, an astonishing 25 percent of today's 6.4 million kids, overwhelmingly boys with developing brains, might be experiencing side effects for no reason. Because he made that assumption long before ADHD became such a popular diagnosis, the number could be far higher now.

Yes, the drugs these children consume may work. They help them focus for longer periods of time. They help them do better in school. But consider this: Stimulants work on just about anyone. "These are powerful drugs," says Bob Schaffer, the former Colorado congressman. "They would work on me. They would make anyone more focused. And everyone's happy because the kid is now under control." The fact that the drugs would help you perform better at work doesn't mean you should take them. And it certainly doesn't mean a seven-year-old boy who doesn't suffer from a psychiatric disorder should be taking them.

Why not, if they help him do better? Because, for one thing, an important study of 4,000 children published last year concluded that children who took stimulants didn't do any better in school than kids who didn't. But also, and perhaps more important, because he might not be the same seven-year-old boy once he starts, and he may never be the same boy again.

Another little-examined feature of these drugs is the global changes in personality that they can cause. Jim Forgan is a psychologist in Jupiter, Florida. The first thing you see on his website is an ad:

"Dr. Jim Forgan's Parent Support System
10 Easy to Use Modules
Over 80 Educational Videos
Downloadable Resources
Online Access 24/7
And Much More!"

The video support system is available for a one-time fee of $49.97. Forgan is the coauthor of a book called *Raising Boys with ADHD,* also available for purchase. He speaks from experience. His son has been diagnosed with ADHD. Forgan knows all the warning signs, and he tells parents about them. He's in favor of drugs when they're administered correctly—starting with low doses, watching vigilantly for side effects, stopping use if the side effects outweigh the benefits.

How do you know if the side effects outweigh the benefits?

"Careful monitoring," says Forgan. "And for me personally, with my son being on the stimulant medications, those are medications you don't have to take every day, so we would give him the holiday breaks on the weekends and spring break and summertime, just so that he didn't have the medication all the time. And yeah, there's a difference, he has more energy. My son doesn't like to take the medications because he feels like it makes him feel flat, and he doesn't like what it does to his personality. And he says he's not the same fun person that he is when he's not on the medication. And some of that fun gets him in trouble at school, because he's funny and knows how to entertain people. But at the same time, he likes that characteristic about himself—that he is fun and knows how to get people laughing and working together and bring energy into a room. Kinda like the life of the party."

I tell Forgan that there is something heartbreaking about the fact that such a lively part of his son's personality disappears when he's on medication, and that his son knows it disappears. "Is it just that he was getting into too much trouble?" I ask.

Forgan pauses and says, "Right. Yup, it gets him in trouble and he hasn't—when he was in elementary school, he didn't have his own ability to have the self-control not to say impulsive things and do impulsive things that other people find funny but the teacher finds very annoying."

"And you see the fun part of him reemerge during breaks from the medicine?"

"Right."

Howard Glasser's biggest fear in life is that a child might grow up not knowing how great a person he is. It keeps Glasser awake at night sometimes, this image of a kid thinking he's no good. It lodges a pit in his throat.

Ned Hallowell, the ADHD expert who has the disorder, writes books about it, has talked about it on *Dr. Oz,* and thinks medication usually gets good results, feels the same. "The medical model is so slanted toward deficits that it excludes strengths—and it also reinforces stigma, that this is shameful, this is bad, this means you're a loser. And that becomes a self-fulfilling prophecy. It's the old line of whether you think you can or you think you can't, you're right. And what breaks my heart is how these kids, and the parents along with them, get broken in school, and they come out of twelfth grade believing that they're stupid. Believing that they're defective. But this trait, these are the people who colonized this country! Just think of it: Who in the world would get on a boat in 1600 and come over here? You had to be some kind of a nut. You had to be a visionary, a dreamer, an entrepreneur—you know, a risk-taker. That's our gene pool. So this country is absolutely full of ADD."

So there is something great about having ADHD. The question is how to treat the difficult parts in a way that pushes the greatness forward.

"I confront kids with their own greatness," Glasser says. "Because that's what I think allows a kid to go from an ordinary life to a purposeful life. To see who they really are. The worst-case scenario in life is that a boy grows up thinking: Who I really am is a kid who annoys everybody."

In 1994 Glasser opened the Center for the Difficult Child in Tucson, his first effort to teach therapists his Nurtured Heart Approach. In 1999 he published *Transforming the Difficult Child,* which has quietly sold nearly 250,000 copies. Today he runs an organization he named the Children's Success Foundation, which is an expanded effort to teach educators and therapists around the United States how to use what he has found from 20 years of practicing the Nurtured Heart Approach.

"It's much more about reaction than attention." That sentence appears on page 10 of *Transforming the Difficult Child.* It's a profound distinction, and there is no deeper nor more simple understanding of a child's needs. Parents of intense boys can shower their children with love and attention, and still the boys might be difficult boys. What's important is how you react to what a child does, good or bad, Glasser says. Mostly, we get animated when our kids do something bad. We get worked up, and we give them energy—negative energy, but energy nonetheless. But when a difficult child is sitting quietly, playing or writing or drawing, not disturbing anyone, not throwing food, not picking on a sibling—we do nothing. We don't acknowledge it at all. The way a difficult child gets a parent's energy, then, is to do something bad.

"Most parenting approaches have you giving a strong punitive consequence that's all energy and that confirms that, as a parent, you're highly available through negativity—you're a toy that works when they push buttons," he says. "And you work if and only if they act out bigger."

Watching Glasser work with a child is a marvel.

He is sitting on the carpeted floor of a family's basement playroom, his lanky frame contorted into what passes for comfort for a 63-year-old man sitting on the floor. He is watching a sandy-haired boy of seven play with his toys. A few minutes before, the boy had been hitting his younger brother, and he had been scolded, hit his brother again, and been banished from the kitchen. Now he plays peacefully.

"I see that you are very calmly building with your Legos," Glasser says to the boy, in a smooth and even voice, as if he were commenting on clouds moving across the sky. "That's really great to see. It shows that you respect your mom and dad, because they love it when you play nicely."

The boy just nods without looking up, like, Sure, thanks mister. So Glasser keeps at it.

"So I assume you heard what I said. And I just want to elaborate a little more. Because here's what's great: You have this wonderful quiet way of thinking things through. I can tell that you're thinking about what it means to be calm. And maybe you don't quite know what calm means. Let me tell you how great calm is. What does it take to be calm?"

The boy looks up now. Words are starting to register with him. His face is blank, but he's thinking. This is unusual for him—getting attention, getting a reaction, for being so good.

"Well, while you're thinking about it, let me tell you. It takes wisdom, for one thing, because you could be yelling. You could be annoying people. Have you ever been annoying? Well, you're not being annoying. You're not running around the lunch table. You're not throwing your food or hitting your brother. All these things that kids your age could do, you're not doing. That's being calm. That shows me you're being thoughtful. That you care about other people, and that you're in control of your body. Being in control takes a lot of concentration and effort. Doesn't it?"

The boy nods, just barely. He is looking right into Glasser's eyes. For years, since he was two, the boy has had trouble controlling his body sometimes. Sometimes the energy inside him is just too much, and it builds like gas trapped in rock until it bursts forth in a violent, painful mess. At times he has driven his parents to a crisis of helplessness. The heartbreaking part is the boy has tried so hard to control his energy, and he's gotten better at it. But sometimes he still just can't. Once, in the middle of the night, when he was four, he wouldn't go to sleep and kept throwing toys at the door until his mother cried and his father yelled, and then through the tears streaming down his tiny cheeks he looked up at his father over the plastic gate that was jammed in his bedroom door and, in a moment of astonishing self-awareness, pleaded, "I need to calm my body down!" When he started school, his parents mentioned to the school psychologist that their son sometimes had an issue with impulsive behavior. The psychologist, who had never met him—who had never met the boy—told the parents that it sounded like he probably had ADHD. The parents had had their son evaluated by child psychologists, pediatricians, teachers, and independent therapists, and not one person had ever suggested ADHD, and in fact, the boy's pediatrician and the rest of the school's counseling, teaching, and professional staff said resolutely the boy showed no signs of it. (When he heard that a school psychologist had said this, Glasser wasn't surprised. "Sure. Your son is intense. If you wanted to go out and get him a prescription for ADHD medication, you could do it tomorrow," he told the parents.)

"That's right," Glasser says to the boy. "It does take a lot of effort. And I want to tell you something: A few minutes ago, you hit your brother. And he started crying, and then you got really upset when your parents told you to stop. You were really mad at him and at them. But look at you now. Look at yourself! You calmed yourself down so beautifully. And that was an amazing, amazing thing to do, because it's hard to calm yourself down when you're so upset. But you figured out how to control your body in a really bad moment. You did that yourself. No one did it for you. And that shows greatness. That shows me and everybody else that you have greatness inside you."

The boy is looking at him still, locked in.

And, slowly at first, the boy begins to smile. And then the smile spreads across his whole, beautiful seven-year-old face. His teeth, missing here and there and sticking out in gaps where he used to suck his thumb, shine across the room, and he lets out a giggle, and the giggle turns into the kind of proud, embarrassed laugh kids do when they haven't learned how to take a compliment. His face is lit up—he is shocked by what he has just heard, and shocked by his own joyful reaction. He's laughing, looking at this man who has just told him that he has greatness within his soul, and the kid slaps the floor, then crosses his skinny arms on top of his head, and smiles with pride. He is euphoric.

It is almost as if he has been drugged.

Critical Thinking

1. How can a parent differentiate between an energetic son and a possible ADHD diagnosis?

2. How do educational policies such as " The No Child Left Behind Act" of 2001 or the recent "Common Core" standards impact rates of ADHD diagnosis and treatment?

3. Are the known side effects of ADHD medications such as Ritalin, Adderall, or Concerta worth the risk to the child?

Internet References

Boys with ADHD may face tougher times as men
http://www.cbsnews.com/news/boys-with-adhd-may-face-tougher-times-as-men

Gender Differences in ADHD Symptoms
http://www.healthline.com/health/adhd/adhd-symptoms-in-girls-and-boys

The Ritalin Explosion
http://www.pbs.org/wgbh/pages/frontline/shows/medicating/experts/explosion.html

Why Boys with ADHD Need Their Dads
http://www.additudemag.com/adhd/article/707.html

Article   Prepared by: Claire N. Rubman, *Suffolk County Community College*

Why Our Approach to Bullying Is Bad for Kids

SUSAN PORTER

Learning Outcomes

After reading this article, you will be able to:

- Describe how the development of the brain's prefrontal cortex and executive functions contributes to bullying behaviors.

- Account for the wide range of statistics that are reported on bullying behaviors.

- Define the "expanded definition of bullying" and its effect on development.

I t's hard to avoid the topic of bullying these days. From parents chatting about it on the soccer field sidelines, to op-ed pieces calling for police presence on school campuses, to the President and First Lady hosting webcasts on the subject—just about everyone with a soapbox, real or virtual, is talking about how to deal with the bullying scourge that is sweeping the nation's schools. And, boy, is it bad.

The next time you've got a spare moment, Google "statistics on bullying" and see for yourself. When I last looked, this is what popped up:

- One in five kids is bullied.
- Twenty-three percent of students say they been bullied several times.
- One in four kids is bullied.
- Fifty percent of kids are bullied, and 10 percent are bullied on a regular basis.
- Seventy-four percent of 8- to 11-year-olds said teasing and bullying occurs at their schools.

- Seventy-seven percent of students say they've been bullied recently.
- It is estimated that *more than half* [emphasis added] of school bullying incidents are never reported.

Despite the fact that the statistics are wildly inconsistent, even the lowest percentages are scary, and they suggest that our kids aren't safe in schools because they're hurting one another at alarmingly high rates. At best, the data suggest that we've got a serious problem on our hands.

Or do we?

Parents often ask me what's behind the rise of bullying among children, and whether or not kids today are different from those of previous generations. As a school counselor, with almost 25 years of experience, I tell parents that kids haven't changed much over the years, but something significant *has* changed recently, and that's how our culture thinks about, talks about, and deals with aggressive childhood behavior. And the change is profound.

A Shift in Definition

A few years ago, a K-12 school asked me to consult on the subject of bullying. This was about the time many schools were implementing "Zero Tolerance Anti-Bullying" policies. In preparation for my presentation, I researched the topic by reviewing local and regional policies on bullying, and articles in the professional literature. I was stunned by what I learned.

First, I discovered that bullying was everywhere. The statistics were as disturbing and wide ranging then as they are today. Admittedly, I was shocked. Here I was, a school counselor with years of experience as both a mental health clinician in schools and a consultant to schools, and somehow I had missed all of this. Of course, I had dealt with cases of bullying in my own work, but the sweeping nature of the phenomenon, as suggested by my research, had eluded me. The ground under my professional feet started to shake. As I digested the information I felt horrible. *How could I have been so blind?*

But then, as I researched further, I learned another important thing about bullying. According to the many definitions I read, the term had come to include not only the classic forms of harassment between children, behaviors such as shaking down a kid for lunch money, beating up a smaller kid in the schoolyard, or repeated hate speech. Now, it also included behaviors such as social exclusion, name-calling, teasing, sarcasm, and being unfriendly. I also noted a corresponding shift in the telltale signs expressed by the victims of bullying, which in addition to extreme symptoms, such as *school phobia* and *depression,* now included symptoms such as *feeling upset* and *being sad.*

As I considered all of this, I realized what I'd missed in my work was not a rise in incidents of classic bullying, but rather the creeping expansion of the definition of bullying, which according to the average anti bullying policy was now a catch-all term for the routine—albeit nasty—selfishness, meanness, and other social misfires that characterize childhood and adolescence. I call this the *expanded definition of bullying.*

As I completed my research, I sensed that this expanded definition of bullying was doing more than just attempting to protect kids. It was also making a lot of normal childhood behaviors seem pathological and dangerous. Many of the behaviors described in the bullying literature were almost inevitable, given brain development, but this didn't seem to matter. What mattered instead was setting unrealistic guidelines for children's behavior in the hopes of preventing them from feeling pain. Lost, it seemed, was the intention of helping kids learn from their mistakes and developing resilience in the face of adversity.

The Preadolescent and Adolescent Brains and Development

The preadolescent and adolescent brains can be characterized in many ways, the most important of which, when it comes to the expanded definition of bullying, is that they are *not yet fully developed.* And the most important part of the brain that has not yet developed is the prefrontal cortex, the part of the brain that deals with functions such as impulse control, judgment, and empathy. These functions are often referred to as *executive functions,* and researchers believe we continue to develop these functions well into our 20s.

This means children, even older teenagers, have brains that are not yet capable of being consistently in control of themselves, even when they try *really, really* hard. As children age, however, the executive functions start to kick in more predictably, and therefore older teenagers can be entrusted, for example, to drive a car or babysit a younger child or do their homework without a nightly battle. That said, the key is *consistency,* and even the best-behaved and seemingly mature teenager can have lapses in judgment and behave without the benefit of fully formed executive functions.

If you consider the expanded definition of bullying in light of brain development, and think about behaviors such as teasing, name-calling, and social exclusion, you can see why kids and teenagers might exhibit these behaviors, given the fact that their brains simply aren't fully formed yet. Being polite, keeping their hands to themselves, not saying everything that pops into their heads, staying on task, and being thoughtful—these are the things kids work on every day, and their brains won't master these tasks for years. The brain constantly makes mistakes as it develops these capacities, and often these mistakes come at the expense of another person's feelings.

Add to this various aspects of development, such as the marked self-consciousness that characterizes adolescence, and you have a recipe for insensitive behavior. When kids walk down school hallways, they aren't thinking about other people's feelings; they're thinking *me, me, me.* This is normal. But this leaves them vulnerable to making big mistakes when it comes to attending to the needs of others, and acting with these needs in mind.

So, regardless of what we'd like, we can't expect kids to sail through childhood and adolescence without blundering—especially given that the average adolescent brain, still under construction, is hardwired to behave in ways that are irritating and selfish at times. This explains, in part, the prevalence of bullying (the expanded version) these days.

There are other reasons why the milder bullying behaviors are rampant (and always have been), and why we can't eradicate them.

First, brains at this age are prone to misinterpreting facial cues, a fact that has huge implications when it comes to social interactions. For example, the teenage brain might interpret a classmate's frown to mean, "She really hates me! She doesn't want to be my friend," when, in fact, it probably means something completely different. A missed cue of this kind, coupled with the self-absorption of the age, can turn a nonsituation into an emotional drama, as the teenager imagines her classmate's expression to be both (A) extremely negative and (B) necessarily about her.

Second, brains at this stage tend to respond very emotionally to social situations. For example, Cathy looks at Susie the wrong way. Unlike an adult, Susie isn't unaffected by Cathy's expression, or simply annoyed by it. Susie takes it personally. She may feel overwrought. This is especially true if Susie believes Cathy's expression indicates that she (Cathy) wishes to exclude her (Susie). Research has shown that the threat of social exclusion is one of the scariest things for a preteen girl's brain to deal with, so Susie's response to Cathy's expression could conceivably cause Susie's brain to initiate a fight-or-flight response, sending Susie on an emotional roller-coaster ride that terrifies her.

An important point to understand about a situation like Susie's is that her reactions and feelings are real *to her*, but that doesn't mean they are an accurate gauge of the outside situation. Our current approach to bullying places so much emphasis on a child's inner experience that I often deal with children (supported by their parents) who believe that their feelings are facts. In today's social climate, Susie's very real, albeit internal and emotional response to Cathy's frown can be sufficient evidence to Susie that Cathy has done something really bad. And, if Susie claimed that Cathy had repeatedly acted this way, and if Susie had some very wounded feelings as evidence, then Cathy could be in big trouble. At the very least, she'd probably get a stern talking-to from a teacher or school administrator. And for what, making a face? But with our expanded definition of bullying, Susie's pain is the trump card.

Finally, bullying is widespread because kids at this age tend to see the world in black and white terms. Their brains are just developing the capacity for abstract thought, and while they may have glimpses of it here and there, for the most part, and especially when it comes to social situations, the world to them is pretty cut and dried. As such, there is little room for a nuanced interpretation of painful situations, so a perceived social attack is usually interpreted in dire terms.

Unfortunately, in our desire to protect perceived victims, we downplay or ignore these essential truths about development such that, over the past decade or so, we have succeeded in redefining many unpleasant childhood behaviors as bullying, and thus the epidemic. With this expanded definition of bullying in place, the average child, behaving in an average way, is statistically likely to be branded a bully at some point, and to become a victim of bullying—and this troubles me.

None of this means that we should ignore children's bad behavior or pain. But our current approach to bullying, which superimposes on the childhood brain an adult-like capacity for intent and self-control, gives little encouragement for growth and change. It also ignores children's capacity for resilience, and it does both through its use of labels.

Code of Conduct for XYZ Academy

Middle School (or High School) is a time of tremendous physical, psychological, and emotional growth and change, and the expectations for XYZ Academy students reflect the capabilities of adolescents (or children) at this developmental stage and the aspirations the community has for them.

All XYZ Academy students are expected to behave in ways that support the well-being, health, and safety of themselves and others. To this end, students should be respectful in their interactions and relationships and learn to recognize how their actions, including their speech, affect others. XYZ students should aim to be courteous, kind, and inclusive, and accept constructive feedback and criticism as being essential parts of learning and membership within the community.

As an educational community, XYZ recognizes that social-emotional development, as any other subject, takes time to master, and involves mistakes and missteps. As such, adults are charged to help students reflect upon their behavioral choices, especially when these choices hurt or deny the rights of others. In cases of severe or repeated negative behavior that falls short of expected conduct, disciplinary action may be taken.

Fixed Mindsets and the Problem with Labels

Labels are everywhere when it comes to bullying, and they are an important part of how antibullying rhetoric aims to educate kids about aggression. Go to any antibullying website, or review antibullying curricula, and you will see what I mean. The labels are ubiquitous: active bully, passive bully, lieutenant, henchman, bystander, ally, hero, and, of course, victim. They constitute the *dramatis personae* of the bully play. In learning about bullying, students are instructed to identify the players, imagine what roles they play, and clearly distinguish between the wrongdoer and the wronged. It's all fixed, perhaps in an effort to simplify what is usually an inherently complicated situation. And with these labels, the painful dynamics that occur among children become carved in stone.

By now, most educators are familiar with the work of Stanford University psychologist Carol Dweck. In *Mindset: The New Psychology of Success*, she describes the two lenses through which we make sense of the world: the fixed mindset and the growth mindset. The fixed mindset is characterized by a belief that personality and intelligence are static qualities, and that they can't be developed. A growth mindset, on the other hand, is characterized by a belief that these qualities *can* change and develop, and that effort leads to learning and therefore growth.

Our approach to bullying is problematic, if for no other reason, because it provides kids (and adults) with little conceptual room to maneuver. When a child misbehaves and is labeled a bully, the label declares something about his character, not just about his behavior. For adults, the bully label affixed to a child sticks in our minds, and encourages us to view the child's behavior—past, present, and future—through this lens. If we consider that children don't develop the capacity for abstract thought until early adolescence (if then), we see how problematic labels are. Children can't see beyond the concrete, so they will take labels like bully or victim and run with them, usually to their own detriment. But adults should know better. Our goal is to facilitate growth and change.

I encourage readers to carefully examine their own schools' and states' antibullying policies and curricula to bring this point home. I have yet to come across a policy that approaches the issue of problematic childhood and adolescent behavior from a growth mindset. These policies, in their presumed effort to protect kids and shape behavior, do little more than make us view children and their behavior in a fixed framework. The formulaic ways in which aggression among kids is described, and a general indifference to context through the use of easy-to-apply labels, let us off the hook for approaching problematic situations between children with compassion for all parties involved.

The use of labels, and the accompanying fixed mindset they engender, does nothing to help us help kids. Children need us to understand their social lives and behavior in dynamic, not static, terms, and to separate their behavior from their characters. Children should be allowed to make mistakes, and these mistakes, even if egregious, should not result in the children receiving labels that limit our ability (and possibly our desire) to help them develop into responsible adults.

But labels aren't bad for just the bullies; they're bad for the victims, too. Remember, mindsets are about whether we see the world through fixed or growth lenses, and the victim label is as fixed and inflexible as the bully one. Both discourage self-exploration and faith in change. The bully has no incentive to change as long as the adults (and children) around him see him in wholly negative terms, while the victim has no incentive to develop resilience if he is continually identified with and reminded of his wounds. In my experience, victims are often the biggest losers when it comes to labeling because, as victims, they are encouraged to identify with their vulnerability,

and as a result, their sense of agency often derives from their feelings of helplessness and pain.

The other labels used in the bully rhetoric—such as bystander, ally, and hero—are also problematic. For starters, they give children, and especially young children, the incorrect impression that they are responsible for preventing other people's pain. In addition, they lead children to believe that they must be vigilant at all times, and know when and how to intervene in complex social situations. Sure, kids should be encouraged to help out other kids, but it is neither their role nor their duty to assume this much responsibility for situations beyond their control, and yet this is the impression our use of labels gives them.

If nothing else, we should abandon labels and the fixed mindset around bullying because they alienate parents, and we need to work closely with parents if we want to help children change their behavior. I routinely tell parents to stop listening if someone (let's say a teacher or another parent) calls their child a bully. Why? Because when adults use the term bully, they have stopped seeing a child's potential, and they aren't focused on helping that child grow. Using the term bully is an easy way out, and it allows adults to avoid the very hard work of helping children change their behavior. This is not just an issue of semantics, as any parent of an accused child can attest. It's about believing in growth or not.

> **Using the term bully is an easy way out, and it allows adults to avoid the very hard work of helping children change their behavior. This is not just an issue of semantics, as any parent of an accused child can attest. It's about believing in growth or not.**

An Alternative Approach

In order to do right by our students, we must first understand brain and psychological development and set reasonable expectations for student behavior. We must recognize that the brain doesn't fully develop for years, and that it makes plenty of mistakes along the way, whether in mathematics or history or relationships. We succeed as educators when we help students solve academic problems. Likewise, we succeed when we help students solve behavioral problems. And just as we avoid labels when it comes to students as academic learners, we should avoid labels when it comes to students as social-emotional learners.

We must also abandon the conceptual frameworks and rhetoric that encourage us to understand childhood aggression in simple and formulaic ways, and we should adopt policies that reflect a growth mindset. To this end, I have included a Code of Conduct statement that approaches behavior and expectations from a growth mindset. You will note that it does not specify certain behaviors or reactions to behaviors, as do most antibullying policies. It is aspirational, open-ended, and doesn't dictate how a school should respond to complex social situations among students.

As educators, it is our job to lead the way. When we stop seeing the potential for growth and change in children, it's time for us to retire.

Critical Thinking

1. How should a parent simultaneously help a child combat bullying while also supporting resilience and autonomy?

2. How does the development of the brain's prefrontal cortex and emerging executive functions contribute to our understanding of solutions to bullying and antisocial behaviors in adolescents and preadolescents?

3. What can parents and teachers do to reduce "labeling" among bullies and victims?

Create Central

www.mhhe.com/createcentral

Internet References

Bullying Statistics.org Bullying Statistics
http://www.bullyingstatistics.org

gov.uk What is Bullying?
http://www.stopbullying.gov/what-is-bullying

Psychology Today.com Sticks and Stones—Hurtful Words Damage the Brain–Verbal abuse in childhood inflicts lasting physical effects on brain structure
http://www.psychologytoday.com/blog/the-new-brain/201010/sticks-and-stones-hurtful-words-damage-the-brain

Reform of anti-social behaviour powers—Bullying—What is the issue?
https://www.gov.uk/government/uploads/system/uploads/attachment_data/file/248751/01_BULLYING_WEB.PDF

Sydney.edu Bullying, Harassment, Discrimination or Antisocial Behaviour
http://sydney.edu.au/student_affairs/complaints/how/harrassment_discrimination.shtml

---

Susan Porter is dean of students at The Branson School (California). Her hook, Bully Nation: Why America's Approach to Bullying Is Bad for Everyone, is scheduled to be released by Paragon Press in the spring of 2013.

Porter, Susan. "Why Our Approach to Bullying is Bad for Kids." *Independent School* 72. 2 (Winter, 2013): 72–78.

Article   Prepared by: Claire N. Rubman,
Suffolk County Community College, Selden, NY

Time to Lower the Drinking Age

A lower age would discourage binge drinking and may help combat sexual assault.

MARY KATE CARY

Learning Outcomes

After reading this article, you will be able to:

- Discuss when and why the laws regarding the legal drinking age were changed.

- Talk about the increase in illegal drug (such as OxyContin, Vicodin, Xanax, and Valium) use since the drinking age was raised.

- Articulate why the author reports that it is time to lower the drinking age.

I was telling my college-age daughter recently that back in the olden days when I went to college, you could fill a red Solo cup with beer at a fraternity party and sip it all night long. No one knew if it was your first beer or your 10th. There was no need for "pregaming"—binge drinking in private apartments or dorms before heading out in public. And unlike today, college kids didn't tend to use fake IDs as much.

That's because when I was an undergrad, the drinking age was 18. Fraternities had kegs out in the open on university property, and student gatherings on campus often included beer. I remember university police regularly strolling through the fraternity parties, making sure everything was under control. That tended to keep a lid on things.

Then, 30 years ago this summer, President Ronald Reagan signed into law the Federal Uniform Drinking Age Act of 1984, which mandated that all states adopt 21 as the legal drinking age over the next five years. States that did not comply faced a cut in their federal highway funds; by 1988, all 50 states had moved the minimum drinking age to 21.

The well-intentioned leaders of Mothers Against Drunk Driving were able to convince politicians that a vote against the bill was a vote in favor of drunken driving, and they succeeded in gaining unanimous passage in both the House and the Senate. According to the MADD website, the National Highway Traffic Safety Administration estimates that the law has saved about 900 lives a year.

Drunken driving deaths have decreased over the last three decades in large part because we now throw the book at drunken drivers in this country: All 50 states currently define a driver's having a blood-alcohol concentration of 0.08 or higher as a crime; 42 states suspend drivers' licenses on the first offense. Every state also now has some type of ignition interlock law, requiring devices to be installed in the vehicles of convicted drunken drivers that prevent a vehicle from starting if the driver breathes into the device and produces a breath-alcohol level above a preset limit. Thanks to MADD, drunken driving isn't the problem it used to be.

The Centers for Disease Control and Prevention reports that in 2010 drug overdoses caused more deaths than motor vehicle crashes among people 25 to 64 years old. The CDC estimates that from 1999 to 2010 drug overdose death rates jumped 102 percent. While first-time use of illegal street drugs such as heroin by young people increased from 90,000 users in 2006 to 156,000 in 2012, it's abuse of prescription drugs that has really skyrocketed. One recent report cited by the Department of Justice says that between 1993 and 2005, the proportion of college students abusing opioids like Vicodin and OxyContin jumped 343 percent and 450 percent for tranquilizers like Xanax and Valium.

Prescription drug use among young people at colleges is, along with binge drinking, part of the epidemic of pregaming. The CDC reported that alcohol is responsible for more than 4,300 deaths annually among underage youth. The CDC also found that young people between the ages of 12 and 20 drink 11 percent of all the alcohol consumed in the U.S., and more than 90 percent of this alcohol is consumed during binge drinking.

Here's the problem with both binge drinking and drug abuse: When you're that impaired, you do things you wouldn't normally do. In an April speech, Dartmouth College's president listed the outrages he now witnesses regularly: "From sexual assaults on campus . . . to a culture where dangerous drinking has become the rule and not the exception . . . to a general disregard for human dignity as exemplified by hazing, parties with racist and sexist undertones, disgusting and sometimes threatening insults hurled on the Internet . . . to a social scene that is too often at odds with the practices of inclusion that students are right to expect on a college campus in 2014." I doubt that list is unique to just one Ivy League school.

President Obama recently announced the creation of the White House Task Force to Protect Students from Sexual Assault, after stating that "1 in 5 women on college campuses has been sexually assaulted during their time there." (If that were true, as one critic pointed out, the crime rates on college campuses would be astronomically higher than America's most violent cities.)

Despite the hyperbole from the White House, we can all agree that sexual assault as a result of alcohol and drug abuse is a very serious problem on America's college campuses. But forming a task force in Washington probably won't help. Allowing states to lower the legal drinking age would. The U.S. is one of only seven nations in the entire world with a drinking age of 21. Most Western democracies allow their citizens to fight in wars, vote in elections and drink alcohol at age 18—as do even China and North Korea.

I'd rather see my kids sipping beer out of a red Solo cup at a well-patrolled fraternity party than drinking shots and popping a Vicodin in someone's basement off campus. Lowering the drinking age will help slow the need for pregaming and bring the college fake ID business to a dead stop. It can't help but reduce the binge drinking, drug overdoses and sexual assaults.

Thirty years ago, drunken driving was the problem. Now that is less true. Let's take a lesson from MADD and make a vote against lowering the drinking age to 18 a vote for drug overdoses and sexual assaults against young women. Times have changed.

Critical Thinking

1. Were women safer on college campuses when the drinking age was lower?
2. Would lowering the drinking age decrease binge drinking episodes?
3. If the drinking age was lowered, would adolescents seek out other thrills instead of alcohol?

Internet References

A Rising Epidemic on College Campuses: Prescription Drug Abuse
https://www.clintonfoundation.org/blog/2014/01/12/rising-epidemic-college-campuses-prescription-drug-abuse

College Drinking
http://www.niaaa.nih.gov/alcohol-health/special-populations-co-occurring-disorders/college-drinking

MADD
http://www.madd.org

Should the Drinking Age Be Lowered from 21 to a Younger Age?
http://drinkingage.procon.org

The Missing Key to Fighting Sexual Assault on Campus
http://www.slate.com/articles/news_and_politics/jurisprudence/2014/05/drinking_and_sexual_assault_on_campus_universities_must_define_when_sex.html

---

MARY KATE CARY is a former White House speechwriter for President George H.W. Bush. She currently writes speeches for political and business leaders, and is a contributing editor for *U.S. News & World Report*.

Unit 5

UNIT

Prepared by: Claire N. Rubman,
Suffolk County Community College, Selden, NY

Development during Adolescence and Young Adulthood

The period of development between childhood and adulthood appears to be changing. What is causing those changes and how do they impact early adulthood? Is it possible that we are becoming more self-centered and more self-indulged than ever before? How do these potential changes impact our careers, our marriage, and our lives? This unit looks at a diverse range of topics including early puberty, college cheats, adolescent crime, and the prospect of marriage.

Perhaps it's the additives in the food that we eat, or it may be the healthier diets that our wealthy societies maintain, but whatever the reason, children are reaching puberty earlier than preceding generations. "The Incredible Shrinking Childhood" by Weil examines "precocious puberty" through the life of Ainsley Sioux who began to show signs of early puberty at age 6. Experts such as Marcia Herman-Giddens and endocrinologist Louise Greenspan chronicled these early maturing cases. They discuss bone loss, emotional development, and "the process of normalizing" or accepting maturation. Weil compares children of divorce noting that their maturation rates are younger suggesting the possibility that stress might be related to early puberty. Weil also notes the relationship between mental health issues such as depression and early puberty. Parents discussed failed methods that they have tried to forestall puberty such as marathon running, additive and hormone free diets, or removing plastics from their homes.

Not all adolescent paths are successful, however, as Ravi Somaiya reports. Some adolescents are prone to lying and attention seeking. "Jackie," as she was referred to, was the University of Virginia undergraduate student who falsely claimed that she was raped at a fraternity party that never actually took place. Her story was told in the prestigious *Rolling Stone* magazine. The magazine had to later rescind the entire story and admit to poor journalistic fact checking. What are the implications for women in the future who are actual victims of sexual violence? How have "Jackie's" actions impacted an entire generation of women? We should also consider the role of the media in our lives. Should we wait for the slow wheels of justice to turn before we accuse potentially innocent fraternity members? It is important to be critical thinkers and trust in our judicial system rather than believing everything we read. As in the field of psychology, it is just an opinion until you can substantiate it with research, or in "Jackie's" case, proof.

Continuing this trend towards a changing generation, let's look to women and their career choices. "The Retro Wife" by Lisa Miller discusses the decline of feminist values and the desire of many women today to focus on one job within the home, that is, raising their children. Miller suggests that "feminism has fizzled, its promise only half fulfilled." In 2011, only 19% of men did housework or laundry. Families with children under 6 reported that men spent 26 minutes on "physical care" like feeding, dressing, or bathing their children.

Whether married women choose a career path or devote their days to raising their children or tending to their home, a successful marriage is important. Foster's article "Will Your Marriage Last?" addresses the problems associated with maintaining a marriage after the honeymoon phase has ended. Psychologist John Gottman recommends "the magic ratio" of five positive interactions for every negative one between couples. Gottman applied his theory to 700 newlyweds with a 94% accuracy rate. Other contributing factors also appear to include whether you are a product of divorce, the age you marry, money, mutual respect, and perceptions about your spouse. In a related article, "Making Marriage Work," Morgan suggests that each spouse should focus on "radical self-acceptance" which may lead to more independent thinking and a happier marriage.

Another key topic in adolescence is the prevalence of cyberbullying. In her article "High-Tech Bullies," Ingrid Sturgis discusses bullying at the college level. Problems on college campuses include cyberstalking, gossiping, and masquerading as another person. Tyler Clemente's tragic cyberbullying case brought this issue to light in 2010 as his Rutger's roommate videotaped him in a sexual encounter that he played on the Internet for all to witness. Unable to withstand the humiliation, Clemente committed suicide by jumping off the George Washington Bridge. Sturgis explores why college students use this perceived anonymity to bully and humiliate their peers. She also explores what college campuses are doing to combat this high tech bullying.

Technology is blamed for yet another deficit in our adolescent and young adult population according to Schnoebelen in her article "Many Professors Say Their Students Lack Professional Qualities for Future Jobs." According to recent surveys, this lack of preparedness for the workforce is a result of a combination of an inflated sense of entitlement and etiquette problems associated with technology. This brief but poignant article should be a wake-up call to many students who hope to enter the workforce.

Returning to the topic of the developing brain in adolescence and young adulthood, Catherine Sebastian explores peer rejection in relation to emerging data on the adolescent brain. Sebastian defines social rejection both as the deliberate exclusion of an individual by a group and as a type of relational aggression. She considers the social environment, the theory of the mind, and emotional development. She acknowledges the pain and emotional sensitivity associated with peer rejection.

"Kids Are Not Adults" looks at the juvenile justice system in light of research on the brain that suggests that maturity occurs around age 25. The idea that adolescents act on the basis of short-term consequences suggests that perhaps our justice system is not set up to adequately address this concept. Sarah Alice Brown highlights the difference between treating adolescents as adults or children within the judicial system. Brown discusses crime rates, the economy and recent findings in brain development to present the case that adolescents should not be treated like adults in the judicial system. She compares policies and trends in states around the country including Arizona, California, Ohio, and Texas. She advocates effective programs such as family functional therapy and aggression-replacement training.

Article   Prepared by: Claire N. Rubman, *Suffolk County Community College*

The Incredible Shrinking Childhood

How Early Is Too Early for Puberty?

Elizabeth Weil

Learning Outcomes

After reading this article, you will be able to:

- Appraise some of the reasons for precocious puberty.
- Suggest several ways that parents can deal with girls who experience early puberty.

One day last year when her daughter, Ainsley, was 9, Tracee Sioux pulled her out of her elementary school in Fort Collins, Colo., and drove her an hour south, to Longmont, in hopes of finding a satisfying reason that Ainsley began growing pubic hair at age 6. Ainsley was the tallest child in her third-grade class. She had a thick, enviable blond-streaked ponytail and big feet, like a puppy's. The curves of her Levi's matched her mother's.

"How was your day?" Tracee asked Ainsley as she climbed in the car.

"Pretty good."

"What did you do at a recess?"

"I played on the slide with my friends."

In the back seat, Ainsley wiggled out of her pink parka and looked in her backpack for her Harry Potter book. Over the past three years, Tracee—pretty and well-put-together, wearing a burnt orange blouse that matched her necklace and her bag—had taken Ainsley to see several doctors. They ordered blood tests and bone-age X-rays and turned up nothing unusual. "The doctors always come back with these blank looks on their faces, and then they start redefining what normal is," Tracee said as we drove down Interstate 25, a ribbon of asphalt that runs close to where the Great Plains bump up against the Rockies. "And I always just sit there thinking, What are you talking about, normal? Who gets pubic hair in first grade?"

Fed up with mainstream physicians, Tracee began pursuing less conventional options. She tried giving Ainsley diindolyl-methane, or DIM, a supplement that may or may not help a body balance its hormones. She also started a blog, the Girl Revolution, with a mission to "revolutionize the way we think about, treat and raise girls," and the accompanying T.G.R. Body line of sunscreens and lotions marketed to tweens and described by Tracee as "natural, organic, craptastic-free products" containing "no estrogens, phytoestrogens, endocrine disrupters."

None of this stopped Ainsley's body from maturing ahead of its time. That afternoon, Tracee and Ainsley visited the office of Jared Allomong, an applied kinesiologist. Applied kinesiology is a "healing art" sort of like chiropractic. Practitioners test muscle strength in order to diagnose health problems; it's a refuge for those skeptical and weary of mainstream medicine.

"So, what brings you here today?" Allomong asked mother and daughter. Tracee stroked Ainsley's arm and said, wistfully, "Precocious puberty."

Allomong nodded. "What are the symptoms?"

"Pubic hair, armpit hair, a few pimples around the nose. Some budding." Tracee gestured with her hands, implying breasts. "The emotional stuff is getting worse, too. Ainsley's been getting super upset about little things, crying, and she doesn't know why. I think she's cycling with me."

Ainsley closed her eyes, as if to shut out the embarrassment. The ongoing quest to understand why her young body was turning into a woman's was not one of Ainsley's favorite pastimes. She preferred torturing her 6-year-old brother and playing school with the neighborhood kids. (Ainsley was always the teacher, and she was very strict.)

"Have you seen Western doctors for this?" Allomong asked.

Tracee laughed. "Yes, many," she said. "None suggested any course of action. They left us hanging." She repeated for

Allomong what she told me in the car: "They seem to have changed the definition of 'normal.'"

For many parents of early-developing girls, "normal" is a crazy-making word, especially when uttered by a doctor; it implies that the patient, or patient's mother, should quit being neurotic and accept that not much can be done. Allomong listened intently. He nodded and took notes, asking Tracee detailed questions about her birth-control history and validating her worst fears by mentioning the "extremely high levels" of estrogen-mimicking chemicals in the food and water supply. After about 20 minutes he asked Ainsley to lie on a table. There he performed a lengthy physical exam that involved testing the strength in Ainsley's arms and legs while she held small glass vials filled with compounds like cortisol, estrogen and sugar. (Kinesiologists believe that weak muscles indicate illness, and that a patient's muscles will test as weaker when he or she is holding a substance that contributes to health problems.)

Finally, he asked Ainsley to sit up. "It doesn't test like it's her own estrogens," Allomong reported to Tracee, meaning he didn't think Ainsley's ovaries were producing too many hormones on their own. "I think it's xeno-estrogens, from the environment," he explained. "And I think it's stress and insulin and sugar."

"You can't be more specific?" Tracee asked, pleading. "Like tell me what crap in my house I can get rid of?" Allomong shook his head.

On the ride back to Fort Collins, Tracee tried to cheer herself up thinking about the teenage suffering that Ainsley would avoid. "You know, I was one of those flat-chested girls at age 14, reading, 'Are You There God? It's Me, Margaret,' just praying to get my period. Ainsley won't have to go through that! When she gets her period, we're going to have a big old party. And then I'm going to go in the bathroom and cry."

In the late 1980s, Marcia Herman-Giddens, then a physician's associate in the pediatric department of the Duke University Medical Center, started noticing that an awful lot of 8- and 9-year-olds in her clinic had sprouted pubic hair and breasts. The medical wisdom, at that time, based on a landmark 1960 study of institutionalized British children, was that puberty began, on average, for girls at age 11. But that was not what Herman-Giddens was seeing. So she started collecting data, eventually leading a study with the American Academy of Pediatrics that sampled 17,000 girls, finding that among white girls, the average age of breast budding was 9.96. Among black girls, it was 8.87.

When Herman-Giddens published these numbers, in 1997 in Pediatrics, she set off a social and endocrinological firestorm. "I had no idea it would be so huge," Herman-Giddens told me recently. "The Lolita syndrome"—the prurient fascination with the sexuality of young girls—"created a lot of emotional interest. As a feminist, I wish it didn't." Along with medical professionals, mothers, worried about their daughters, flocked to Herman-Giddens's slide shows, gasping as she flashed images of possible culprits: obesity, processed foods, plastics.

Meanwhile, doctors wrote letters to journals criticizing the sample in Herman-Giddens's study. (She collected data from girls at physicians' offices, leaving her open to the accusation that it wasn't random.) Was the age of puberty really dropping? Parents said yes. Leading pediatric endocrinologists said no. The stalemate lasted a dozen years. Then in August 2010, the conflict seemed to resolve. Well-respected researchers at three big institutions—Cincinnati Children's Hospital, Kaiser Permanente of Northern California and Mount Sinai School of Medicine in New York—published another study in Pediatrics, finding that by age 7, 10 percent of white girls, 23 percent of black girls, 15 percent of Hispanic girls and 2 percent of Asian girls had started developing breasts.

Now most researchers seem to agree on one thing: Breast budding in girls is starting earlier. The debate has shifted to what this means. Puberty, in girls, involves three events: the growth of breasts, the growth of pubic hair and a first period. Typically the changes unfold in that order, and the process takes about two years. But the data show a confounding pattern. While studies have shown that the average age of breast budding has fallen significantly since the 1970s, the average age of first period, or menarche, has remained fairly constant, dropping to only 12.5 from 12.8 years. Why would puberty be starting earlier yet ending more or less at the same time?

To endocrinologists, girls who go through puberty early fall into two camps: girls with diagnosable disorders like central precocious puberty, and girls who simply develop on the early side of the normal curve. But the line between the groups is blurring. "There used to be a discrete gap between normal and abnormal, and there isn't anymore," Louise Greenspan, a pediatric endocrinologist and co-author of the August 2010 Pediatrics paper, told me one morning in her office at Kaiser Permanente in San Francisco. Among the few tools available to help distinguish between so-called "normal" and "precocious" puberty are bone-age X-rays. To illustrate how they work, Greenspan pulled out a beautiful old book, Greulich and Pyle's "Radiographic Atlas of Skeletal Development of the Hand and Wrist," a standard text for pediatric endocrinologists. Each page showed an X-ray of a hand illustrating "bone age." The smallest hand was from a newborn baby, the oldest from an adult female. "When a baby is born, there's all this cartilage," Greenspan said, pointing to large black gaps surrounding an array of delicate white bones. As the body grows, the pattern of black and white changes. The white bones lengthen, and the black interstices between them, some of which is cartilage, shrink. This process stops at the end of puberty, when the growth plates fuse.

One main risk for girls with true precocious puberty is advanced bone age. Puberty includes a final growth spurt, after which girls mostly stop growing. If that growth spurt starts too early in life, it ends at an early age too, meaning a child will have fewer growing years total. A girl who has her first period at age 10 will stop growing younger and end up shorter than a genetically identical girl who gets her first period at age 13.

That morning one of Greenspan's patients was a 6 ½-year-old girl with a bone age of 9. She was the tallest girl in her class at school. She started growing pubic hair at age 4. No one thought her growth curve was normal, not even her doctors. (Eight used to be the age cutoff for normal pubic-hair growth in girls; now it's as early as 7.) For this girl, Greenspan prescribed a once-a-month shot of the hormone Leuprolide, to halt puberty's progress. The girl hated the shot. Yet nobody second-guessed the treatment plan. The mismatch between her sexual maturation and her age—and the discomfort that created, for everybody—was just too great.

By contrast, Ainsley was older, and her puberty was progressing more slowly, meaning she wasn't at much of an increased risk for short stature or breast cancer. (Early periods are associated with breast cancer, though researchers don't know if the risk stems from greater lifetime exposure to estrogen or a higher lifetime number of menstrual cycles, or perhaps something else, like the age at which a girl has her growth spurt.) In cases of girls Ainsley's age, Greenspan has been asked by parents to prescribe Leuprolide. But Greenspan says this is a bad idea, because Leuprolide's possible side effects—including an increased risk of osteoporosis—outweigh the benefits for girls that age. "If you have a normal girl, a girl who's 8 or 9, there's a big ethical issue of giving them medicine. Giving them medicine says, 'Something is wrong with your body,' as opposed to, 'This is your body, and let's all find a way to accept it.'"

> **"'Giving them medicine says, Something is wrong with your body, as opposed to, This is your body, and let's all find a way to accept it.'"**

"I would have a long conversation with her family, show them all the data," Greenspan continues. Once she has gone through what she calls "the process of normalizing"—a process intended to replace anxiety with statistics—she has rarely had a family continue to insist on puberty-arresting drugs. Indeed, most parents learn to cope with the changes and help their daughters adjust too. One mother described for me buying a drawer full of football shirts, at her third-grade daughter's

request, to hide her maturing body. Another reminded her daughter that it's O.K. to act her age. "It's like when you have a really big toddler and people expect the kid to talk in full sentences. People look at my daughter and say, 'Look at those cheekbones!' We have to remind her: 'You may look 12, but you're 9. It's O.K. to lose your cool and stomp your feet.'"

"We still have a lot to learn about how early puberty affects girls psychologically," says Paul Kaplowitz, chief of endocrinology at Children's National Medical Center. "We do know that some girls who start maturing by age 8 progress rapidly and have their first period before age 10, and many parents prefer that we use medications to slow things down. However, many girls do fine if they are simply monitored and their parents are reassured that they will get through it without major problems."

In some ways early puberty is most straightforward for families like those of the kindergartner on Leuprolide. She has a diagnosis, a treatment plan. In Greenspan's office, I asked the girl's father at what age he might choose to take his child off the drugs and let her puberty proceed. He laughed. Then he spoke for most parents when he said, "Would it be bad to say 22?"

So why are so many girls with no medical disorder growing breasts early? Doctors don't know exactly why, but they have identified several contributing factors.

Girls who are overweight are more likely to enter puberty early than thinner girls, and the ties between obesity and puberty start at a very young age. As Emily Walvoord of the Indiana University School of Medicine points out in her paper "The Timing of Puberty: Is It Changing? Does It Matter?" body-mass index and pubertal timing are associated at age 5, age 3, even age 9 months. This fact has shifted pediatric endocrinologists away from what used to be known as the critical-weight theory of puberty—the idea that once a girl's body reaches a certain mass, puberty inevitably starts—to a critical-fat theory of puberty. Researchers now believe that fat tissue, not poundage, sets off a feedback loop that can cause a body to mature. As Robert Lustig, a professor of clinical pediatrics at the University of California, San Francisco's Benioff Children's Hospital, explains, fatter girls have higher levels of the hormone leptin, which can lead to early puberty, which leads to higher estrogen levels, which leads to greater insulin resistance, causing girls to have yet more fat tissue, more leptin and more estrogen, the cycle feeding on itself, until their bodies physically mature.

In addition, animal studies show that the exposure to some environmental chemicals can cause bodies to mature early. Of particular concern are endocrine-disrupters, like "xeno-estrogens" or estrogen mimics. These compounds behave like steroid hormones and can alter puberty timing. For obvious ethical reasons, scientists cannot perform controlled studies proving the direct impact of these chemicals on children, so researchers instead look for so-called "natural experiments," one of which occurred in 1973 in Michigan, when cattle were accidentally fed grain contaminated with an estrogen-mimicking chemical, the flame retardant PBB. The daughters born to the pregnant women who ate the PBB-laced meat and drank the PBB-laced milk started menstruating significantly earlier than their peers.

One concern, among parents and researchers, is the effect of simultaneous exposures to many estrogen-mimics, including the compound BPA, which is ubiquitous. Ninety-three percent of Americans have traces of BPA in their bodies. BPA was first made in 1891 and used as a synthetic estrogen in the 1930s. In the 1950s commercial manufacturers started putting BPA in hard plastics. Since then BPA has been found in many common products, including dental sealants and cash-register receipts. More than a million pounds of the substance are released into the environment each year.

Family stress can disrupt puberty timing as well. Girls who from an early age grow up in homes without their biological fathers are twice as likely to go into puberty younger as girls who grow up with both parents. Some studies show that the presence of a stepfather in the house also correlates with early puberty. Evidence links maternal depression with developing early. Children adopted from poorer countries who have experienced significant early-childhood stress are also at greater risk for early puberty once they're ensconced in Western families.

Bruce Ellis, a professor of Family Studies and Human Development at the University of Arizona, discovered along with his colleagues a pattern of early puberty in girls whose parents divorced when those girls were between 3 and 8 years old and whose fathers were considered socially deviant (meaning they abused drugs or alcohol, were violent, attempted suicide or did prison time). In another study, published in 2011, Ellis and his colleagues showed that first graders who are most reactive to stress—kids whose pulse, respiratory rate and cortisol levels fluctuate most in response to environmental challenges—entered puberty earliest when raised in difficult homes. Evolutionary psychology offers a theory: A stressful childhood inclines a body toward early reproduction; if life is hard, best to mature young. But such theories are tough to prove.

Evolutionary psychology offers a theory: A stressful childhood inclines a body toward early reproduction; if life is hard, best to mature young.

Social problems don't just increase the risk for early puberty; early puberty increases the risk for social problems as well. We know that girls who develop ahead of their peers tend to have lower self-esteem, more depression and more eating disorders.

They start drinking and lose their virginity sooner. They have more sexual partners and more sexually transmitted diseases. "You can almost predict it"—that early maturing teenagers will take part in more high-risk behaviors, says Tonya Chaffee, associate clinical professor of pediatrics at University of California, San Francisco, who oversees the Teen and Young Adult Health Center at San Francisco General Hospital. Half of the patients in her clinic are or have been in the foster system. She sees in the outlines of their early-developing bodies the stresses of their lives—single parent or no parent, little or no money, too much exposure to violence.

Some of this may stem from the same social stresses that contribute to early puberty in the first place, and some of it may stem from other factors, including the common nightmare of adolescence: being different. As Julia Graber, associate chairwoman of psychology at the University of Florida, has shown, all "off-time" developers—early as well as late—have more depression during puberty than typically-developing girls. But for the late bloomers, the negative effect wears off once puberty ends. For early bloomers, the effect persists, causing higher levels of depression and anxiety through at least age 30, perhaps all through life. "Some early-maturing girls have very serious problems," Graber told me. "More than I expected when I started looking for clinical significance. I was surprised that it was so severe."

Researchers know there's a relationship between pubertal timing and depression, but they don't know exactly how that relationship works. One theory is that going through puberty early, relative to other kinds of cognitive development, causes changes in the brain that make it more susceptible to depression. As Elizabeth Sowell, director of the Developmental Cognitive Neuroimaging Laboratory at Children's Hospital Los Angeles, points out, girls in general tend to go through puberty earlier than boys, and starting around puberty, girls, as a group, also experience more anxiety and depression than boys do. Graber offers a broader hypothesis, perhaps the best understanding of the puberty-depression connection we have for now. "It may be that early maturers do not have as much time as other girls to accomplish the developmental tasks of childhood. They face new challenges while everybody else is still dealing with the usual development of childhood. This might be causing them to make less successful transitions into adolescence and beyond."

Over the past year, I talked to mothers who tried to forestall their daughters' puberty in many different ways. Some trained with them for 5K runs (exercise is one of the few interventions known to help prevent early puberty); others trimmed milk and meat containing hormones from their daughters' diets; some purged from their homes plastics, pesticides and soy. Yet sooner rather than later, most threw up their hands. "I'm empathetic with parents in despair and wanting a sense of agency," says Sandra Steingraber, an ecologist and the author of *Raising Elijah: Protecting Our Children in an Age of*

Environmental Crisis. "But this idea that we, as parents, should be scrutinizing labels and vetting birthday party goody bags—the idea that all of us in our homes should be acting as our own Environmental Protection Agencies and Departments of Interior—is just nuts. Even if we could read every label and scrutinize every product, our kids are in schools and running in and out of other people's homes where there are brominated flame retardants on the furniture and pesticides used in the backyard."

Adding to the anxiety is the fact that we know so little about how early puberty works. A few researchers, including Robert Lustig, of Benioff Children's Hospital, are beginning to wonder if many of those girls with early breast growth are in puberty at all. Lustig is a man prone to big, inflammatory ideas. (He believes that sugar is a poison, as he has argued in this magazine.) To make the case that some girls with early breast growth may not be in puberty, he starts with basic science. True puberty starts in the brain, he explains, with the production of gonadotropin-releasing hormone, or GnRH. "There is no puberty without GnRH," Lustig told me. GnRH is like the ball that rolls down the ramp that knocks over the book that flips the stereo switch. Specifically, GnRH trips the pituitary, which signals the ovaries. The ovaries then produce estrogen, and the estrogen causes the breasts to grow. But as Lustig points out, the estrogen that is causing that growth in young girls may have a different origin. It may come from the girls' fat tissue (postmenopausal women produce estrogen in their fat tissue) or from an environmental source. "And if that estrogen didn't start with GnRH, it's not puberty, end of story," Lustig says. "Breast development doesn't automatically mean early puberty. It might, but it doesn't have to." Don't even get him started on the relationship between pubic-hair growth and puberty. "Any paper linking pubic hair with early puberty is garbage. Garbage. Pubic hair just means androgens, or male hormones. The first sign of puberty in girls is estrogen. Androgen is not even on the menu."

Frank Biro, lead author of the August 2010 Pediatrics paper and director of adolescent medicine at Cincinnati Children's Hospital, began having similar suspicions last spring after he flew to Denmark to give a lecture. Following his talk, Biro looked over the published data on puberty of his colleague Anders Juul. In Juul's study, some of the girls with early breast development had unexpectedly low levels of estradiol, the predominant form of estrogen in women's bodies from the onset of puberty through menopause. Biro had seen a pattern like this in his data, suggesting to him that the early breast growth might be coming from nonovarian estrogens. That is to say, the headwaters for the pubertal changes might not be in the girls' brains. He is now running models on his own data to see if he can determine where the nonovarian estrogens are coming from.

The possibility that these early "normal" girls are reacting to estrogens that are not coming from their ovaries is compelling.

Part of the comfort is that a girl who is not yet in puberty may not have developed an adolescent brain. This means she would not yet feel the acute tug of her own sexual urges. She would not seek thrills and risk. Still, the idea that there are enough toxins or fat cells in a child's body to cause breast development is hardly consoling. Besides, some of the psychosocial problems of early puberty derive from what's happening inside a girl's body; others, from how people react to her. "If a girl is 10 and she looks 15, it doesn't make any difference if her pituitary is turned on or if something else caused her breast growth," Biro says. "She looks like a middle adolescent. People are going to treat her that way. Maybe she's not interested in reciprocal sex, but she might be pressured into sex nonetheless, and her social skills will be those of a 10-year-old."

So what are families of early bloomers to do? Doctors urge parents to focus on their daughters' emotional and physical health rather than on stopping or slowing development. In this way, the concept of a new normal is not just a brushoff but an encouragement to support a girl who is vulnerable.

"I know they can't change the fact that their daughter started developing early, but they can change what happens downstream," Louise Greenspan, the pediatric endocrinologist at Kaiser Permanente, told me. Parents can keep their daughters active and at healthy body weights. They can treat them the age they are, not the age they look. They can defend against a culture that sells push-up bikinis for 7-year-olds and otherwise sexualizes young girls. "Most of the psychological issues associated with early puberty are related to risk-taking behaviors," Greenspan continued, and parents can mitigate those. "I know it sounds corny and old-fashioned, but if you're in a supportive family environment, where you are eating family meals and reading books together, you actually do have control." Early breast growth may be just that—early breast growth: disconcerting, poorly understood, but not a guarantee of our worst fears. "You don't go directly from the first signs of early puberty to anorexia, depression, drinking and early sexual debut."

In Fort Collins, Tracee, Ainsley's mother, tried to stay focused on the positive. At one point during my visit, she disappeared into her basement, the headquarters for her company, T.G.R. Body, and returned with a pink hat box filled with chemical-free samples of Peppermint Pimple Popper and Bad Hair Day Miracle Powder. "I just want to be part of the solution," Tracee said, rubbing a sample of silver hair-streaking gel on my wrist. "I'm so tired of running away. I need to have something Ainsley is moving toward."

Mothers who have been through it urge candor. "Be honest with her, and by honest I mean brutally honest"—about what's going to happen to her body—"while still being kind," says the mother of a girl who recently turned 10 but who first showed signs of developing what she calls "a shape" at age 3. "You don't want your daughter experiencing something for which she's unprepared."

Patience and perspective may be the greatest palliatives. "The thing with puberty is that everybody is going to go through it at some point," another mother told me. Three years ago this woman was installing small trash cans in her third-grade girl's school bathroom stalls so that her daughter could discreetly throw away menstrual pads. But now that daughter is 12, in the sixth grade; her body seems less strange. "I feel so much better, and so does she. By another two or three years down the road, all the other girls will have caught up."

Critical Thinking

1. Why do some researchers insist that there is no puberty without the production of gonadotropin-releasing hormone (GnRH)?

2. Identify sources of environmental estrogens that may cause breast development in preadolescents.

3. How are cognitive development and depression correlated in females who experience early puberty? What might explain this correlation?

Create Central

www.mhhe.com/createcentral

Internet References

Link between Body Fat and the Timing of Puberty
http://pediatrics.aapublications.org/content/121

Lolita Syndrome
www.hindustantimes.com/Entertainment/Wellness

Onset of Puberty in Girls Has Fallen
www.theguardian.com/society/2012/oct/21/puberty

Physical Development in Girls: What to Expect
www.healthychildren.org/English/ages-stages/gradeschool

Article

Prepared by: Claire N. Rubman,
Suffolk County Community College, Selden, NY

Rolling Stone Article on Rape at University of Virginia Failed All Basics, Report Says

RAVI SOMAIYA

Learning Outcomes

After reading this article, you will be able to:

- Discuss the events that led to the printing of this false rape allegation in *Rolling Stone* magazine in 2014.

- Elaborate on the impact of this false rape allegation on other women who may be legitimate victims of sexual abuse on a college campus.

*R*olling Stone magazine retracted its article about a brutal gang rape at a University of Virginia fraternity after the release of a report on Sunday that concluded the widely discredited piece was the result of failures at every stage of the process.

The report, published by the Columbia Graduate School of Journalism and commissioned by *Rolling Stone,* said the magazine failed to engage in "basic, even routine journalistic practice" to verify details of the ordeal that the magazine's source, identified only as Jackie, described to the article's author, Sabrina Rubin Erdely.

On Sunday, Ms. Erdely, in her first extensive comments since the article was cast into doubt, apologized to *Rolling Stone*'s readers, her colleagues and "any victims of sexual assault who may feel fearful as a result of my article."

In an interview discussing Columbia's findings, Jann S. Wenner, the publisher of *Rolling Stone,* acknowledged the piece's flaws but said that it represented an isolated and unusual episode and that Ms. Erdely would continue to write for the magazine. The problems with the article started with its source,

Mr. Wenner said. He described her as "a really expert fabulist storyteller" who managed to manipulate the magazine's journalism process. When asked to clarify, he said that he was not trying to blame Jackie, "but obviously there is something here that is untruthful, and something sits at her doorstep."

The Columbia report cataloged a series of errors at *Rolling Stone,* finding that the magazine could have avoided trouble with the article if certain basic "reporting pathways" had been followed. Written by Steve Coll, the Columbia journalism school's dean; Sheila Coronel, the dean of academic affairs; and Derek Kravitz, a postgraduate research scholar at the university, the report, at nearly 13,000 words, is longer than the 9,000-word article, "A Rape on Campus."

After its publication last November, the article stoked a national conversation about sexual assault on college campuses and roiled the university.

The police in Charlottesville, Va., said last month they had "exhausted all investigative leads" and found "no substantive basis" to support the article's depiction of the assault. Jackie did not cooperate with the police and declined to be interviewed for the Columbia report. She also declined, through her lawyer, Palma Pustilnik, to be interviewed for this article. She is no longer in touch with some of the advocates who first brought her to the attention of *Rolling Stone,* said Emily Renda, a rape survivor working on sexual assault issues at the University of Virginia.

In a statement responding to the report, the University of Virginia's president, Teresa A. Sullivan, described the article as irresponsible journalism that "unjustly damaged the reputations of many innocent individuals and the University of Virginia."

Mr. Wenner said Will Dana, the magazine's managing editor, and the editor of the article, Sean Woods, would keep their jobs.

In an interview, Mr. Dana said he had reached many of the same conclusions as the Columbia report in his own efforts to examine the article, but he disagreed with the report's assertion that the magazine had staked its reputation on the word of one source. "I think if you take a step back, our reputation rests on a lot more than this one story," he said.

Ms. Erdely first heard Jackie's account in a phone conversation last July, the report said. Jackie told her she had been lured to a darkened room at a fraternity party in September 2012, and raped by seven men, the article said, led by her date for the evening, a lifeguard at the university's aquatic center identified only as Drew. Ms. Erdely hung up the phone "sickened and shaken," the report said.

Despite some misgivings about the vividness of some of the details, which included a smashed glass coffee table and an assault with a beer bottle in the published account, Ms. Erdely interviewed Jackie seven more times between July and October of last year.

The first misstep during the reporting process, the Columbia report said, was that Ms. Erdely did not seek to independently contact three of Jackie's friends, who were quoted in the piece, using pseudonyms, expressing trepidation at the idea of Jackie telling the authorities that she had been assaulted. The quotes came from Jackie's recollection of the conversation. Those friends later cast doubt on Jackie's story in interviews with *The Washington Post* and denied saying the words *Rolling Stone* had attributed to them. The three told the report's authors that they would have made the same denials to *Rolling Stone* if they had been contacted.

Rolling Stone, the report said, also did not provide the fraternity with enough information to adequately respond to questions from the magazine. Later, when the article had been published, the fraternity, Phi Kappa Psi, said it did not host a function on the weekend Jackie had specified.

And the magazine failed to identify Jackie's attacker, the report said. It was content to give him a pseudonym, Drew, when Jackie resisted Ms. Erdely's request to help find him. The fraternity, *The Post* and the police have been unable to find anyone who matches Jackie's description of Drew.

The reporting errors by Ms. Erdely were compounded by insufficient scrutiny and skepticism from editors, the report said. And the fact-checking process relied heavily on four hours of conversations with Jackie.

Ms. Erdely, a contributing editor at *Rolling Stone* who has also written for *GQ* and *The New Yorker,* declined to be interviewed for this article. She said in her apology that reading the report was "a brutal and humbling experience." She also acknowledged that she did not do enough to verify Jackie's account.

Rolling Stone's fundamental mistake, Mr. Dana said, was in suspending any skepticism about Jackie's account because of the sensitivity of the issue. "We didn't think through all the implications of the decisions that we made while reporting the story, and we never sort of allowed for the fact that maybe the story we were being told was not true," he said. That was compounded by the fact that any reporting on any purported crime that has not been reported to the authorities is difficult, he said.

"Ultimately, we were too deferential to our rape victim," Mr. Woods, the article's editor, said in the report. "We honored too many of her requests in our reporting. We should have been much tougher, and in not doing that, we maybe did her a disservice."

Ms. Erdely, Mr. Wenner said, "was willing to go too far in her effort to try and protect a victim of apparently a horrible crime. She dropped her journalistic training, scruples and rules and convinced Sean to do the same. There is this series of falling dominoes."

Mr. Dana said that the report was punishment enough for those involved, and that they did not deserve to lose their jobs because the article "was not the result of patterns in the work of these people." The full report was posted on *Rolling Stone*'s website, and an edited version will appear in the print magazine. Mr. Dana has also written an editor's note.

Both Mr. Dana and Mr. Wenner said that newsroom practices had been amended. "We are not going to cut those corners even for the most sympathetic reasons," Mr. Wenner said. The article, and the ensuing scandal, may have discouraged some women from coming forward with their accounts of sexual assault, said John D. Foubert, a former dean at the University of Virginia and the current president of One in Four, a rape prevention charity. Ms. Renda, the expert at the university on sexual assault issues, said she hoped that one effect of the Columbia report would be that such a chilling effect would dissipate.

"In the long term I don't think people are going to look back at this story and say, 'This is why women are not coming forward,' " Mr. Dana said. "At the same time, it's certainly not helping things immediately."

Ms. Renda, who was interviewed for the Columbia report, offered another reason that she felt the *Rolling Stone* article was flawed: The magazine was drawn toward the most extreme story of a campus rape it could find. The more nuanced accounts, she suggested, seemed somehow "not real enough to stand for rape culture. And that is part of the problem."

Critical Thinking

1. What can colleges do differently to address the culture of rape or abuse on their campus?

2. Does "Greek Life" on a college campus increase the rates of rape and harassment complaints?

Internet References

Campus Rape Reports Are Up, and Assaults Aren't the Only Reason

http://www.npr.org/2014/04/30/308276181/campus-rape-reports-are-up-and-there-might-be-some-good-in-that

Is College Sexual Assault a Fraternity Problem?

http://op-talk.blogs.nytimes.com/2015/01/29/is-college-sexual-assault-a-fraternity-problem

Sexual Violence on College Campuses

https://www.clevelandrapecrisis.org/resources/statistics/sexual-violence-on-college-campuses

Article

Prepared by: Claire N. Rubman, *Suffolk County Community College*

Will Your Marriage Last?

What social scientists have learned from putting couples under the microscope.

BROOKE LEA FOSTER

Learning Outcomes

After reading this article, you will be able to:

- Identify three things that make some couples more likely to divorce than other couples.

- Describe three things that make some couples less likely to divorce than other couples, and explain why.

- Explain the paradox of less, then more, happiness in a marriage with children.

My husband, John, and I lived together for four years before we got engaged. He's Filipino; I'm white. And we have a two-year-old. Can you guess which of these things makes us more likely to divorce than other couples?

The answer: all of the above.

People who live together before marriage are more likely to divorce than those who move in together after their engagement. Mixed-race couples don't fare as well as couples of the same race or ethnicity: According to the National Center for Health Statistics, 41 percent of couples who intermarry will divorce before the ten-year mark. And as for kids, let's just say the research doesn't paint a rosy picture of marriage post-baby.

Psychologists have been trying for decades to figure out why some marriages last while others fail. It's easy to be cynical about marriage. With the conventional wisdom saying about half of all couples will divorce, it's hard to go to a wedding without wondering if a couple will make it. At age 36, I already know several people who split up within a few years of getting married. I've got bets on others.

The secret to long-lasting relationships is particularly confounding considering that most couples start in the same place: madly in love. What happens after the wedding that alters the course of so many relationships?

It turns out that the initial years of marriage are particularly telling. Once the honeymoon is over and the fairy dust settles, the work of merging two lives begins. Talking gas bills and car payments can kill the mood. Sometimes one partner might feel disappointed in the relationship, and bad habits can form.

"The first two years are supposed to be a honeymoon," says Barry McCarthy, a professor of psychology at American University and coauthor of *Sexual Awareness: Your Guide to Healthy Couple Sexuality.* "But research says they're quite difficult. You're figuring out sexually and emotionally how to be a couple."

Most divorces happen within the first several years of marriage in part because, McCarthy says, "many couples just can't figure these things out and they end up fighting all of the time." Those who make it through aren't exactly in the clear—racking up marital years isn't the same as having a happy and fulfilling marriage.

Last December, the University of Virginia's National Marriage Project analyzed a survey of more than 1,400 couples between ages 18 and 46 about the key to a happy marriage. The project found that couples who reported higher levels of generosity toward each other also reported happier marriages. The study defined generosity as "being affectionate and forgiving of your spouse."

Is the key to marital happiness as easy as making your partner breakfast each morning—or simply saying "I love you"?

"It's not that simple," laughs the study's lead author, W. Bradford Wilcox, director of the National Marriage Project. But the study did reveal that playing nice improves your sex life, another key factor in a couple's happiness. Respondents who reported high levels of generosity, commitment, religious faith, and quality time together also said they had increased sexual satisfaction. Interestingly, women were more sexually satisfied when husbands shared the housework. Says Wilcox: "It seems that what happens outside of the bedroom has a lot to do with what happens inside the bedroom."

Pioneering marriage researcher John Gottman, a psychology professor at the University of Washington, has been trying to figure out the secret to a happy marriage for decades. He calls one of his most famous theories "the magic ratio." Gottman believes that couples who have at least five positive interactions for every negative one are more likely to make it.

In 1992, Gottman did a study of 700 newlywed couples, inviting them in for a 15-minute videotaped conversation. He counted how many positive and negative interactions they had during the interview. Based on his 5-to-1 ratio, he predicted which couples would be together ten years later and which would be divorced. In a 2002 follow-up study, his findings were astounding: He had a 94-percent accuracy rate, which means he could predict marital happiness for strangers in a quarter of an hour.

A clue to how happy your marriage is may lie in the way you talk about it. Last year, researchers at the University of California at Berkeley found that middle-aged and older couples who used words such as "we," "our," and "us" tended to treat each other better and were better at resolving conflicts. Couples who emphasized their "separateness"—using pronouns such as "I," "me," and "you"—tended to be less happy.

Do you have couple friends? If not, you should get some. Professor Geoffrey Greif and associate professor Kathleen Holtz Deal of the University of Maryland's School of Social Work recently authored a book, *Two Plus Two: Couples and Their Couple Friendships*. After interviewing 123 couples, they found that those who had a social network of couple friends reported higher levels of marital happiness. The researchers said that having couple friends promotes marital satisfaction because it increases attraction to each other and allows couples to observe how other couples interact and resolve differences.

Everyone brings some baggage to a relationship, but a parent's divorce greatly affects marital quality. If your parents split up when you were a kid, you have a 50-percent greater chance of getting divorced yourself. If you and your spouse are both children of divorce, you have a 200-percent higher risk of divorce, says Nicholas Wolfinger, an associate professor of family and consumer studies at the University of Utah and author of a book called *Understanding the Divorce Cycle: The Children of Divorce in Their Own Marriages*.

People who live together before getting engaged tend to "slide" into a lifelong commitment.

Children of divorce are also more likely to live together before marriage or to marry young—both of which increase the chance of divorce. You'd think cohabiting partners would have lower divorce rates—isn't the whole point of moving in together to test the waters, to give couples a chance to try each other on as life partners?

Apparently, it doesn't work. Researchers say that people who live together before getting engaged tend to "slide" into a lifelong commitment rather than choose it. In other words, they've already got the house, the patio furniture, and someone to split the bills with—why wouldn't they take the next step?

Experts say this inertia doesn't bode well for lasting happiness. Scott Stanley, a psychologist at the University of Denver, found that 19 percent of couples who lived together before their engagement suggested divorce at least once over the course of the five-year study, compared with only 10 percent who moved in together after the big day.

But cohabitation doesn't always spell doom: Couples who move in together after their engagement—but before marriage—appear to fare just as well as couples who moved in together after saying "I do."

As for having kids, the jury is out on whether they strain or enrich a marriage. "There's a dip in marital happiness after the birth of your first child," says the Marriage Project's W. Bradford Wilcox. A study by Texas A&M University and the University of Denver of 218 couples in their mid-twenties—roughly two-thirds of whom welcomed their first child within eight years of marrying and a third of whom had no children—showed that couples with kids were less happy than childless couples. While the study showed that overall marital happiness decreased over time for both those with kids and those without, the couples with children reported a more sudden drop in marital dissatisfaction; the childless couples' happiness levels decreased more slowly over time.

Still, Wilcox says that couples with kids often rebound and report higher levels of happiness later in life. Longitudinal data show that marital satisfaction increases as children get older and leave home. In other words, while individuals love their children and glean much happiness from them, their marriages benefit when their kids enter college and they're able to spend more quality time together.

There doesn't seem to be a magic age for getting married. Even so, couples who wed later tend to report higher levels of education, leading to greater affluence and greater marital satisfaction. If you have a college degree, you're 66 percent less likely to divorce. "It's partly because people with college degrees make more money and do better in the professional world," says Wilcox, "but it's also because many have the social skills needed to navigate married life more successfully."

Money makes a big difference in a couple's life. Research cited in a 2009 article by Jeffrey Drew of the National Marriage Project found that wives with higher incomes and assets are happier in their marriages; they're also less likely to get a divorce. Couples who reported fighting about money once a week were 30 percent more likely to split up than couples who argued about finances a few times a month. And couples with no assets at the beginning of a three-year period were 70 percent likelier to divorce than couples with at least $10,000 in assets.

But while having money can help, it's not a good sign if either spouse is too motivated by it. A Brigham Young University study of 1,734 married couples found that those who said money wasn't important scored 10 to 15 percent better on marriage stability than couples in which one or both said they highly valued "having money and lots of things."

"Couples where both spouses are materialistic were worse off on nearly every measure we looked at," says Jason Carroll, a BYU professor of family life.

A second study cited in Drew's National Marriage Project article found that perceptions of how well one's spouse handles money can also cause strain. If you feel your husband or wife doesn't handle money well, you probably have a lower level of marital happiness. "In one study, feeling that one's spouse spent money foolishly increased the likelihood of divorce by 45 percent for both men and women. Only extramarital affairs and alcohol/drug abuse were stronger predictors of divorce," Drew writes.

What do happy couples have in common? They respect each other. They don't nitpick, criticize, or put each other down. And yes, they go out of their way to be nice. Says Wilcox: "Being an affectionate and engaging spouse is going to make both of you happier."

My husband and I may be of different ethnicities and we may have a kid, but I think we're going to make it. Here's why: When my feet are cold in winter, he'll always let me warm them up on his legs. I kiss him hello every day when he gets home. He encourages me to take time for myself when he sees I'm feeling drained. In other words, we're kind to each other—and as the studies show, that counts for a lot.

Critical Thinking

Don't nitpick, critize or put eachother down makes both happier.

1. Why does "playing nice" improve a couple's sex life?

2. What are some of the positive interactions that contribute to the 5-to-1 ratio of positive-to-negative interactions that predict marital success?

3. How does the desire for money and lots of things decrease the chances of marital success? *Because your never content.*

Create Central

www.mhhe.com/createcentral

Internet References

Child Out of Wedlock: Huffington Post
www.huffingtonpost.com/tag/child-out-of-wedlock

Does Living Together before Marriage Increase Chances of Divorce?
www.eharmony.com/blog/2013/07/24/does-living-together-before-marriage-increase-chances-of-divorce

The Downside of Cohabitating before Marriage
www.nytimes.com/2012/04/15/opinion/Sunday

U.S. Rate of Interracial Marriage Hits Record High
http://usatoday30.usatoday.com/health/news/2012-02-16

Foster, Brooke Lea. From *Washingtonian*, December 2012, pp. 74–76. Copyright © 2012 by Brooke Lea Foster. Reprinted by permission of the author.

Article Prepared by: Claire N. Rubman, *Suffolk County Community College*

The Retro Wife

Feminists who say they're having it all—by choosing to stay home.

LISA MILLER

Learning Outcomes

After reading this article, you will be able to:

- Contrast traditional women's roles (stay home and nurture husband/children) with the liberated women's roles (independence, career).

- Explain why women who expect their husbands to fully share housework, child care, and money-making in careers are frequently disappointed.

When Kelly Makino was a little girl, she loved to go orienteering—to explore the wilderness near her rural Pennsylvania home, finding her way back with a compass and a map—and the future she imagined for herself was equally adventuresome. Until she was about 16, she wanted to be a CIA operative, a spy, she says, "like La Femme Nikita." She put herself through college at Georgia State working in bars and slinging burgers, planning that with her degree in social work, she would move abroad, to India or Africa, to do humanitarian work for a couple of years. Her husband would be nerdy-hip, and they'd settle down someplace like Williamsburg; when she eventually had children, she would continue working full time, like her mother did, moving up the nonprofit ladder to finally "run a United Way chapter or be the CEO." Kelly graduated from college magna cum laude and got an M.S.W. from Penn, again with honors, receiving an award for her negotiating skills.

Now Kelly is 33, and if dreams were winds, you might say that hers have shifted. She believes that every household needs one primary caretaker, that women are, broadly speaking, better at that job than men, and that no amount of professional success could possibly console her if she felt her two young children—Connor, 5, and Lillie, 4—were not being looked after the right way.

The maternal instinct is a real thing, Kelly argues: Girls play with dolls from childhood, so "women are raised from the get-go to raise children successfully. When we are moms, we have a better toolbox." Women, she believes, are conditioned to be more patient with children, to be better multitaskers, to be more tolerant of the quotidian grind of playdates and temper tantrums; "women," she says, "keep it together better than guys do." So last summer, when her husband, Alvin, a management consultant, took a new position requiring more travel, she made a decision. They would live off his low-six-figure income, and she would quit her job running a program for at-risk kids in a public school to stay home full time.

Kelly is not a Martha Stewart spawn in pursuit of the perfectly engineered domestic stage set. On the day I met her, she was wearing an orange hoodie, plum-colored Converse low-tops, and a tiny silver stud in her nose. In the family's modest New Jersey home, the bedroom looked like a laundry explosion, and the morning's breakfast dishes were piled in the sink. But Kelly's priorities are nothing if not retrograde. She has given herself over entirely to the care and feeding of her family. Undistracted by office politics and unfettered by meetings or a nerve-fraying commute, she spends hours upon hours doing things that would make another kind of woman scream with boredom, chanting nursery rhymes and eating pretend cake beneath a giant *Transformers* poster. Her sacrifice of a salary tightened the Makinos' upper-middle-class budget, but the subversion of her personal drive pays them back in ways Kelly believes are priceless; she is now able to be there for her kids no matter what, cooking healthy meals, taking them hiking and to museums, helping patiently with homework, and devoting herself to teaching the life lessons—on littering, on manners, on good habits—that she believes every child should know. She introduces me as "Miss Lisa," and that's what the kids call me all day long.

Alvin benefits no less from his wife's domestic reign. Kelly keeps a list of his clothing sizes in her iPhone and, devoted to his cuteness, surprises him regularly with new items, like the dark-washed jeans he was wearing on the day I visited. She tracks down his favorite recipes online, recently discovering one for pineapple fried rice that he remembered from his childhood in Hawaii. A couple of times a month, Kelly suggests that they go to bed early and she soothes his work-stiffened muscles with a therapeutic massage. "I love him so much, I just want to spoil him," she says.

Kelly calls herself "a flaming liberal" and a feminist, too. "I want my daughter to be able to do anything she wants," she says. "But I also want to say, 'Have a career that you can walk away from at the drop of a hat.'" And she is not alone. Far from the Bible Belt's conservative territories, in blue-state cities and suburbs, young, educated, married mothers find themselves not uninterested in the metaconversation about "having it all" but untouched by it. They are too busy mining their grandmothers' old-fashioned lives for values they can appropriate like heirlooms, then wear proudly as their own.

Feminism has fizzled, its promise only half-fulfilled. This is the revelation of the moment, hashed and rehashed on blogs and talk shows, a cause of grief for some, fury for others. American women are better educated than they've ever been, better educated now than men, but they get distracted during their prime earning years by the urge to procreate. As they mature, they earn less than men and are granted fewer responsibilities at work. Fifty years after the publication of *The Feminine Mystique,* women represent only a tiny fraction of corporate and government leaders, and they still earn only 77 cents on the male dollar.

What to do? One solution is to deny the need for broader solutions or for any kind of sisterly help. It's every woman for herself, and may the best one win. "I don't, I think, have, sort of, the militant drive and, sort of, the chip on the shoulder that sometimes comes with that," said Yahoo CEO Marissa Mayer in an interview with PBS, in which she declined to label herself a "feminist." "I think it's too bad, but I do think that *feminism* has become in many ways a more negative word." (*I went to Stanford, worked at Google, got pregnant, and still became the chief executive of a Fortune 500 company,* she seemed to say. *If you're smart enough, so can you.*) But others, as you may have read, believe it's time for women to resume the good fight. In her much-discussed *Atlantic* piece, Anne-Marie Slaughter, by profession a policy wonk (now at Princeton, formerly at the State Department), calls for better workplace programs: more parental leave, more part-time and flextime options. Facebook COO Sheryl Sandberg, in her new book, *Lean In,* acknowledges the need for better policies, but argues that the new revolution needs to start with women themselves, that what's needed to equalize U.S. workplaces is a generation of women tougher, stronger, wilier, more honest about their ambition, more strategic, and more determined to win than American women currently are.

But what if all the fighting is just too much? That is, what if a woman isn't earning Facebook money but the salary of a social worker? Or what if her husband works 80 hours a week, and her kid is acting out at school, and she's sick of the perpetual disarray in the closets and the endless battles over who's going to buy the milk and oversee the homework? Maybe most important, what if a woman doesn't have Sandberg-Slaughter-Mayer-level ambition but a more modest amount that neither drives nor defines her?

Reading *The Feminine Mystique* now, one is struck by the white-hot flame of Betty Friedan's professional hunger, which made her into a prophet and a pioneer. But it blinded her as well: She presumed that all her suburban-housewife sisters felt as imprisoned as she did and that the gratification she found in her work was attainable for all. That was never true, of course; the revolution that Friedan helped to spark both liberated women and allowed countless numbers of them to experience financial pressure and the profound dissatisfactions of the workaday grind. More women than ever earn some or all of the money their family lives on. But today, in the tumultuous 21st-century economy, depending on a career as a path to self-actualization can seem like a sucker's bet.

Meanwhile, what was once feminist blasphemy is now conventional wisdom: Generally speaking, mothers instinctively want to devote themselves to home more than fathers do. (Even Sandberg admits it. "Are there characteristics inherent in sex differences that make women more nurturing and men more assertive?" she asks. "Quite possibly.") If feminism is not only about creating an equitable society but also a means to fulfillment for individual women, and if the rewards of working are insufficient and uncertain, while the tug of motherhood is inexorable, then a new calculus can take hold: For some women, the solution to resolving the long-running tensions between work and life is not more parent-friendly offices or savvier career moves but the full embrace of domesticity. "The feminist revolution started in the workplace, and now it's happening at home," says Makino. "I feel like in today's society, women who don't work are bucking the convention we were raised with . . . Why can't we just be girls? Why do we have to be boys and girls at the same time?" She and the legions like her offer a silent rejoinder to Sandberg's manifesto, raising the possibility that the best way for some mothers (and their loved ones) to have a happy life is to make home their highest achievement.

"What these women feel is that the trade-offs now between working and not working are becoming more and more unsustainable," says Stacy Morrison, editor-in-chief of BlogHer, a network of 3,000 blogs for and by women. "The conversation we hear over and over again is this: 'The sense of calm and control that we feel over our lives is so much better than what is currently on offer in our culture.' And they're not wrong." The number of stay-at-home mothers rose incrementally between 2010 and 2011, for the first time since the downturn of 2008. While staying home with children remains largely a privilege of the affluent (the greatest number of America's SAHMs live in families with incomes of $100,000 a year or more), some of the biggest increases have been among younger mothers, ages 25 to 35, and those whose family incomes range from $75,000 to $100,000 a year.

This is not the retreat from high-pressure workplaces of a previous generation but rather a more active awakening to the virtues of the way things used to be. Patricia Ireland, who lives on the Upper West Side, left her job as a wealth adviser in 2010 after her third child was born. Now, even though her husband, also in finance, has seen his income drop since the recession, she has no plans to go back to work. She feels it's a privilege to manage her children's lives—"not just what they do, but what they believe, how they talk to other children, what kind of story we read together. That's all dictated by me. Not by my nanny or my babysitter." Her husband's part of the arrangement is to go to work and deposit his paycheck in the joint account. "I'm really grateful that my husband and I have fallen into traditional gender roles without conflict," says Ireland. "I'm not bitter that I'm the one home and he goes to work. And he's very happy that he goes to work."

A lot of the new neo-traditionalists watched their own mothers strain under the second shift, and they regard Sandberg's lower-wattage mini-mes, rushing off to Big Jobs and back home with a wad of cash for the nanny, with something like pity. They don't want a return to the confines of the fifties; they treasure their freedoms, but see a third way. When Slaughter tours the lecture circuit, she is often approached, she says, by women younger than 30 who say, "I don't see a senior person in my world whose life I want." In researching her 2010 book *The Unfinished Revolution: Coming of Age in a New Era of Gender, Work and Family,* New York University sociologist Kathleen Gerson found that, in spite of all the gains young women have made, about a quarter say they would choose a traditional domestic arrangement over the independence that comes with a career, believing not just "that only a parent can provide an acceptable level of care" but also that "they are the only parent available for the job."

The harried, stressed, multiarmed Kali goddess, with a laptop in one hand and homemade organic baby food in the other,

has been replaced with a domestic Madonna, content with her choices and placid in her sphere. "I was . . . blessed," wrote one woman on the UrbanBaby message boards recently, "with the patience to truly enjoy being home with my kids and know that in the end family is what is important in life—not pushing papers at some crap job." When the UB community fired back with a fusillade of snark, the poster remained serene. "It's sacred work but not for everyone," she wrote. "I will never have regrets." In season three of *The Good Wife,* Caitlin D'arcy, the law firm's ambitious and strategically minded female associate, unexpectedly quits her job when she becomes pregnant, saying she wants to be a full-time wife and mother. Her mentor, Alicia Florrick—separated from her husband and a mother of two—tries to dissuade her. "You're smart and clever," she says. "If you give this up for someone, even someone important to you, you'll regret it."

"I'm not giving it up for my fiancé," says Caitlin. "I'm giving it up for myself. I like the law, but I love my fiancé."

"But you don't need to choose," protests Alicia. "There's no reason why you can't work, be a wife and a mother."

"But I want to choose," says Caitlin. "Maybe it's different for my generation, but I don't have to prove anything. Or if I have to, I don't want to. I'm in love."

In Friedan's day, housewives used novel technologies such as the automatic washing machine to ease the burden of their domestic work; today, technology helps them to avoid the isolation of their grandmothers and to show off the fruits of their labor. Across the Internet, on a million mommy blogs and Pinterest pages, these women—conceptual cousins of the bearded and suspendered artisanal bakers and brewers who reside in gentrified neighborhoods—are elevating homemaking to an art, crocheting baby hats, slow-roasting strawberries for after-school snacks ("taste like Twizzlers!"), and making their own laundry soap from scratch. Young mothers fill the daytime upholstery and pattern-making courses at Third Ward, a craftspace in Williamsburg, and take knitting classes at the Brooklyn Yarn Café in Bushwick while their kids are in school.

Home, to these women, is more than a place to watch TV at the end of the day and motherhood more than a partial identity. It is a demanding, full-time endeavor, requiring all of their creativity, energy, and ingenuity. Kelly Makino set up a giant mothers' group in northern Jersey, using her M.S.W. to help other parents pool time and resources. (Such "side projects," she says, have the added benefit of "keeping us sane.") Home-schooling, once the province of Christian conservatives, is now increasingly chosen by lefty families; in New York City, the number of children being taught in their apartments rose by nearly 10 percent over the past year.

For Rebecca Woolf, maternal ambition led to the creation of her website, Girl's Gone Child, in 2005, when she was 23 and had just given birth to her son Archer. She has since had three more children (a girl, Fable, and twins named Reverie and Boheme), and every day she posts staged photos of her kids that make her family life look like one big, wholesome-but-funky romp. Here are the twins wearing adorable handmade animal hats with ears! Here is a lesson in at-home bang trimming! Woolf, who lives in Los Angeles and whose husband is a television producer, points out that as the founder of a thriving blog, she does have a job. But the image of home life she presents for popular consumption is as glossy and idealized as the mythical feminine perfection Friedan rebelled against. It is perhaps no wonder that in the world of mommy blogs, tattooed Fort Greeners and Mormons unknowingly collide, trafficking the same sites and trading recipes on the same message boards. They may vote different tickets, but on the centrality of home and family to a satisfying life, their interests are aligned.

Before they marry, college students of both genders almost universally tell social scientists that they want marriages in which housework, child care, professional ambition, and moneymaking will be respectfully negotiated and fully shared. According to a 2008 report by the Families and Work Institute, two thirds of people younger than 29 imagine for themselves partnerships not defined by traditional gender roles. Maybe she'll change the lightbulbs; maybe he'll go part time for a while after the birth of the baby. Seventy-four percent of American employees say they believe that women who work outside the home can be as good at mothering as those who don't. The institute's data also indicates that "men today view the 'ideal' man as someone who is not only successful . . . but also involved as a father, husband/partner, and son." Once married, the research shows, men are more contented over the long term, and women are happiest in an egalitarian union—so long as both parties agree about what egalitarian means.

That, of course, is where things get tricky. Despite their stated position, men still do far less housework than their spouses. In 2011, only 19 percent spent any time during the average day cleaning or doing laundry; among couples with kids younger than 6, men spent just 26 minutes a day doing what the Bureau of Labor Statistics calls "physical care," which is to say bathing, feeding, or dressing children. (Women did more than twice as much.) In her research, Gerson found that in times of stress men overwhelmingly revert to the traditional provider role, allowing them to justify punting on the dishes. "All [men]," she says, "agree that no matter what the gender revolution prescribes, it is still paramount for men to earn a living and support their families, which also implies taking a backseat as caregiver." As a romantic college student, a man may imagine he will request an extended paternity leave, but

it's very likely that he won't. The average amount of time a man takes off after the birth of a child is five days. "That's exactly what happened to me!" exclaimed Kelly Makino when I relayed that stat to her. Alvin had planned on taking a two-week leave after Lillie was born but was back at the office after half that time.

All those bachelors' vows of future bathroom cleanings, it turns out, may be no more than a contemporary mating call. "People espouse equality because they conform to the current normative values of our culture," says University of Texas evolutionary psychologist David Buss. "Any man who did not do so would alienate many women—yes, espousing values is partly a mating tactic, and this is just one example." At least in one area, there's scant penalty for this bait and switch. Last year, sociologists at the University of Washington found that the less cooking, cleaning, and laundry a married man does, the more frequently he gets laid.

Feminism has never fully relieved women from feeling that the domestic domain is theirs to manage, no matter what else they're juggling. There is a story, possibly apocryphal yet also believable, of an observer looking over Secretary of State Madeleine Albright's shoulder during a Cabinet meeting in the late nineties. On the pad before her, the secretary had written not "paths to peace in the Middle East" but "buy cottage cheese." (Albright declined to comment for this story, but while promoting a book in 2009, she told an audience that all her life she made it a point always to answer phone calls from her children, no matter what else she was doing. "Every woman's middle name is guilt," she said.) Those choices have a different tenor now, one that upholds the special importance of the maternal role. "My sense," says Buss, "is that younger women are more open to the idea that there might exist evolved psychological gender differences." Among my friends, many women behave as though the evolutionary imperative extends not just to birthing and breast-feeding but to administrative household tasks as well, as if only they can properly plan birthday parties, make doctors' appointments, wrap presents, communicate with the teacher, buy the new school shoes. A number of those I spoke to for this article reminded me of a 2010 British study showing that men lack the same mental bandwidth for multitasking as women. Male and female subjects were asked how they'd find a lost key, while also being given a number of unrelated chores to do—talk on the phone, read a map, complete a math problem. The women universally approached the hunt more efficiently. Joanna Goddard, who runs the women's lifestyle blog A Cup of Jo, says she hears this refrain among her friends. "I'll just do it. It'll be easier. I'll just do it. It'll be faster. I'll do the dishes. I know where everything goes."

Psychologists suggest that perhaps American women are heirs and slaves to some atavistic need to prove their worth through domestic perfectionism: "So many women want to control their husbands' parenting," says Barbara Kass, a therapist with a private practice in Brooklyn. "'Oh, do you have the this? Did you do the that? Don't forget that she needs this. And make sure she naps.' Sexism is internalized." Perhaps this mentality explains the baffling result of a survey that the Families and Work Institute conducted last spring for *Real Simple* magazine. Women said they yearned for more free time and that they hated doing most housework. But when they got free time, they used it to do housework—convinced that no one else could do it as well.

If women and men are at odds with themselves over what they value most, if a woman says she wants a big job but also needs to be home by 5:30 to oversee homework, and her husband promises to pick up the kids from chess club but goes instead to the meeting with the boss, how can marriages with two working parents not wind up conflict-ridden? From Kelly Makino's perspective, it was a no-brainer. "Some days I just have to pinch myself," she says. "It's so easy, it's so rewarding to live this way."

Kelly and Alvin decided to change their lives one night last spring during a mini-vacation to Washington, D.C. They were there to see the cherry blossoms, and Kelly was aware, all weekend long, of the ebbing of her anxiety. "I didn't have to worry about 500 people's lives. I had to worry about four people's lives."

Connor had been in a fight at school. Lillie had been having nightmares. After the kids were in bed, the Makinos retired to the bathroom of their hotel room. "We realized that neither one of us were happy. We were sleep deprived and stressed out all the time," says Kelly. If they scaled back, they reasoned, they could live on Alvin's salary. But first Kelly had to come to terms with her unfulfilled ambition—"I knew I had it in me to be the best"—and the disapproval of her parents. Her father worried that she'd be bored out of her mind. Her mother accused her of "mooching." It took Kelly three months to quit her job.

Sitting at their kitchen table, littered with the detritus from a birthday-party goody bag, the Makinos retrace how their relationship turned out the way it has. They met at a biker bar where Kelly was waitressing, and at first, when Alvin envisioned their collective future, he thought, "*Oh, it's totally not going to be like my parents. We're going to do things equally. Both of us are working, and we'll take care of the kids together.* It just seemed so simple in my mind."

"I remember you said you wanted us to be a power couple," says Kelly.

But there was tension. Alvin earned a lot more money. Kelly felt that her job contributed more good to the world, that its emergencies were more urgent. One time, she remembers, she was just leaving work when she found herself face-to-face with an anguished child. "It's 4:30, this 12-year-old girl tells me she has been raped." Kelly attended to the girl and contacted the school authorities; after she got home, she put her own kids to bed and then was on the phone making a report to protective services until midnight. It was exhausting work but gratifying. "Honestly, before I had kids," she says, "I kind of looked down on stay-at-home moms a little. I thought, *You can't hack it.* It was a prejudice that was wrong. I thought, *Why can't you do it? You must've sucked at your job if you stay home.*"

Kelly's commitment to her career "put a lot more pressure on me to make sure I could pick up the kids and I could feed the kids," says Alvin. "As much as I tried to be really supportive, there were conflicts with schedule, with availability, with resource time. We would get home at 6:30 or 7:00, then we'd have to think about dinner. It's a rush to get the kids to bed. The time either of us had with the kids was short, hectic, stressful. Day to day, managing our schedules—sometimes my meeting would last two hours instead of twenty minutes—it put a lot of strain on our relationship." They got fat on takeout. At bedtime, they talked about "bills, plans, schedules, the next day, everything but spending time together," says Alvin. They never had sex, remembers Kelly. They rarely had any fun at all.

In 2006, British researchers studied work–life conflict in five European countries. They found a lot of strife in France, despite a high percentage of women in the workforce and widespread government policies aimed at helping women remain employed when their children are young: subsidized nursery schools, day-care collectives, and the like. What's more, the French expressed progressive, optimistic ideals about gender roles. Seventy-four percent of full-time employees in France disagreed with the following statement: "A man's job is to earn money, a woman's job is to look after the home and family."

The explanation for the disconnect, the researchers surmised, was that French people, like Americans, lie to themselves about what they want. French women (like their American counterparts) do the bulk of the domestic work, and the majority also work full time. Quoting from colleagues' earlier work, the sociologists showed that sexism in France is as much a part of the culture as great bread, wine, and a long lunch hour. In France, "there were numerous men who were available to look after children during the week when their partner was employed . . . but nevertheless did not take responsibility for child care even when they were free." They were saying one thing and doing another, which in marriage, says the historian Stephanie Coontz, is "a recipe for instability and unhappiness."

That same year, an American sociologist published a paper describing similar results. Predictors of marital unhappiness, found Bradford Wilcox at the University of Virginia, included wives who earned a large share of household income and wives who perceived the division of labor at home as unfair. Predictors of marital happiness were couples who shared a commitment to the institutional idea of marriage and couples who went to religious services together. "Our findings suggest," he wrote, "that increased departures from a male-breadwinning-female-homemaking model may also account for declines in marital quality, insofar as men and women continue to tacitly value gendered patterns of behavior in marriage." It's an idea that thrives especially in conservative religious circles: The things that specific men and women may selfishly want for themselves (sex, money, status, notoriety) must for the good of the family be put aside. Feminists widely critiqued Wilcox's findings, saying it puts the onus on women to suck it up in marriage, when men should be under more pressure to change. But these days you'll find echoes of Wilcox's thesis in unlikely places. "We look at straight people," a gay friend said to me recently as we were comparing anecdotes about husbands, "and we think marriage must be so much easier for them."

When I look at Kelly and Alvin Makino, I feel the same way. I have worked full time for almost all my daughter's nine years, and only very rarely have I ever felt that nature required anything else of me. I love my job and have found work to be gratifying and even calming during periods when other parts of my life are far less so. Like 65 percent of American couples, my husband and I both work to pay our bills, but my commitment to my career extends way beyond financial necessity. My self-sufficiency sets a good example for my daughter (or so we tell ourselves), which is one reason why even if we were to win the lotto, staying at home would not likely be a course I'd choose.

And yet. I am not immune to the notion that I have powers and responsibilities as a mother that my husband does not have. I prepare our daughter's lunch box every morning with ritualistic care, as if sending her off to school with a bologna sandwich made by me can work as an amulet against all the pain of my irregular, inevitable absences. I believe that I have a special gift for arranging playdates, pediatrician appointments, and piano lessons, and I yearn sometimes for the vast swaths of time Kelly Makino has given herself to keep her family's affairs in order. In an egalitarian marriage, every aspect of home life is open to renegotiation. When two people need to leave the house at 6 A.M., who gets the children ready for school? When two people have to work late, who will meet that inflexible daycare pickup time? And who, finally, has the energy for those constant transactions?

Two of the fastest-growing religious movements in America are Mormonism and Orthodox Judaism, which clearly define gender roles along traditional lines. It's difficult not to see the appeal—if only as a fleeting fantasy. How delicious might our weeknight dinners be, how straight the part in our daughter's hair, how much more carefree my marriage, if only I spent a fraction of the time cultivating our domestic landscape that I do at work.

This veneration of motherhood is fed by popular culture. On critically praised TV shows, ambitious women are nutty and single (Claire Danes in *Homeland,* Tina Fey on *30 Rock*), while good mothers are chopping veggies with a big glass of Chardonnay at their elbow. Beyoncé and Marissa Mayer never explain how they do it all, I suspect, because they have teams of nannies and housekeepers on the payroll—and realize that outing themselves as women who rely on servants will taint them, somehow, as bad parents. (Sandberg places this feeling within "the holy trinity of fear: the fear of being a bad mother/wife/daughter.") In my Facebook feed, Michelle Obama is an object of obsession not for the causes she's pursued as First Lady but for her child-rearing tactics: two mandatory sports (one chosen by them and one chosen by her) and no screen time on weeknights. When her husband first ran for president, he delivered speeches proclaiming the heroism of the working mother: "I don't accept an America that makes women choose between their kids and their careers." Four years later, against an opponent whose home life looked like a Disney production, Obama took a sanctity-of-motherhood tack: There is "no tougher job than being a mom."

Even Anne-Marie Slaughter would say that her maternal drive ultimately superseded her professional one, which is why she was unable to achieve more in her huge State Department job. She had a troubled kid at home. Thus the policy solutions she proposes do not dispel the mind-sets that continue to haunt American couples: In a world where men still run things and women still feel drawn to the kitchen and the nursery, an army of flextime females might lock in a second-class tier of workers who will never be able to compete with men for the top jobs. "That's the criticism of my piece that I worry most about," Slaughter says. "If that turns out to be true, I'll have to live with it forever."

Even as she enjoys her new life, Kelly Makino misses certain things about her old one. She misses getting dressed for work in clothes that have buttons and hems and sexy shoes to match. She misses "eating lunch with chopsticks," a euphemism for a universe of cuisine beyond chopped fruit and yogurt cups. She acknowledges the little luxuries of an office: a desk, a quiet cup of coffee, sick days. She misses her work friends—it is vexing trying to find the same hours free—and the validation that bosses and colleagues offer for a job well done. "There is no way my wonderful, loving family can fill that need," she says. In February, a few months after I met the Makinos at their home in New Jersey, they moved to the suburbs of Washington, D.C., for Alvin's job. Out of her element and detached from her old network, she is, for the first time since quitting work, bored.

Kelly loved her old profession and does not want to be painted as betraying the goals of feminism. She prefers to see herself as reaching beyond conventional ideas about what women should do. "I feel like we are evolving into something that is not defined by those who came before us," she says. By making domesticity her career, she and the other stay-at-home mothers she knows are standing up for values, such as patience, and kindness, and respectful attention to the needs of others, that have little currency in the world of work. Professional status is not the only sign of importance, she says, and financial independence is not the only measure of success.

I press her on this point. What if Alvin dies or leaves her? What if, as her children grow up, she finds herself resenting the fact that all the public accolades accrue to her husband? Kelly wrestles with these questions all the time, but for now she's convinced she's chosen the right path. "I know this investment in my family will be paid back when the time is right." When her kids don't need her anymore, she'll figure out what she wants to pursue next. Someday, she's sure, she'll have the chance to "play leapfrog" with Alvin; she'll wind up with a brilliant career, or be a writer, or go back to school. "You have to live in the now. I will deal with later when later comes. I'll find a way," she says. "Who knows? Maybe I will be home for ever and ever. Maybe I will have the best-kept lawn on the block for the rest of my life."

Critical Thinking

1. If a woman is benign in her confrontations, yet assertive, will her husband fully share housework and child care in a dual-career marriage? Why or why not?

2. Why are women more nurturing and men more assertive? Are these traits biological or learned?

3. What attributes foster creativity, energy, and ingenuity in child caregiving?

Create Central

www.mhhe.com/createcentral

Internet References

Genderless Child-Rearing
www.feminagination.com/1365/genderless-childrearing

How Involved Are Fathers in Raising Children?
www.prb.org/Publications/Articles/2000

Is Aggression Genetic?
www.salon.com/2012/05/28/is_aggression_genetic

Is There a Genetic Contribution to Cultural Differences?
http://scan.oxfordjournals.org/content/5/2-3/203.long

Article   Prepared by: Claire N. Rubman, *Suffolk County Community College*

Kids Are Not Adults

Brain research is providing new insights into what drives teenage behavior, moving lawmakers to rethink policies that treat them like adults.

SARAH ALICE BROWN

Learning Outcomes

After reading this article, you will be able to:

- Detail why adolescents differ from adults in their decision-making processes.

- Explain the RECLAIM program.

- Discuss why 19 is a critical age in relation to violence.

J uvenile justice policy is at a crossroads. Juvenile crime has decreased. Recent brain and behavioral science research has revealed new insights into how and when adolescents develop. And state budgets remain tight. Together, these factors have led many lawmakers to focus on which approaches can save money, yet keep the public safe and treat young offenders more effectively.

Why Now?

When youth violence reached a peak more than 20 years ago, the country lost confidence in its ability to rehabilitate juveniles. Legislatures responded by passing laws allowing more young offenders to be tried as adults. Since then, however, juvenile crime has steadily declined.

Between 1994 and 2010, violent crime arrest rates decreased for all age groups, but more for juveniles than for adults. More specifically, the rates dropped an average of 54 percent for teenagers 15 to 17, compared to 38 percent for those between 18 and 39. And while arrest rates for violent crimes were higher in 2010 than in 1980 for all ages over 24, the rates for juveniles ages 15 to 17 were down from 1980.

With the steady decline in juvenile violence, the current state of the economy and new information on how brain development

shapes teens' behavior, some lawmakers are reconsidering past assumptions.

Legislatures across the country are working on their juvenile justice policies, from passing individual measures to revamping entire codes. Arkansas revised its juvenile justice code in 2009; Georgia and Kentucky are considering doing so, and many other states are at various stages of making changes in juvenile justice.

"It's time to bring the juvenile code back to current times and find methods that work by looking at best practices nationally," says Georgia Representative Wendell Willard (R), who introduced a bill to revise the code this session. "We need to incorporate key items, such as instruments to assess risks, and put interventions in place within communities for young people involved in the system," says Willard.

Last year, lawmakers in Kentucky formed a task force to study juvenile justice issues. The group will recommend whether to amend any of the state's current juvenile code in 2013. "Frankly, our juvenile code is out of date, but this task force will give the legislature the foundation to change that and reflect best practices nationwide," says Representative John Tilley (D), co-chair of the task force.

Changes are not always easily made, and states are at different stages of reform. Among the various viewpoints and depths of changes, however, is the generally agreed-upon belief that juveniles are different from adults.

For Adults Only

Research distinguishing adolescents from adults has led states to re-establish boundaries between the criminal and juvenile justice systems. New policies reflect the growing body of research on how the brain develops, which has discovered teens' brains do not fully develop until about age 25, according to the John D. & Catherine T. MacArthur Foundation's

Research Network on Adolescent Development and Juvenile Justice. Other social science and behavioral science also shows that kids focus on short-term payoffs rather than long-term consequences of their actions and engage in immature, emotional, risky, aggressive and impulsive behavior, and delinquent acts.

Dr. David Fassler, a psychiatry professor at the University of Vermont College of Medicine, has testified before legislative committees on brain development. He says the research helps explain—not excuse—teenage behavior.

"It doesn't mean adolescents can't make rational decisions or appreciate the difference between right and wrong. But it does mean that, particularly when confronted with stressful or emotional circumstances, they are more likely to act impulsively, on instinct, without fully understanding or considering the consequences of their actions."

"Every single adult has been a teenager, and many have also raised them. We all know firsthand the mistakes teens can make simply without thinking. Now we have the science that backs this up," says North Carolina Representative Marilyn Avila (R). She is working to increase the age at which teenagers can be tried as adults from 16 to 18 in her state.

Other states are considering similar changes. Lawmakers in Colorado passed significant changes in 2012, barring district attorneys from charging juveniles as adults for many low- and mid-level felonies. For serious crimes, they raised the age at which offenders can be tried as adults from 14 to 16.

In Nevada, Mississippi and Utah, lawmakers now leave it up to the juvenile courts to decide whether to transfer a juvenile to adult court. The Oklahoma Legislature upped the age limit at which offenders can be tried as adults for misdemeanors to 18 and one-half. And Ohio now requires a judicial review before transferring anyone under age 21 to an adult jail.

Counsel Is Key

A related trend in the past decade is to increase due process protections to preserve the constitutional rights of young offenders to ensure that youths understand the court process, make reasonable decisions regarding their case, and have adequate counsel. At least 10 states now have laws requiring qualified counsel to accompany juveniles at various stages of youth court proceedings. For juveniles appealing their cases, Utah created an expedited process. And two new laws in Pennsylvania require that all juvenile defendants be represented by counsel and that juvenile court judges state in court the reasoning behind their sentences.

To protect the constitutional rights of young offenders, Massachusetts Senator Karen Spilka (D) says "it is important for states to ensure that juveniles have access to quality counsel." The Bay State created juvenile defense resource centers that provide leadership, training and support to the entire Massachusetts juvenile defense bar.

Legislators are also enacting laws on determining the competency of juvenile offenders to stand trial. At least 16 states—Arizona, California, Colorado, Delaware, Florida, Georgia, Idaho, Kansas, Louisiana, Maine, Michigan, Minnesota, Nebraska, Ohio, Texas, and Virginia—and the District of

Supreme Court Rulings Set Stage

Significant rulings by the U.S. Supreme Court have also reshaped juvenile justice policies. The high court abolished the death penalty for juveniles in 2005 in *Roper v. Simmons,* citing findings by the MacArthur Research Network that adolescents can be less culpable than adults for their crimes.

Its 2010 ruling in *Graham v. Florida* ended life sentences without parole for crimes other than homicide committed by juveniles. Then last summer, in *Miller v. Alabama,* the court ruled that imposing mandatory life sentences without the possibility of parole for juveniles violates the Eighth Amendment of cruel and unusual punishment. Justice Anthony Kennedy wrote that juveniles have less culpability and, as a result, are "less deserving of the most severe punishments."

The Court went on to state in the ruling that life without parole for juveniles is especially harsh because it removes all hope. It makes it so "that good behavior and character improvement are immaterial. When compared with the reality that juveniles are more likely to change than are adults, juveniles who have demonstrated substantial improvement should be given the opportunity for parole."

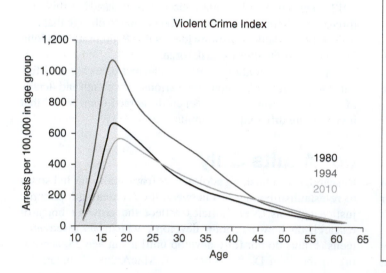

Violent Crime Index

1980
1994
2010

Columbia, now specifically address competency in statute. For example, Idaho lawmakers established standards for evaluating a juvenile's competency to proceed. Maine passed a similar measure that defines "chronological immaturity," "mental illness," and "mental retardation" for use in determining juvenile competency.

Between 65 percent and 70 percent of the 2 million young people arrested each year in the United States have some type of mental health disorder. Newer policies focus on providing more effective evaluations and interventions for youths who come into contact with the juvenile justice system. This includes proper screening, assessment, and treatment services for young offenders. Some states have special mental health courts to provide intensive case management as well.

New mental health assessments in Louisiana and Pennsylvania give a wide range of professionals the means to reliably ascertain youths' needs. And other states such as Colorado, Connecticut, Ohio, and Texas have passed comprehensive juvenile mental health reform laws.

Family Matters

"Show me it will work, and then I am all for it!" says North Carolina's Avila. "As a legislator, I am very much in favor of evidence-based programming, because I want to invest in what will work." She cites the effectiveness of three kinds of programs that have passed the evaluation test and are being used in at least 10 states. They include the families in the treatments young offenders receive to address specific behaviors to improve positive results for the whole family.

- Multi-systemic therapy teaches parents how to effectively handle the high-risk "acting out" behaviors of teenagers.
- Family functional therapy focuses on teaching communication and problem-solving skills to the whole family.
- Aggression-replacement training teaches positive ways to express anger as well as anger control and moral reasoning.

Massachusetts Senator Spilka believes these kinds of programs are important because "instead of simply focusing on the child's behavior, they look to effectively treat and help the entire family."

Communities Are Key

Policymakers across the country are searching for ways to keep the public safe while reducing costs. Many are looking at effective policies that divert young offenders away from expensive, secure correctional facilities and into local community programs. According to the U.S. Office of Juvenile Justice and Delinquency Prevention, incarceration is a costly and ineffective way to keep delinquent juveniles from committing more serious crimes. Researchers suggest, instead, in investing in successful and cost-effective programs that have undergone rigorous evaluations.

For example, RECLAIM Ohio is a national model for funding reform that channels the money saved from fewer juvenile commitments into local courts to be used in treating and rehabilitating young people. The program not only has reduced juvenile commitments to detention facilities and saved money, but also has cut down on the number of young people re-entering the justice system. The cost of housing 10 young people in a Department of Youth Services' facility is $571,940 a year versus $85,390 a year for RECLAIM Ohio programs.

Realignment shifts responsibility for managing young offenders from states to the counties. Such strategies are based on the premise that local communities are in the best position to provide extensive and cost-effective supervision and treatment services for juvenile offenders, and that youth are more successful when supervised and treated closer to their homes and families.

Illinois lawmakers, for example, passed major changes in 2004 that created Redeploy Illinois, which encourages counties to develop community programs for juveniles rather than confine them in state correctional facilities.

The program gives counties financial support to provide comprehensive services in their home communities to delinquent youths who might otherwise be sent to the Illinois Department of Juvenile Justice. The program has been so successful that it is expanding statewide and has become a model for other states.

Several other states, from California and Georgia, to New York and Texas, are also looking at ways to effectively and safely redirect fiscal resources from state institutions to community services.

"Getting kids out of the correctional centers and treated in the community is obviously the best practice," says Georgia's Willard. "You have to close these large infrastructures and the overhead that goes with it, so you can redirect that money to treating youth in the community. When you go about such an exercise in your own communities, you will accomplish the goal of saving money."

States also are shortening the time juveniles are confined in detention centers, usually while they wait for a court appearance or disposition. A recent Mississippi law, for example, limits it to 10 days for first-time nonviolent youth offenders. And Georgia decreased it from 60 to 30 days. Illinois lawmakers increased the age of kids who can be detained for more than 6 hours in a county jail or municipal lockup from age 12 to 17.

Texas Moves Away from Youth Detention

Texas lawmakers responded quickly to reports of physical and sexual abuse by staff at juvenile detention facilities in 2006. During the following session, the Legislature passed laws to address these incidents and improve the overall administration of juvenile justice. The changes included creating the Independent Ombudsman's office to investigate and review allegations of misconduct, monitoring detention facilities with cameras and on-site officials, and barring juveniles from serving time in detention facilities for committing misdemeanors.

Legislators continued to focus on juvenile justice during the next two sessions, passing laws in 2009 that strengthened support and funding for local and county programs that monitor juveniles closer to their homes. And in 2011, to consolidate oversight of young offenders and improve communication among different levels of government, lawmakers merged the Probation Commission, and the Youth Commission to create the Texas Juvenile Justice Department.

The laws appear to be making a difference. The number of juveniles in state-run detention facilities dropped from nearly 5,000 in 2006 to around 1,200 in 2012, with more participating in county and local programs. The state has closed nine facilities and may close more during the coming biennium. In addition, verified complaints of abuse dropped 69.5 percent from 2008 to 2011.

Challenges with safety within facilities, however, persist. Early in 2012, the Independent Ombudsman reported incidents of youth-on-youth violence in the state's largest remaining detention facility. Executive Director Mike Griffiths, on the job since September 2012, believes that "there needs to be a foundation of safety and security to be effective. We are light years ahead of where we were in 2007, and the success of the community-based programs is encouraging, but safety needs to be a continued focus." Subsequent reports indicate improvements in the culture of the facilities.

One way Texas is tackling violence in its facilities is by placing the most challenging juveniles in The Phoenix Program, which focuses on preventing high-risk youth from becoming reoffenders. It holds the kids in the program "accountable for the actions of each individual, and provides a staffing ratio of one to four, as opposed to the regular one to 12," says Griffiths.

Texas continues to work on improving its juvenile justice system. "My challenge moving forward is to find additional dollars for local community programs, while making sure the overall system is secure," says Griffiths. "It's important to give the staff the support they need, while letting them know that they are accountable."

—*Richard Williams, NCSL*

Young Offenders Grow Up

Violence toward others tends to peak in adolescence, beginning most often around age 16, according to Emory University psychiatrist Peter Ash. However, if a teenager hasn't committed a violent crime by age 19, he's unlikely to become violent later, Ash says. The promising news is that 66 to 75 percent of violent young people grow out of it. "They get more self-controlled."

Realizing that teens who commit delinquent acts don't always turn into adult criminals, more states are protecting the confidentiality of juvenile records for future educational and employment opportunities to help them make successful transitions into adulthood.

In 2011, Delaware lawmakers passed legislation allowing juvenile criminal cases that are dismissed, acquitted or not prosecuted to be expunged from a young person's record. "Children who are charged with minor crimes that are dismissed or dropped should not have these charges following them around

for the rest of their lives," says Representative Michael A. Barbieri (D), sponsor of the bill.

And in 2012, eight states—California, Colorado, Hawaii, Louisiana, Ohio, Oregon, Vermont, and Washington—enacted laws vacating or expunging any prostitution charges juvenile victims of sex trafficking may have received.

A Bipartisan Issue

These recent legislative trends reflect a new understanding of adolescent development. Investing in alternative programs in the community instead of incarceration and adopting only proven intervention programs are among the examples of how state legislators hope to better serve youth and prevent juvenile crime.

"Reforming juvenile justice is definitely a bipartisan issue that all legislators can get behind. It is the right time. All the research says it makes sense and will save money," says Representative Avila from North Carolina.

Critical Thinking

1. Should the adolescent judicial system differ from the adult system? If adolescents under the age of 25 act on the bases of short-term consequences, then should we offer short-term punishments for them rather than adult sentences?

2. If the adolescent brain is still growing, how can we protect our adolescent population and prevent them from committing serious crimes?

3. Why don't all adolescents commit crimes—is there a profile?

Create Central

www.mhhe.com/createcentral

Internet References

aspe.hhs.gov What Challenges Are Boys Facing, and What Opportunities Exist To Address Those Challenges? Fact Sheet
http://aspe.hhs.gov/hsp/08/boys/factsheets/jd/report.pdf

multiplying connections.org The Amazing Adolescent Brain: What Every Educator, Youth Serving Professional, and Healthcare Provider Needs to Know
http://www.multiplyingconnections.org/sites/default/files/Teen%20Provider%20article%20(2)_0.pdf

news.discovery.com The Teen Brain on Rage: How It's Different
http://news.discovery.com/human/teen-brain-rage-violence-120229.htm

NJJN.org National Juvenile Justice Network
http://www.njjn.org/library/search-results?subject=7

Yale.edu Juvenile Delinquency Cause and Effect
http://www.yale.edu/ynhti/curriculum/units/2000/2/00.02.05.x.html

Brown, Sarah Alice. "Kids Are Not Adults." *Juvenile Justice Bulletin* 39. 4 (April, 2013): 20–23.

Article | Prepared by: Claire N. Rubman, *Suffolk County Community College*

High-Tech Bullies

Suicides have made administrators aware that acts of aggression in the wireless, viral world of the Internet demand action to protect targeted students.

INGRID STURGIS

Learning Outcomes

After reading this article, you will be able to:

- Identify the most vulnerable members of our society who are most prone to bullying.
- Describe what colleges and universities are doing to combat cyberbullying.

Cases of cyberbullying have made headlines over the past decade, raising awareness about the number of young people who have committed suicide or otherwise been harmed as a result of being on the receiving end of constant Internet harassment or shaming.

Bullying that started in email and chat rooms in the early days of the Internet has evolved into other forms—mostly social networking sites and instant messaging, as well as video and pictures, Justin W. Patchin, PhD, co-director of the Cyberbullying Research Center at the University of Wisconsin-Eau Claire, agrees.

"It's constantly changing," he said. "The bullies are pretty creative. Now there is a level of permanence that is not evident in traditional bullying. Early adopters are most likely to use new technology. It's amazing how creative some can be to cause harm."

Patchin, author of *Words Wound: Delete Cyberbullying and Make Kindness Go Viral* (Free Spirit Publishing, December 2013), has been studying cyberbullying among secondary students for more than a decade, starting in 2001. He has surveyed nearly 15,000 students across the United States.

Most cases seem to involve middle school or high school students, whom experts say, are in the primary age group for such behavior.

However, as social media continues its pervasive intrusion into everyday lives, cyberbullying is trickling up to college campuses and even into the workplace. Researchers, law-enforcement lawyers, college officials, and students say there are more reported incidents of acts of cyberbullying cropping up on campus and a rise in incidents of teenage suicide has coincided with the rise in incidents of cyberbullying. In fact, the suicide of Rutgers University freshman Tyler Clementi in 2010, who was the target of a campaign of intimidation by his roommate, put universities on notice that what might have once been treated as a college prank could lead to suicide for vulnerable students. Clementi jumped off the George Washington Bridge after learning that his roommate spied on him during a romantic encounter with a man using a webcam. Clementi also learned that his roommate conspired to "out" him by alerting Twitter followers to a second viewing.

Attacking the Vulnerable

Cyberbullies often target gays, women or people of color. Students who are different in some way (race, ethnicity, sexual orientation, religion, or appearance) or high-profile students (athletes, student government officers) are often the most vulnerable.

Jiyoon Yoon, associate professor and director of the elementary education program at University of Texas at Arlington, said via email that while nearly anyone can be a victim, most victims are targeted because of perceived differences from a group and weaknesses.

"Students who do not fit in may become the prime targets of cyberbullying," she said. "In many contexts, students of minority status and/or lower economic privilege may be more susceptible to the abuse."

Yoon said victims of such bullying are more likely to report feelings of depression than other groups of students, which interfere with their scholastic achievement, social skills, and sense of well-being. She has conducted research with Dr. Julie Smith on cyberbullying among college students and says it is increasing. According to survey responses conducted by Yoon and Smith within a Midwestern university system, 10.1 percent of the students said they experienced cyberbullying by another student; 2.9 percent of the students had been cyberbullied by instructors, and 27.5 percent of the students witnessed cyberbullying behavior by a student toward another student.

This is consistent with other studies on cyberbullying. In one study conducted at Indiana State University, 22 percent of college students reported being cyberbullied, and 9 percent reported cyberbullying someone.

"People thought cyberbullying happened mostly among teenagers who are familiar with and willingly use electronic technology," Yoon said. "However, as portability and accessibility of technology for distance learning increases daily in higher education, incidents of cyberbullying are rising on college campuses."

Dawn Harner, a training coordinator and counselor at Salisbury University, said a potent mix of 24/7, always-on communication lends itself to abuses. She cited the pervasive use of connected mobile devices, multiple social media profiles from Facebook to Twitter to Instagram, growth in text messaging and decline in phone conversations, the illusion of anonymity and the international reach of the Internet, coupled with students' immaturity and newly found freedom.

"It is much more common for students to be connected to social media," Harner said. "Now, as opposed to seven years ago, phones connect to Internet as well."

Researchers are just starting to examine the rise in university-level bullying. Today, universities are obligated to face the problem before another student is hurt. First, they must define cyberbullying.

"A lot of times as academics, we debate definitions," said Patchin. "What's the difference between hazing, bullying and harassing? All could be the same behaviors. We don't focus on it until something happens. We have to focus on behaviors that repeatedly cause harm to another person." Although definitions vary, cyberbullying can be defined as acts of aggression and subterfuge against someone that gain power through digital technology.

The problems can range from the use of gossip sites like JuicyCampus, College Anonymous Confessions Board or College Wall of Shame to "revenge porn sites," in which former lovers upload photos of ex-girl friends and to stalking by emails and text messages. Some of the most popular vehicles

for cyberbullying, said Yoon, are Facebook texting, email, Twitter, and YouTube. Other technologies or applications and online gaming technologies, such as AOL Instant Messenger, MSN Messenger MySpace and League of Legends, as well as online forums, message boards, blogs, are also used. Researchers have identified several types of aggression, which include online stalking, flaming, fights, and arguments; posting embarrassing or incriminating photos of a victim; outing, revealing secrets; exclusion and masquerading as someone else.

Aggressors may send mean text messages or emails, spread rumors by email or social networking sites, and they may post videos, put up embarrassing websites, or create fake profiles of a victim. The use of technology means that victims can be exposed to an audience of millions and may be unable to escape scrutiny.

Students also face dangers from impersonation, fraud and trickery online. In one infamous incident, Manti Te'o, the Notre Dame star linebacker and a finalist for the Heisman Trophy, became a victim of "catfishing." He met someone online who pretended to become his "girlfriend" even though they had never met. The ruse was uncovered by a sports website after she was reported to have died. Similarly, MTV's reality TV show called "Catfish" focuses on deceptions in online dating and is popular among college students.

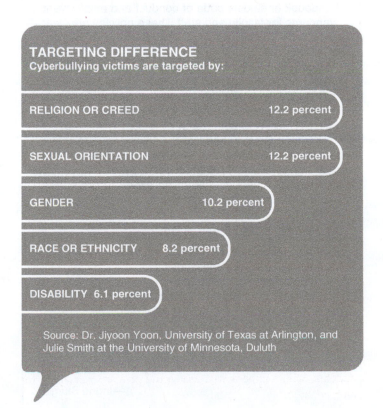

TARGETING DIFFERENCE
Cyberbullying victims are targeted by:

RELIGION OR CREED	12.2 percent
SEXUAL ORIENTATION	12.2 percent
GENDER	10.2 percent
RACE OR ETHNICITY	8.2 percent
DISABILITY	6.1 percent

Source: Dr. Jiyoon Yoon, University of Texas at Arlington, and Julie Smith at the University of Minnesota, Duluth

Handling the Cyberbully

Colleges and universities are developing courses, starting anti-bully campaigns and offering mentoring relationships and other tools to deal with the emerging social issue of cyberbullying. Rutgers University opened the Tyler Clementi Center to help students adjust to college life. Other colleges and universities are developing anti-bullying policies and taking other actions to combat problems of cyberbullying and "online incivility."

In many states, schools are required to address cyberbullying in their anti-bullying policy. Some state laws also cover off-campus behavior that creates a hostile school environment. Some universities also address direct punishment of the cyberbullying and provide special reporting tools when cyberbullying is exhibited.

University instructors/faculty are also required to report cyberbullying incidents. University IT staffs record and track incidences and courses on college campuses contain "netiquette" rules in syllabi. As most colleges and universities realize the seriousness of cyberbullying on campus, said Dr. Jiyoon Yoon, associate professor and director of the elementary education program at University of Texas at Arlington, they start to incorporate anti-cyberbullying policies into the student handbook or student code of conduct and employment standards for faculty and staff. These policies are clear about what constitutes cyberbullying and what the penalties may be.

Dawn Harner, a training coordinator and counselor at Salisbury University, said the university has a program training first-year students as leaders and asking them to refer students to a counseling center if they are experiencing anxiety or depression as related to bullying.

Whitney Gibson, head of the Internet crises group for Vorys, Sater, Seymour, and Pease LLP, s said victims should tell someone at school or get help by talking to police or school officials or an expert to get screen shots of the offending posts, chats, messages, videos, or emails.

Yoon recommends that victims:

- Take immediate action but do not respond or forward cyberbullying messages.
- Keep evidence of cyberbullying.
- Learn how to use privacy settings to block the bully.
- Report cyberbullying to the social media site, law enforcement officials, the school and online service providers.
- Review the terms and conditions of service at social media sites and Internet service providers.

—Ingrid Sturgis

One of the main characteristics of the cyberbullying is that bullies believe they can act anonymously, said Yoon. "They can harass their victims without the victims ever knowing who or why they are being cyberbullied," she said. "The various forms of current professional technology on campus allow the victims to be continually victimized without identifying the perpetrators." Experts can determine the identities of the abusers, however. The pervasiveness of social media, said Elaine Heath, PhD, dean for Student Services at Howard University, and the fact that the reasoning capabilities in adolescents do not fully mature until age 25, makes students emotionally ill equipped to handle the consequences of being a bully or being bullied.

"They are not mature enough to pick up social cues to determine this is inappropriate behavior," Heath said. "They are shocked when you tell them. Young people don't understand the boundaries and the appropriateness of how to use it."

Heath said bullying often reveals a degree of anger and deep-seated emotions. "It will start within the person and then triggers an outward manifestation," she said. "Anger or emotional problems will be acted out. They will continue the conversation with social media. It's a lack of impulse control."

When Heath asks students why they do it, she said many have given no thought to their actions. "Bottom line, people don't think about it," she said. "They are angry and want to get their story and their say out. These children live in reality TV."

"It's about power and control to instill fear," she said. "People don't fear the consequences. There is a lack of empathy, lack of control, and immaturity around relationships. A lot people don't know how to have healthy relationships."

Patchin of the Cyberbullying Research Center said parents and teachers who may not use social media sometimes underestimate the seriousness of the issue. He said some adults ask cyberbullied students questions like, "Why can't you turn it off?"

"For high school and college students, it's a big part of their social lives," he said. "If you don't know anything about it, it's not a big problem."

Cyberbullying can have implications beyond the campus and maybe even have long-lasting legal ramifications for students. Whitney Gibson, a partner at Vorys, Sater, Seymour, and Pease LLP and head of the firm's Internet crises group, works with schools to help them educate students about the unintended consequences of Internet use.

"What I see is a lot of students using technology," he said. "A lot of students don't think what they are doing is a big deal . . . They don't understand how quickly that goes viral, and they can never get it down. There is a rise of serious damage being done to people on the Internet. People are dying. Kids are getting arrested for felony."

Gibson said students often don't realize that their online behavior, including posting pictures while drinking or using marijuana, as well as acts of bullying, can affect their scholarships or job prospects as more recruiters check social media sites. In addition, Gibson said, college students think they can conceal their identities with fake names.

"They don't realize that it is very hard to remain anonymous on the Internet," he said. "They end up getting in big trouble."

Critical Thinking

1. How much supervision and monitoring is appropriate at the college level?
2. Where do we draw the line between teasing and cyberbullying?
3. How does technology like instagram, vine, and flikr contribute to cyberbullying?

Create Central

www.mhhe.com/createcentral

Internet References

buzzfeed.com 9 Teenage Suicides In The Last Year Were Linked to Cyber-Bullying on Social Network Ask.fm
   http://www.buzzfeed.com/ryanhatesthis/a-ninth-teenager-since-last-september-has-committed-suicide

cyberpsychology.eu Cyberbullying in Adolescent Victims: Perception and Coping
   http://www.cyberpsychology.eu/view.php?cisloclanku=2011121901

Huffingtonpost.com 8 Scary Social Networking Sites Every Parent Should Know
   http://www.huffingtonpost.com/michael-gregg/8-scary-social-network-sites-every-parents-should-know_b_4178055.html

thementalelf.net Bullying and Cyberbullying Increase the Risk of Suicidal Ideation and Suicide Attempts in Adolescents
   http://www.thementalelf.net/populations-and-settings/child-and-adolescent/bullying-and-cyberbullying-increase-the-risk-of-suicidal-ideation-and-suicide-attempts-in-adolescents

tylerclementi.org The Tyler Clementi Foundation
   http://www.tylerclementi.org/

Ingrid Sturgis is an author, journalist, and assistant professor specializing in new media in the Department of Media, Journalism and Film at Howard University.

Sturgis, Ingrid. "High-Tech Bullies." *Diverse: Issues in Higher Education, Convergence Supplement.* (February, 27, 2014): 19–23.

Article   Prepared by: Claire N. Rubman, *Suffolk County Community College*

Many Professors Say Their Students Lack Professional Qualities for Future Jobs

ANN SCHNOEBELEN

Learning Outcomes

After reading this article, you will be able to:

- Describe the relationship between technology use among students and poor professional skills.

- Explain how a sense of entitlement relates to a lack of professional qualities.

In a recent survey of college and university professors, more than one-third (38.3 percent) said they felt that fewer than half of their upper-level students exhibited qualities associated with being professional in the workplace, and nearly as many (37.5 percent) reported a drop over the past 5 years in the percentage of students demonstrating professionalism.

The survey was conducted by the Center for Professional Excellence at York College of Pennsylvania, which over the past four years has conducted an annual study of employers' views of the professionalism of recent college graduates in the workplace.

This year the study was expanded to include a survey of faculty views of the state of professionalism on campuses. More than 400 professors in various disciplines at more than 330 2- and 4-year institutions across the country participated in the survey.

According to a report describing the survey's findings, "2012 Professionalism on Campus," the qualities the respondents most strongly associated with being professional included having good interpersonal skills, being focused and attentive, being dependable in completing tasks on schedule, and displaying a work ethic.

Of those who viewed their students as failing to exhibit professionalism, almost 30 percent blamed that view on a heightened sense of entitlement among students. Entitlement was defined in the survey as "expecting rewards without putting in the work or effort to merit the rewards."

"In unaided questioning," the report says, "22.2 percent of the respondents included a sense of entitlement in their description of unprofessional qualities in students," and nearly two-thirds said they believed there had been an increase in students' sense of entitlement.

"There is obviously something happening on college campuses when it comes to students exhibiting a sense of entitlement," the report states.

Multitasking Blamed

Technology was blamed by 75.6 percent of those surveyed for interrupting student focus, and many said the problem was getting worse. According to 96.7 percent of respondents, information-technology etiquette problems and abuses—such as texting or inappropriate use of the Internet and cellphones during class, poorly written e-mails, and substituting digital communication for in-person communication—had increased or stayed the same over the past 5 years. More than half of respondents also saw students' attempts at multitasking as a factor contributing to a lack of focus.

The faculty survey's findings mirror results the Center for Professional Excellence has consistently seen in its survey of employers about the professionalism of their first-year employees who are recent college graduates.

According to a report describing the findings of the latest employer survey, "2013 Professionalism in the Workplace," 35.9 percent of the employers said the percentage of new employees exhibiting professionalism had fallen.

Deborah D. Ricker, dean of academic services at York College and a coauthor of the report on the faculty survey, said the center decided to poll professors this year after seeing no significant improvement over the past four years in employers' views of the level of professionalism in the workplace among newly hired college graduates.

"Seeing that," Ms. Ricker said in an e-mail message, "we chose to turn back the clock, if you will, to explore their level of professionalism in college before they graduate and enter their career."

The researchers hypothesized that "professional behaviors that are honed in college would be similar to those professional behaviors new graduates take into the workplace," she said, and they found that, "indeed, there were a number of consistencies."

"The overarching consistency," she wrote, "was that declining professionalism among both current college students and newly hired college graduates in the workplace was attributed to a heightened sense of entitlement, a change in culture/values, declining communication skills, and a lack of motivation and focus."

Asked if she expected that trend to continue, Ms. Ricker said, "In the workplace, yes."

Critical Thinking

1. What constitutes professional conduct in the workplace and which skills are most valued by employers?
2. How have today's students developed this "sense of entitlement"?
3. Which skills do our students lack and is this a cross-cultural phenomenon?

Create Central

www.mhhe.com/createcentral

Internet References

CNN.com Generation Y: Too demanding at work?
http://www.cnn.com/2007/LIVING/worklife/12/26/cb.generation

facultyfocus.com Student Entitlement: Six Ways to Respond
http://www.facultyfocus.com/articles/teaching-and-learning/student-entitlement-six-ways-to-respond/

quintcareers.com What Do Employers *Really* Want? Top Skills and Values Employers Seek from Job-Seekers
http://www.quintcareers.com/job_skills_values.html

timeshighereducation.co Students' Sense of Entitlement Angers Academics
http://www.timeshighereducation.co.uk/news/students-sense-of-entitlement-angers-academics/405460.article

Schnoebelen, Ann, "Many Professors Say Their Students Lack Professional Qualities for Future Jobs." *The Chronicle of Higher Education* 59. 29 (March, 29, 2013): A21–A21.

Article   Prepared by: Claire N. Rubman, *Suffolk County Community College*

Don't Leave Me Out!

Adolescents are anecdotally sensitive to peer rejection. Many people can vividly recall, even as adults, instances during their teenage years in which they were excluded by a particular clique or left 'out of the loop' about parties or social plans. Rejection is undoubtedly part of the social landscape in adolescence, but why do young people find it quite so distressing? One possibility is that ongoing brain development in regions involved in emotional processing, emotion regulation, and social cognition may contribute to this phenomenon. This development could have far-reaching implications, not just for how adolescents respond to rejection, but for mental health during this crucial and formative stage of development.

CATHERINE SEBASTIAN

Learning Outcomes

After reading this article, you will be able to:

- Explain how the amygdala, ventral striatum, and prefrontal cortex contribute to adolescent thought and behavior.

- Describe how the author used the "cyberball" paradigm to explore adolescent rejection.

The idea that the brain continues to develop during adolescence has now entered popular consciousness. For example, the excellent *Blame My Brain* by Nicola Morgan (2005) describes for teenagers and their parents alike how changes going on in the brain may at least partially underlie stereotypically 'teenage' behaviours, such as risk-taking in the presence of peers, mood swings, sleeping late, and thrill-seeking. In the equally fascinating *Teenagers: A Natural History*, David Bainbridge (2010) suggests that this protracted period of brain development and plasticity is what allows the human brain to achieve adult levels of abstract thinking and social complexity. This positive spin on adolescence is a welcome antidote to the often negative portrayal of young people in the media, for example during coverage of the recent riots in England.

Thinking about adolescence seems to involve striking a balance: recognising that there are certain features of adolescent biology and cognition that need to be understood, without falling into the trap of stigmatising or patronising young people.

In my PhD, I was interested in the link between ongoing brain development and social and emotional behaviour; in particular, how do young people respond to social rejection, and might ongoing brain development contribute to this response? And conversely, what do differences in behaviour and cognition tell us about how the brain develops?

"How do young people respond to social rejection?"

The Teenage Brain

The last decade or so has seen an upsurge in the study and understanding of adolescence. The availability of safe and non-invasive neuroimaging techniques means we now have access to a wealth of data showing that the brain continues to develop well into the second decade of life, and likely into the mid-twenties as well. Particularly influential has been data suggesting that different brain regions mature at different rates and with differing trajectories. For example, Shaw et al. (2008) showed that evolutionarily older parts of the brain, such as the limbic system, mature in a simpler linear trajectory than regions that evolved more recently, such as the neocortex. There is additional evidence that the dopaminergic system, involved in the processing of reward signals, undergoes substantial remodelling during adolescence (Steinberg, 2008).

These data have led to the development of a number of models of how ongoing brain development may help paint the picture of a 'typical' teenager. Several models have been proposed (Nelson et al., 2005; Steinberg, 2008; Casey et al., 2008), with all having in common the idea of a 'developmental mismatch' between parts of the brain involved in processing emotional and reward signals (including brain regions such as the amygdala and ventral striatum), and those responsible for regulating these responses (e.g., parts of the prefrontal cortex). During adolescence, the development of the latter lags behind the former, leaving the adolescent brain in a similar state to a 'fast car with poor brakes'.

Is There More to It Than That?

Of course, adolescents don't develop in a vacuum, and the social environment is vitally important in shaping the adolescent brain (Blakemore, 2008). Adolescence is a time of social transition: early adolescents spend more time with parents than peers, but by mid-late adolescence, this pattern is reversed (Steinberg & Silverberg, 1986). Adolescents' ability to think abstractly about themselves and other people means they have a much more sophisticated understanding of complex social phenomena such as reputation, social hierarchy, personality traits, and how others see them (the 'looking glass self') than do younger children (Harter, 1990; Parker et al., 2006; Sebastian et al., 2008).

Indeed, while until recently it was assumed that theory of mind (understanding others' thoughts, beliefs, and intentions) develops by around age four, evidence now suggests that some aspects of theory of mind continue to develop until late adolescence. For example, Dumontheil et al. (2009) found that the ability to automatically use what we know about another person's point of view during social interaction is still improving between late adolescence (14–17 years) and adulthood. The idea that social cognitive abilities undergo substantial development in adolescence is also supported by neuroimaging studies. In a recent review, Blakemore (2008) noted that across four recent functional magnetic resonance imaging (fMRI) studies using a range of social cognition tasks, all showed a reduction in brain activity between adolescence and adulthood in a region of the brain called medial prefrontal cortex. While the meaning of this reduction in computational terms is unclear (e.g., Does it relate to ongoing anatomical development? Could it index increasing efficiency of processing between adolescence and adulthood?), it does seem that important social cognitive development is ongoing in adolescence.

One of the things I aimed to do in my PhD was to reconcile models of adolescent emotional and social development into a single framework. For example, in Sebastian, Viding et al.

(2010), I discussed how 'developmental mismatch' between emotion processing and regulation mechanisms could interact with ongoing social cognitive development to account for social behaviours specific to adolescence; in particular, sensitivity to social rejection.

Adolescent Social Rejection

Social rejection, or ostracism, refers to being deliberately ignored or excluded by an individual or a group (Williams, 2007). In adolescence, social rejection is often used as a form of relational aggression or bullying, with one recent study (Wang et al., 2009), reporting that 27.4 percent of adolescent girls had been excluded or ignored by a group of peers while at school. (Although boys do use relational aggression, there is evidence that girls are both more likely to use it as a bullying tactic and to be more upset by its consequences (Crick et al., 2002, Wang et al., 2009)). Several self-report studies had also shown that adolescents might be more sensitive to social rejection than both adults and younger children in everyday life (Kloep, 1999; O'Brien & Bierman, 1988). However, when I started my PhD, the processes underlying these effects were unclear.

In Sebastian, Viding et al. (2010), I investigated whether adolescent sensitivity to social rejection could be replicated under laboratory conditions. If so, this would suggest that the phenomenon could not be explained as an artefact of the adolescent social environment (e.g., strict social hierarchies at school, or the transition to secondary school). I used the Cyberball paradigm (Williams et al., 2000), in which participants think they are playing a game of 'catch' over the internet with two other players, whereas in fact the actions of the other players can be pre-programmed to either include or exclude the participant.

Relative to adult females, both young (11–13 years) and mid (14–15 years) adolescents reported lower overall mood following the rejection condition, with the young adolescents also reporting greater anxiety. The mid-adolescents did report high anxiety following rejection, but anxiety was also high following inclusion (relative to a baseline condition before they had played either game). This led to the intriguing possibility that social interaction in general can be anxiety-provoking at this age. Indeed evidence suggests that the mean age of onset for social phobia occurs in mid-adolescence at age 15 (Mancini et al., 2005). In contrast, all groups (young adolescents, mid-adolescents, and adults) reported that they had been excluded by the other players to a similar degree, and reported the experience as feeling equally real. This suggests increased emotional responsivity to rejection in the adolescents, in the absence of objective differences in the perception of the rejection episode.

The Rejected Brain

Given that sensitivity to rejection in adolescence could be elicited in a brief online encounter when there were no lasting consequences for social reputation, I investigated whether this phenomenon might be associated with differences in how the brain processes social rejection between adolescence and adulthood. Work by Naomi Eisenberger and colleagues (2003) suggested that the adult brain processes social pain in a similar way to physical pain, and that a brain region called right ventrolateral prefrontal cortex may be involved in regulating or controlling distress associated with social rejection. This was followed up by the same laboratory with an fMRI study using Cyberball with 23 adolescents aged 12–13 (Masten et al., 2009). This study suggested some intriguing differences in the adolescent neural response to rejection, compared with previous studies in adults. However, this study did not compare adults and adolescents directly.

In Sebastian et al. (2011), we used a modified version of the Cyberball paradigm in an fMRI study directly comparing 19 adolescents (aged 14–16), and 16 adults. Regardless of age, all participants activated a network of regions involved in social evaluation and negative emotion. Of most interest was a group difference in right ventrolateral prefrontal cortex, with the adult group showing a greater response in this region during rejection than during inclusion, but the adolescent group showing no difference between conditions.

In the same fMRI session, we also gave participants a rejection emotional Stroop task, in which they indicated the ink colour of rejection-, acceptance-, and neutral-themed words. By using this task, we aimed to look at the way the brain processes rejection-related information implicitly, as opposed to the very overt and explicit social rejection scenario in the Cyberball game. Despite these important differences between the tasks, we again found a reduced response in ventrolateral prefrontal cortex in adolescents relative to adults during the processing of rejection-related words compared with neutral and acceptance words (Sebastian, Roiser et al., 2010).

It seems that across both tasks, the regulatory response of the ventrolateral prefrontal cortex was attenuated in adolescents relative to adults. While speculative, it may be that poor regulation of distress associated with social rejection contributes to adolescent sensitivity to this phenomenon.

However, it is still unclear why this brain region should be responding suboptimally in adolescence. Is it due to ongoing anatomical maturation of the prefrontal cortex? What about connections between ventrolateral prefrontal cortex and other brain regions involved in generating feelings of rejection-related distress? Can differences between groups be explained by adults having more experience over time in dealing with rejection effectively? While there are unanswered questions,

our research suggests that there should be a greater focus on training adolescents to regulate their emotions effectively, particularly within the social context.

Social Rejection and the Autism Spectrum

While most people are likely to experience social rejection at some point during adolescence, it can be an unfortunately common occurrence for individuals whose social skills may not keep pace with those of their peers; for example, adolescents with high-functioning autism or Asperger's syndrome. There is evidence that adolescents with autism spectrum conditions (ASC) perceive themselves to hold lower peer approval than their typically developing peers, while placing the same emphasis on its importance (Williamson et al., 2008). At the same time, individuals with ASC often report a desire for friendship (Frith, 2004), while experiencing greater levels of loneliness (Bauminger & Kasari, 2000) and bullying (Van Roekel et al., 2010) than their peers. Given this picture, it is surprising that very little research has addressed the question of how individuals with ASC experience and process social rejection.

Using the Cyberball paradigm, we found that adolescent males with ASC and matched controls (mean age 16.9) reported very similar reactions to social rejection (Sebastian et al., 2009). According to Williams' (1997) need-threat model, social rejection threatens four fundamental social needs: self-esteem, belonging, control, and a sense of meaningful existence. These needs are threatened reflexively, and are not necessarily modulated by context; for example, Zadro et al. (2004) showed that these needs are threatened even when we know that the Cyberball game is controlled by a computer. Adolescents with ASC reported similar or greater levels of need-threat across all four needs compared with controls; and also showed similar modulation of anxiety levels between inclusion and rejection conditions. The only difference between groups was seen for self-reported mood, for which controls showed a greater reduction in mood following exclusion than did individuals with ASC.

While this study explored responses to social rejection behaviourally, three recent follow-up studies have used neuroimaging techniques to investigate responses to social rejection in adolescents with ASC (Bolling et al., 2011; Masten, Colich et al., 2011; McPartland et al., 2011). All found a similar picture of preserved self-reported responses to rejection, but reduced responses in brain regions activated by social rejection, relative to control groups. This is interesting, as it suggests that the picture is more complex than a case of responses to rejection being either "preserved" or "deficient" in ASC. It is clear, however, that adolescents with ASC find social rejection distressing.

Since data suggest that this group are more likely to experience social rejection than are their peers, it makes sense to focus on bullying prevention in this group, as well as on helping these individuals to develop effective coping strategies for dealing with social rejection in everyday life.

Conclusions

Social rejection is painful at any age, but it seems that adolescents may be particularly sensitive to the emotional consequences of social rejection, possibly due to a mismatch in the timing of development of regions involved in emotion processing versus emotion regulation. While for most adolescents, social rejection will have no more than a transitory impact, some will experience more prolonged relational bullying (including rejection), which can feed into feelings of low self-esteem, depression and even, in extreme cases, to suicide. But even responses to a single rejection episode can be informative. One recent fMRI study showed that the way in which the adolescent brain responds to rejection can be used to predict depressive symptoms one year later (Masten, Eisenberger et al., 2011). Future research should focus on the processes by which responses to negative social experiences in adolescence feed into adverse mental health outcomes. With adolescence being a key time for the onset of both internalising and externalising conditions (Kessler et al., 2005; Paus et al., 2008), efforts focused on understanding and prevention at this early stage are likely to be particularly effective.

Questions

1. How do negative social experiences feed into the development of mental illness in adolescence?
2. Why do some young people cope with rejection and bullying better than others?

Resources

Williams, K.D. (2007). Ostracism. *Annual Review of Psychology, 58,* 425–452.

www.kidscape.org.uk (anti-bullying charity)

http://teenagebrain.blogspot.co.uk (blog about teenage brain development)

References

Bainbridge, D. (2010). *Teenagers: A natural history.* London: Portobello Books.

Bauminger, N. & Kasari, C. (2000). Loneliness and friendship in high-functioning children with autism. *Child Development, 71,* 447–456.

Blakemore, S.J. (2008). The social brain in adolescence. *Nature Reviews Neuroscience, 9*(4), 267–277.

Bolling, D.Z., Pitskel, N.B., Deen, B. et al. (2011). Enhanced neural responses to rule violation in children with autism. *Developmental Cognitive Neuroscience, 1*(3), 280–294.

Casey, B., Jones, R.M. & Hare, T.A. (2008). The adolescent brain. *Annals of the New York Academy of Sciences, 1124*(1), 111–126.

Crick, N.R. & Nelson, D.A. (2002). Relational and physical victimization within friendships. *Journal of Abnormal Child Psychology, 30*(6), 599–607.

Dumontheil, I., Apperly, I.A. & Blakemore, S.J. (2009). Online usage of theory of mind continues to develop in late adolescence. *Developmental Science, 13*(2), 331–338.

Eisenberger, N.I., Lieberman, M.D. & Williams, K.D. (2003). Does rejection hurt? *Science, 302*(5643), 290.

Frith, U. (2004). Emanuel Miller Lecture: Confusions and controversies about Asperger syndrome. *Journal of Child Psychology and Psychiatry, 45,* 672–686.

Harter, S. (1990). Developmental differences in the nature of self-representations. *Cognitive Therapy & Research, 14*(2), 113–142.

Kessler, R.C., Berglund, P., Demler, O. et al. (2005). Lifetime prevalence and age-of-onset distributions of DSM-IV disorders in the National Comorbidity Survey Replication. *Archives of General Psychiatry, 62*(6), 593–602.

Kloep, M. (1999). Love is all you need? Focusing on adolescents' life concerns from an ecological point of view. *Journal of Adolescence, 22,* 49–63.

Mancini, C., Van Ameringen, M., Bennett, M. et al. (2005). Emerging treatments for child and adolescent social phobia: A review. *Journal of Child and Adolescent Psychopharmacology, 15*(4), 589–607.

Masten, C.L., Colich, N.L., Rudie, J.D. et al. (2011). An fMRI investigation of responses to peer rejection in adolescents with autism spectrum disorders. *Developmental Cognitive Neuroscience, 1*(3), 260–270.

Masten, C.L., Eisenberger, N.I., Borofsky, L.A. et al. (2009). Neural correlates of social exclusion during adolescence: Understanding the distress of peer rejection. *Social Cognitive and Affective Neuroscience, 4*(2),143–157.

Masten, C.L., Eisenberger, N.I., Borofsky, L.A. et al. (2011). Subgenual anterior cingulate responses to peer rejection. *Development and Psychopathology, 23*(1), 283–892.

McPartland, J.C., Crowley, M.J., Perszyk, D.R. et al. (2011). Temporal dynamics reveal atypical brain response to social exclusion in autism. *Developmental Cognitive Neuroscience, 1*(3), 271–279.

Morgan, N. (2005). *Blame my brain.* London: Walker Books.

Nelson, E.E., Leibenluft, E., McClure, E.B. & Pine, D.S. (2005). The social reorientation of adolescence. *Psychological Medicine, 35*(2), 163–174.

O'Brien, S.F. & Bierman, K.L. (1988). Conceptions and perceived influence of peer groups: Interviews with preadolescents and adolescents. *Child Development, 59*(5), 1360–1365.

Parker, J.G., Rubin, K.H., Erath, S.A. et al. (2006). Peer relationships, child development, and adjustment. In D. Cicchetti & D.J. Cohen (Eds.) *Developmental psychopathology. Vol. 1: Theory and Methods* (2nd edn, pp. 96–161). New York: Wiley.

Paus, T., Keshavan, M. & Giedd, J.N. (2008). Why do many psychiatric disorders emerge during adolescence? *Nature Reviews Neuroscience, 9*(12), 947–957.

Sebastian, C., Blakemore, S.J. & Charman, T. (2009). Reactions to ostracism in adolescents with autism spectrum conditions. *Journal of Autism and Developmental Disorders, 39,* 1122–1130.

Sebastian, C., Burnett, S. & Blakemore, S.J. (2008). Development of the self concept during adolescence. *Trends in Cognitive Sciences, 12*(11), 441–446.

Sebastian, C.L., Roiser, J.P., Tan, G.C. et al. (2010). Effects of age and MAOA genotype on the neural processing of social rejection. *Genes Brain & Behavior, 9,* 628–637.

Sebastian, C.L., Tan, G.C.Y., Roiser, J.P. et al. (2011). Developmental influences on the neural bases of responses to social rejection: Implications of social neuroscience for education. *NeuroImage, 57*(3), 686–694.

Sebastian, C., Viding, E., Williams, K.D. & Blakemore, S.J. (2010). Social brain development and the affective consequences of ostracism in adolescence. *Brain and Cognition, 72,* 134–145.

Shaw, P., Kabani, N.J., Lerch, J.P. et al. (2008). Neurodevelopmental trajectories of the human cerebral cortex. *Journal of Neuroscience, 28*(14), 3586–3594.

Steinberg, L. (2008). A social neuroscience perspective on adolescent risk-taking. *Developmental Review, 28*(1), 78–106.

Steinberg, L. & Silverberg, S.B. (1986). The vicissitudes of autonomy in early adolescence. *Child Development 57,* 841–851.

Van Roekel, E., Scholte, R.H. & Didden, R. (2010). Bullying among adolescents with autism spectrum disorders. *Journal of Autism and Developmental Disorders, 40,* 63–73.

Wang, J., Iannotti, R.J. & Nansel, T.R. (2009). School bullying among adolescents in the United States. *Journal of Adolescent Health, 45,* 368–375.

Williams, K.D. (1997). Social ostracism. In R.M. Kowalski (Ed.) *Aversive interpersonal behaviors* (pp.133–170). New York: Plenum.

Williams, K.D. (2007). Ostracism. *Annual Review of Psychology, 58,* 425–452.

Williams, K.D., Cheung, C.K. & Choi, W. (2000). Cyberostracism: Effects of being ignored over the internet. *Journal of Personality and Social Psychology, 79*(5), 748–762.

Williamson, S., Craig, J. & Slinger, R. (2008). Exploring the relationship between measures of self-esteem and psychological adjustment among adolescents with Asperger syndrome. *Autism, 14*(4), 391–402.

Zadro, L., Williams, K.D. & Richardson, R. (2004). How low can you go? Ostracism by a computer is sufficient to lower self-reported levels of belonging, control, self-esteem, and meaningful existence. *Journal of Experimental Social Psychology, 40,* 560–567.

Critical Thinking

1. Why do adolescents respond differently than adults to emotions such as rejection?

2. What could the reduced role of the medial prefrontal cortex as adolescents shift into adulthood mean in terms of development?

3. How can we help adolescents to cope with rejection and other emotions while their brains are still maturing?

Create Central

www.mhhe.com/createcentral

Internet References

academia.edu The Social Brain in Adolescence: Evidence from Functional Magnetic Resonance Imaging and Behavioural Studies
http://www.academia.edu/415376/The_social_brain_in_adolescence_Evidence_from_functional_magnetic_resonance_imaging_and_behavioural_studies

apa.org Grantee Spotlight: Studying Social Rejection in Adolescence
http://www.apa.org/monitor/2013/12/grantee-spotlight.aspx

Medscape.com Social Cognitive and Affective Neuroscience Adolescent Social Cognitive and Affective Neuroscience Past, Present, and Future
http://www.medscape.com/viewarticle/757839

NCBI.MLN.NIH.gov Special issue on the teenage brain: Sensitivity to social evaluation
http://www.ncbi.nlm.nih.gov/pmc/articles/PMC3992953/

Psychologytoday.com 10 Surprising Facts About Rejection Research Finds that Rejection Affects Intelligence, Reason, and More
http://www.psychologytoday.com/blog/the-squeaky-wheel/201307/10-surprising-facts-about-rejection

CATHERINE SEBASTIAN is a Lecturer in the Department of Psychology, Royal Holloway, University of London catherine.sebastian@rhul.ac.uk

Sebastian, Catherine. "Don't leave me out!" *The Psychologist* 25. 11 (November, 2012): 820–823.

Unit 6

UNIT

Prepared by: Claire N. Rubman,
Suffolk County Community College, Selden, NY

Development during Middle and Late Adulthood

The focus shifts from our children and our spouse in this unit. Now the spotlight shifts to ourselves and how we change as we age. This collection of articles focuses primarily on retirement, declines in our brain as we age, and elder abuse. Do we plan properly for our retirement? Can we plan for the inevitable declines in our cognitive capacity and physical wellbeing? What can we do to delay that inevitable decline in our brains and how can we enjoy living our life to the fullest extent even as we age? Finally, how can we identify and prevent the abuse of the elderly in our society?

As our aging population focuses on retirement, they have to contend with a lack of, or change in, routine. Retirement today has increased in time as a result of an increase in life expectancy for both men and women. The impact of more education, more years in the workforce and more retirement years is discussed in Clark's article titled "Pick Your Path to Retirement."

As we retire from our working life, this can be a trigger for depression. One possible cure for depression is suggested in "The Switched-On Brain" by Amy Barth. Barth explores the potential for optogenetics as a cure for severe depression. Optogenetics involes the "switching on and off" of neural pathways in the brain. Optogenetics founder, Deisseroth, worked on mice and addiction but his paradigm has inspired researchers around the world.

During the normal course of development our brain will age along with our body. Robert Epstein discusses the particulars of what we can expect as we age. Our brain will shrink, we lose dopamine and our dendrites lose their connectivity. We also face a deterioration in our myelin sheath that insulates our neural pathways. The four domains of decline according to Epstein in his article "Brutal Truths about the Aging Brain" include our senses, our memory, our knowledge base, and our intelligence.

On a more upbeat note, Beth Howard outlines "10 easy ways to stay sharp forever" in the article titled "Age-Proof Your Brain." Howard's recommendations range from proper vitamin intake to finding a purpose and a social life!

This unit ends with a discussion on the tragic subject of elder abuse. Lois Bowers is shocked to discover elder abuse in assisted living facilities. She suggests ways to combat physical, psychological, and sexual abuse including neglect, medication errors, and inappropriate behaviors. Sorenson also discusses ways that the elderly are abused in the final article titled "Elder Abuse Identification: A Public Health Issue." She also discusses warning signs that elder abuse is occurring. She discusses the federal law passed in 2011 on elder abuse prevention. She acknowledges that elder abuse is a difficult topic to discuss but emphasizes the importance of the conversation. She offers a myriad of resources for the reader.

Article

Prepared by: Claire N. Rubman,
Suffolk County Community College, Selden, NY

PICK Your PATH to Retirement

Once, retirement meant hitting the golf course or sitting by the pool. The new retirement? Whatever you want it to be.

JANE BENNETT CLARK

Learning Outcomes

After reading this article, you will be able to:

- Explain what is meant by the term "the new retirement."
- Articulate 6 tips that may lead to a more enjoyable retirement.

Look up *retire* in the dictionary and here's what you'll find: "To retreat from action or danger. To withdraw for privacy, to recede. To conclude a career."

Retreat, recede, conclude are not words in Priscilla Jackman's vocabulary. In 2008, she retired from a 33-year teaching career in the Steel Valley school district, outside Pittsburgh, and immediately returned to the same district as a consultant on literacy programs. Four years later, she "retired" from that gig and took a five- to seven-hour-a-week job mentoring student teachers at a nearby university. Now 61, Jackman enjoys mentoring, but she says, "I don't see myself doing it until I'm 70." She definitely sees herself doing "something else"—maybe tutoring elementary school kids as a volunteer.

The beauty of Jackman's setup is that with a shorter work schedule, she has plenty of time to take guitar and violin lessons, act as social director for her extended family, sing in a volunteer hospital program and explore back roads with her husband, Tom, who is also retired. "We set the GPS and see where it takes us," she says. "We love finding great little towns and great diners." Rather than define her postcareer life as a slow fade into the sunset, she says, "I'm in awe of what it's possible to do as a retiree."

In fact, demographic changes have turned the standard definition of retirement upside down. Life expectancy has increased steadily over the decades. Now, a man who reaches 65 can expect to live another 18 years; a 65-year-old woman can expect to live 20 years. Plus, people work longer than in past decades, thanks to better health and a higher level of education, which generally leads to more gratifying, less-strenuous work.

With more time and opportunities, many retirees are phasing in and out of work, taking part-time, seasonal or consulting jobs or acting as entrepreneurs. Some post-66-ers work because they need the money, but the majority are taking advantage of the resources they have (including Social Security, savings and maybe a pension) to seek work that is more enjoyable and less stressful than their career was, says Nicole Maestas, a senior economist at the Rand Corp. who has studied older workers. For many, "retirement connotes a broader set of options," she says. "It's a new phase of life."

Explore the Possibilities

Having more time to work and play may sound delightful, but figuring out how to do it over 20 or 30 years is no last-minute exercise. Experiment by pursuing hobbies, volunteering at places where you might want to work, and thinking carefully about whether you want to downsize or move to another city altogether, says Larry Rosenthal, a certified financial planner in Manassas, Va. "People retire to a place and then think, *The grandkids are back where we were,* and they want to move back. Or they discover that Florida gets really hot in the summer."

One way to get a sense of what you want to do a few years hence is through a "practice retirement." That idea, proposed by investment firm T. Rowe Price, has you continue to work at your career job but back off on saving for retirement—say, by contributing only enough to your 401(k) to get the company match. Then you can use the money you've freed up (plus vacation time) to try out your ideas, such as traveling cross-country or turning your hobby into a side business.

Cutting back on contributions to savings in your early sixties may sound like heresy, but the key is staying on the job and waiting to take Social Security until full retirement age (66 until 2021) or later. For each year you delay taking Social Security after 66 until age 70, you get an 8% bump in benefits. And while you're still pulling in a paycheck, you can let your retirement savings grow, even if you're not contributing to your accounts. "It's a way to stay in the workforce and have a little fun while doing it," says Judith Ward, a senior financial planner at T. Rowe Price.

Plan to Work Longer

In most professions, employers can no longer require you to retire at a certain age, but keeping yourself relevant in your current career or attractive to your next employer is on you, says Catherine Collinson, president of the Transamerica Center for Retirement Studies. That includes keeping your skills up-to-date, maintaining and expanding your network, staying on top of the job market, and taking classes or going to school for another degree.

Peter Sefton of Alexandria, Va., accepted the challenge and took it to a whole new level. After working for the U.S. Census Bureau for 24 years, he enrolled in a master's degree program at the University of Virginia, leaving his wife, Linda, to hold down the fort in Alexandria for the next two years. "My retirement party was on Friday. I packed up my desk, and on Monday morning, I was in Charlottesville with the 25-year-olds," says Sefton, who was then 59. A federal pension provided financial underpinning. In addition, he was awarded a fellowship to help pay for his degree in architectural history, an extension of his longtime interest in historic preservation. Now 63, he works about 25 hours a week as a consultant on building preservation (and is happily back in Alexandria with his wife).

Look into phasing out

Not interested in reinventing yourself? Consider staying at the job you have but changing from full-time to part-time work or to a less demanding role. Some employers offer formal phased-retirement programs that let you cut your hours or work only part of the year, or trade managerial responsibilities for a mentoring role. The federal government recently launched a program in which eligible employees can work half-time, training less-experienced employees.

If your employer has no formal program, scope out the feasibility of making your own arrangement. Start by checking with the human resources department. "Have a clear vision of what you want and be very specific," says Collinson. Some companies only want full-time employees, she says; proposing

anything else is a nonstarter. "There's homework to be done before you even have a conversation with your boss," she says.

While you're talking to HR, find out how changing from full-time to part-time status would affect your eligibility for employee benefits. Only half of the employers who offer 401(k) allow part-time employees to participate in the plan, according to a recent survey by the Transamerica Center. And a report by the Employee Benefit Research Institute shows that fewer than half of large employers (those with 200 or more employees) and one-third of smaller employers offer health coverage to part-time workers.

If you continue to work past 65, you'll have to coordinate your health coverage with Medicare. At 65, you qualify for Medicare Part A, which covers hospital services and is free. At that point, you can also enroll in Medicare Part B (for doctor visits) and buy Medicare supplemental coverage and Part D (for prescription drugs), or enroll in a Medicare Advantage plan, which combines the two and offers other benefits.

If your company has 20 or more employees, employer-based coverage pays first, and you can stay on it if you work enough hours to be eligible. In that case, just sign up for Part A; when you do retire, you can sign up for Part B and the other coverage without penalty or having to wait for open enrollment. If your company has fewer than 20 employees, Medicare becomes your primary insurance, even if your employer offers its own coverage—so if you don't sign up for Medicare, you may not be covered at all. Be sure to talk to your employer about what your options are.

Line Up Your Finances

Whether you figure on working well past retirement age or kicking back on day one, anticipate how you'll handle ongoing expenses plus potential curveballs, such as a downturn in the stock market or a health problem that could force you to retire early. Mark Thorndyke, a Merrill Lynch wealth management adviser in Chicago, works with clients who are three to five years out to put together a financial plan and plug in what-if scenarios. "That helps clients get a good idea of what's achievable and what kind of planning they need to do now."

Start with a budget for necessary expenses, including food, housing and health care, as well as nice-to-haves, such as travel and trips to see the grandkids. Match the need-to-haves with guaranteed income, such as Social Security, pensions and maybe an annuity, and plan to tap your retirement portfolio to pay for the wants.

Many retirement planners recommend that you withdraw no more than 4% of total assets the first year and the same amount, adjusted for inflation, every year after that. But working longer lets you leave more of your savings intact and makes it easier to defer Social Security (and collect a bigger benefit). And because your earning power offsets risk, you can afford to take more risk in how you invest, says Matt Sadowsky, director of retirement at TD Ameritrade. "Instead of a traditional balanced portfolio in retirement—say, 50% stocks and 50% bonds—you might allocate 60% or more of your portfolio to stocks."

Not everyone delays taking Social Security. In fact, most people take it before 66. Be aware that your benefit is reduced based on the number of months you take it before full retirement age. Start taking it as soon as you turn 62 and it gets dinged by 25%. If you keep working after claiming Social Security but before you reach full retirement age, you'll also be subject to an earnings test, in which $1 is deducted from your benefit for every $2 you earn above the annual limit—$15,720 in 2015. (In the year you reach full retirement age, $1 is deducted in benefits for every $3 you earn above a higher limit, which is $41,880 in 2015.)

Another option: Claim Social Security at 66 but keep working and use your benefit checks to, say, travel or pay for college for the grandkids. "All of a sudden you get a couple of thousand dollars a month coming in—there's a lot you can do with that," says Rosenthal.

Don't forget about taxes

Up to 85% of your Social Security benefits may be subject to tax. That becomes almost a certainty if you're pulling in a paycheck while collecting benefits. Working can also put you in a higher tax bracket or keep you there, meaning you'll owe more on distributions from your pretax retirement accounts. From a tax perspective, you might be better off if you delay claiming Social Security until 70 and hold off on tapping pretax accounts until you turn 70½, when you are required to take minimum distributions.

Or keep your options open by funneling money into a Roth IRA. As long as you're older than 59½ and have had the account for at least five years, distributions, including earnings, are tax-free (you can withdraw contributions tax-free at any time). If most of your money is in a tax-deferred account, consider paying the necessary tax bill to convert a chunk of that money each year into a Roth. If you convert $10,000 a year from age 60 to 70, at 70 you will have $100,000 plus earnings sitting in a tax-free account. By about that time, says Rosenthal, "you're on Social Security and taking required minimum distributions, and you can take tax-free dollars to minimize the taxes."

Retire, Rinse, Repeat

Almost 20 years ago, Gregory Contro, now 52, had a frenetic, lucrative career as the head of a futures brokerage group on the Chicago Mercantile Exchange. By age 37, he was ready to move on. An avid tennis player, he retired from his first career and became a tennis coach for young, highlevel players in the Chicago area, a job he had already been doing on the side. "I had achieved a lot of my goals on the exchange and was going to try this new challenge."

Most people don't have the resources to retire at 52, much less 37. In making the transition, Contro had the luxury of knowing he could afford to hang up his career altogether. "I was able to save and got familiar with the concept of wealth management early. When I left the Merc, I knew I could pretty much do what I wanted if I didn't mess it up." He managed his assets conservatively, working with financial adviser Gayle Ronan, who has since retired. "She made me understand what I needed to live on comfortably, taking into account shocks that investments go through and shocks in your personal life that you have to account for," he says. "You have to build in some safety nets"—including, in his case, umbrella insurance because he works with kids in a physically demanding setting.

Contro could still retire if he chose to. "I work because I like to work," he says. But, like others his age, he has started preparing for a next act. Inspired by his relationship with companies including Fila sportswear and Wilson Racquet Sports, Contro is working toward a master's degree at Northwestern University in sports marketing, a career he hopes will last him until he fully retires. "Going back to school has been incredibly exhilarating for me mentally," says Contro, who is by far the oldest in his class.

Contro's experience reflects the growing awareness that productivity doesn't stop when a career ends. "You think, I want to make enough money to get out of the game, and then you realize, I'm just too young to retire—there are a lot of challenges out there," says Contro. "You become thirsty for something different."

So when does he actually plan to retire? He's not sure. "The one thing I do know is, I don't want to sit still."

Critical Thinking

1. Why has the concept of retirement changed in the twenty-first century?

2. What advice should be given to adolescents and young adults to allow them to plan for the optimal retirement experience?

Internet References

A Timeline of the Evolution of Retirement in the United States
http://scholarship.law.georgetown.edu/cgi/viewcontent.cgi?article=1049&context=legal&sei-redir=1&referer=http%3A%2F%2Fwww.bing.com%2Fsearch%3Fq%3Dthe%2520history%2520of%2520retirement%26qs%3Dn%

26form%3DQBRE%26pq%3Dthe%2520history%2520of%2520retirement%26sc%3D8-25%26sp%3D-1%26sk%3D%26cvid%3D583F98DAC8E4425BB4814B4178DB15F9#search=%22history%20retirement%22

Retirement Planning Advice for Teens to 50+
http://hereandnow.wbur.org/2014/04/03/jaffe-rethinking-retirement

Retirement in the 21st Century
https://www.jrf.org.uk/report/retirement-21st-century

Retirement Planning in the 21st Century
https://www.piu.org/communicators/retirement-planning-in-the-21st-century

Article   Prepared by: Claire N. Rubman, Suffolk *County Community College*

The Switched-On Brain

AMY BARTH

Learning Outcomes

After reading this article, you will be able to:

- Evaluate the research on optogenetics and defeating mental illness.

- Predict what illnesses may be abbreviated or alleviated in the near future with more knowledge about opsins and light therapy.

Stopped at a red light on his drive home from work, Karl Deisseroth contemplates one of his patients, a woman with depression so entrenched that she had been unresponsive to drugs and electroshock therapy for years. The red turns to green and Deisseroth accelerates, navigating roads and intersections with one part of his mind while another part considers a very different set of pathways that also can be regulated by a system of lights. In his lab at Stanford University's Clark Center, Deisseroth is developing a remarkable way to switch brain cells off and on by exposing them to targeted green, yellow, or blue flashes. With that ability, he is learning how to regulate the flow of information in the brain.

Deisseroth's technique, known broadly as optogenetics, could bring new hope to his most desperate patients. In a series of provocative experiments, he has already cured the symptoms of psychiatric disease in mice. Optogenetics also shows promise for defeating drug addiction. When Deisseroth exposed a set of test mice to cocaine and then flipped a switch, pulsing bright yellow light into their brains, the expected rush of euphoria—the prelude to addiction—was instantly blocked. Almost miraculously, they were immune to the cocaine high; the mice left the drug den as uninterested as if they had never been exposed.

Today, those breakthroughs have been demonstrated in only a small number of test animals. But as Deisseroth pulls into his driveway he is optimistic about what tomorrow's work could bring: Human applications, and the relief they could deliver, may not be far off.

> **For all its complexity, the brain in some ways is a surprisingly simple device. Neurons switch off and on, causing signals to stop or go. Using optogenetics, Deisseroth can do that switching himself. He inserts light-sensitive proteins into brain cells. Those proteins let him turn a set of cells on or off just by shining the right kind of laser beam at the cells.**

That in turn makes it possible to highlight the exact neural pathways involved in the various forms of psychiatric disease. A disruption of one particular pathway, for instance, might cause anxiety. To test the possibility, Deisseroth engineers an animal with light-sensitive proteins in the brain cells lying along the suspected pathway. Then he illuminates those cells with a laser. If the animal begins cowering in a corner, he knows he is in the right place. And as Deisseroth and his colleagues illuminate more neural pathways, other researchers will be able to design increasingly targeted drugs and minimally invasive brain implants to treat psychiatric disease.

Optogenetics originally emerged from Bio-X, a multidisciplinary project spearheaded in part by Stephen Chu, then a Stanford physicist and now the U.S. Secretary of Energy. Bio-X takes some of Stanford's best engineers, computer scientists, physicists, chemists, and clinicians and throws them together in the Clark Center, where an open, glass-clad structure makes communication unavoidable. Deisseroth, whose beat-up jeans and T-shirt practically define the universal academic wardrobe, proved a natural at working across disciplines. Over the past decade, his omnivorous quest has filtered far beyond Bio-X into a thousand institutions around the world.

Although his Bio-X work involves esoteric genetics and animal experiments, Deisseroth has never forgotten the human needs that motivated him in the first place. He still divides his time between his basement lab and the psychiatry patients who desperately need his research to pay off.

Psychiatry's Core Dilemma

Karl Deisseroth was 27 when he first brushed past the curtains of the psychiatry ward at Palo Alto's VA hospital in northern California. It was 1998 and he had just completed his first two years of Stanford Medical School, where he had earned a PhD in brain cell physiology, exploring the electrical language of neuron communication. As part of his medical training, he was required to complete a rotation in psychiatry—a hazy specialty, he felt, much less compelling than the brain surgery that was his career goal.

Several patients in the ward lay in narrow beds lined up before him, awaiting a treatment called electroconvulsive therapy (ECT). After the anesthesiologist on duty put them under, the attending psychiatrist placed pads on the patients' temples and walked from bed to bed, pressing a small button on each person's control box, sending volts of electricity into their brains. Their bodies tensed and their brains rattled with seizures for a full minute. The recipients risked losing large swaths of memory, but if things went well, the current would reset their neurons, purging their depression and providing months of relief.

From that experience, Deisseroth determined that he would spend his life solving a core puzzle of psychiatric disease: A brain could appear undamaged, with no dead tissue or anatomical deformities, yet something could be so wrong it destroyed patients' lives. Perhaps because the damage was invisible, the available therapies were shockingly crude. ECT was lifesaving but usually temporary; although it was likely that just a small set of cells caused the patient's troubles, the shock jolted neurons throughout the brain. Psychoactive drugs, targeting general brain regions and cell types, were too broad as well. And scientists were so uncertain about what chemical imbalances impacted which neural circuits that one-third of people with major depression did not respond to drugs at all.

Deisseroth pondered the problem through a subsequent psychiatry residency, where he oversaw more than 200 ECT procedures over four years. Then, in 2004, he became a principal investigator at Stanford and was given his own lab. As a clinician treating patients, his arsenal was limited. But with his scientific imagination roaming free and a brand-new lab sparkling with empty chairs and beakers to fill, he began to envision elegant new strategies. One stood out: a concept first suggested by Francis Crick, the legendary genetics and consciousness researcher.

Crick's idea was that light, with its unparalleled speed and precision, could be the ideal tool for controlling neurons and mapping the brain. "The idea of an energy interface instead of a physical interface to work with the brain was what was so exciting," Deisseroth says. He thought creating a light-sensitive brain was probably impossible, but then an idea floated up: What about tapping the power of light-sensitive microbes, single-celled creatures that drift in water, turning toward or away from the sun to regulate energy intake? Such brainless creatures rely on signals from light-sensitive proteins called opsins. When sunlight hits the opsin, it instantly sends an electric signal through the microbe's cell membrane, telling the tiny critter which way to turn in relation to the sun.

Deisseroth wondered if he could insert these opsins into targeted mammalian brain cells in order to make them light-sensitive too. If so, he could learn to control their behavior using light. Shining light into the brain could then become the tool Crick imagined, providing a way to control neurons without electric shocks or slow-acting, unfocused drugs.

Lighting the Brain

The necessary tools were already out there. The first opsin—the light-sensitive protein made by microbes—had been identified in 1971, the same year Deisseroth was born. Bacteriorhodopsin, as it was called, responded to green light, and scientists have since found it in microbes living in saltwater all over the world. The next opsin, halorhodopsin, which responds to yellow light, was discovered in 1977. Like bacteriorhodopsin, it was found in bacteria living in salty lakes and seas.

Deisseroth, who read everything he could about opsins, realized that light-sensitive microbes speak the same basic language as neurons: When light hits the opsin, gates in the cell membrane open, allowing charged particles called ions to flow in and out. In microbes, ion flow tells the organism which way to turn. In neurons, ions flowing through the cell wall initiate action, setting off a string of communications that tell organisms like us how to feel and behave. This similarity suggested to Deisseroth that opsins could be manipulated to switch brain cells on and off.

Deisseroth was still mulling this over in 2003, when German biologists Georg Nagel and Peter Hegemann announced a new light-sensitive microbe, a green alga called *Chlamydomonas reinhardtii*. The 10-micrometer-wide microbe has a small eye-spot, which Deisseroth describes as "kind of cute," that spins around to detect light. It makes a protein called channelrhodopsin-2 (ChR2) that acts as an antenna to receive blue light and convert it to an ion flow. When a light shines on ChR2, the cell becomes active and tells the microbe where to turn.

Deisseroth immediately wanted ChR2. The other opsins might do the trick, but because his goal—putting them into a brain and getting that brain to respond—was so tricky and success so improbable, he needed to try as many options as possible. He wrote to Nagel in the spring of 2004, requesting a copy of the gene and explaining he planned to try inserting it into neurons. "I was realistic enough to know it was worth testing but probably a long ways away from being useful," he says. "If I'd told him I was going to cure depression with it, I'm sure he would have thought I was crazy."

Deisseroth realized that even the first step of his plan—inserting the microbial opsin molecule into a mammalian neuron and getting the two to sync up—was a long shot. For one thing, there was a good chance the mammalian immune system would reject the foreign protein. Even if the opsin was tolerated, there was no way to know whether it could toggle mammalian cells in the same way it controlled algae. The opsin's electric signals would need to fire and shut down within milliseconds of the stimulus to communicate as quickly as neurons; Deisseroth doubted that the simple biology of algae required such speed.

To run the necessary tests, Deisseroth had to hire staff for his lab, and fast. Someone would have to provide expertise in handling viruses—specifically, a virus to serve as a vector, or Trojan horse, to cart algal genes into mammalian cells. The gene for the opsin would need to be inserted into the virus, which would infect the neurons, transferring the opsin gene to them. If all went as planned, mammalian neurons would then produce light-sensitive microbial opsins as if they were proteins of their own.

A Team Is Born

Luck was on Deisseroth's side that summer of 2004. As a new Stanford faculty member, he had moved into an office that had been occupied by Steven Chu, who had recently left Stanford to become director of the Lawrence Berkeley National Laboratory. Deisseroth's door still had Chu's name on it. One afternoon, a disoriented young chemistry student named Feng Zhang wandered in, looking for Chu. "I can still remember looking at him—he was a little surprised to see me," Deisseroth says. But the two started talking. Zhang wanted to understand the chemical imbalances underlying depression. He also had the skills to help Deisseroth with viruses: At age 15 he had started working with viral vectors, a project that won him the top prize at the Intel International Science and Engineering Fair. Now an aspiring Stanford PhD, he decided to join Deisseroth's team.

Next, Deisseroth required someone skilled at patch clamping, a technique that uses an electrode to record ions passing through cells. This would allow him to record when neurons fired or shut down, indicating whether they were responding to light. For this he hired Ed Boyden, a newly minted neuroscience PhD at Stanford. Boyden was brilliant and energetic, with an aggressiveness that was sometimes off-putting but was ideal for tackling nearly impossible experiments and getting them published. He also had expertise in electrophysiology, another skill required for Deisseroth's nascent optogenetics project.

That fall Deisseroth set to work with his new team. First they inserted the ChR2 opsin into a harmless retrovirus that Zhang had harvested. Then they added the engineered virus to a culture of rat neurons in a petri dish. As hoped, Zhang's virus penetrated the neurons and delivered the light-sensitive gene. The final step was observing whether the cell actually fired quickly in response to light. Boyden hooked up one neuron to a glass electrode that could also deliver light. The other end of the electrode was attached to a computer. When the cell was quiet, a steady line appeared on the computer screen; when it was active, the line jumped up in a spike.

To Deisseroth's elation, the effort was a success: As Boyden poked the electrode into the cell, Deisseroth saw pulses of bright blue light in the culture dish and spikes precisely matching those pulses on the computer screen. "For the next nine months we worked frenetically to publish it. We wanted to move quickly," Deisseroth says. The paper, published in *Nature Neuroscience* in August 2005, chronicled the first time anyone had managed to control brain cells with light.

The cell cultures still did not prove whether optogenetics would apply to brain cells inside living, freely moving mammals, however. The effort to find out required expanding the team. By 2006 Deisseroth had a tight-knit group of 15 who took frequent excursions to local Indian buffets and In-N-Out Burger when they were not working intensely side by side.

Cracking the Animal Code

In cell culture, only a small number of mild virus particles were needed to deliver the opsin gene to targeted neurons. But inserting genes into mammalian neurons inside an intact brain required a larger number of more virulent viruses. Zhang worked tirelessly on this challenge, developing a highly concentrated but still-safe retrovirus derived from HIV; in essence, he removed HIV's toxic genes and replaced them with a version of ChR2. He could brew the virus from scratch in just three days.

Deisseroth also needed a miniature flashlight that could be surgically inserted in the brain to turn cells on and off at close range. Mice weigh only about 20 grams, less than two tablespoons of sugar, so the device could not be big or heavy. And although the light needed to be 100 times as bright as room light, the system could not heat the brain as it delivered the beam. The team's solution was to implant a fiber-optic cable in the brain and connect it to a miniature laser affixed to the animal's head. The contraption was small and light enough to travel with the mouse wherever it went.

Finally, Deisseroth needed a way to tag the specific neurons he wanted to study so that only those cells would become activated in response to the light. Other brain researchers had identified certain cell types and areas of the brain associated with fear, reward, addiction, and depression. But they had no way of knowing exactly which neurons within these regions were driving a particular behavior. Deisseroth strove to find out. He used snippets of DNA called promoters to link ChR2 genes with DNA found only in the specific neurons he wanted to study. When he shined his light, it would not disturb the entire region but just the relevant cells.

Only then was Deisseroth ready to test optogenetics in a living animal. He charged Zhang with conducting a study of hypocretin neurons, sleep-related cells located deep in the brain's hypothalamus. The cells are crucial for arousal during sleep–wake cycles and are thought to play a key role in narcolepsy.

Zhang did the research at Stanford Sleep Center, where he could record brain waves of snoozing mice. He targeted ChR2 to the sleep cells and then, using optical fiber, delivered light directly to the mice's brains. In early 2007 his team placed a ChR2-altered mouse in a sleeping chamber with two implants in its skull. One was the optical fiber; the other consisted of four wires that measured the animal's brain waves.

Deisseroth vividly remembers the moment when an excited postdoc summoned him to the room. "I walked in and he whispered to me, 'Be quiet.'" A mouse was peacefully dreaming in his chamber. But when the laser was turned on, they saw a slight change on the brain-wave monitor and the animal began to twitch. It was waking up in response to a light signal inside its brain. For the first time ever, Deisseroth's team had used optogenetics to control behavior in a living animal.

Soon after, in March 2007, their results were more dramatic still. Deisseroth implanted an optical fiber in the cortex of a mouse with ChR2 in its motor neurons. When he flashed blue light through the cable, a meandering mouse began running to the left. When the laser was switched off, the mouse resumed wandering aimlessly. "You can turn it on and off and the animal isn't distressed. It's comfortable. You're just reaching in there with the fiber-optic, controlling the cells, and you're causing its behavior," Deisseroth says. "That was the moment I knew this would be amazing."

In the five years since, the Deisseroth lab, dubbed the D-lab, has expanded into an entire brain-control research center, with more than 40 scientists on the job. Molecular biologists, neuroscientists, engineers, and physicists from all over the world rush through his cavernous laboratories, tinkering with microscopes, lasers, viral soups, electrodes, and rodent brains. Located in the heart of Silicon Valley, the D-lab feels like an entrepreneurial start-up. Members enthusiastically talk among themselves, build and invent together—there is a palpable sense of enthusiasm and urgency.

One of the team's greatest accomplishments was spearheaded by Kay Tye, a former postdoc who now works at MIT. In a lab near Deisseroth's office, Tye inserted a fiber-optic cable into a mouse's little brain at just the right spot, leaving enough slack for the animal to run around. Tye was studying anxiety circuits and needed to put the cable into a specific part of the amygdala. For decades, researchers have known that the amygdala is associated with fear and anxiety but did not know exactly which neurons in what part of the amygdala played a role. Tye used data from previous studies to home in on a likely circuit, then carefully positioned the cable to deliver light right there. As the targeted neurons were stimulated, she watched to see how the mouse's behavior changed. If it suddenly became bolder, that would be a good sign that she had found a neuron set involved in anxiety.

Mice are naturally fearful of exploring open spaces, where they are vulnerable to predators. When placed in Tye's four-armed maze, they would spend most of their time in the two arms protected by high walls, occasionally poking a nose out to explore. But when Tye switched on the light and activated the circuit in her subject's brain, the mouse ventured out, exploring the open part of the maze with no visible anxiety. The results suggested that Tye had located an anxiety circuit in the brain that could someday be targeted by drugs.

Breaking the cycle of addictive behavior was another goal for the D-team. Again working with mice, they built a three-chamber cage in which one room became a designated drug den. Mice in that room received a shot of cocaine. Animals typically formed a positive association between the effects of the cocaine and the room, just as a person addicted to alcohol might form an association between feeling good and the pop of a cork. Left to their own devices, the mice hung around the room long after the cocaine wore off, even when they were free to wander elsewhere.

But when mice were injected with cocaine and also treated with halorhodopsins and light—in this case a yellow pulse sent directly to the brain's reward center—the rush of euphoria was blocked. Those mice never formed a positive association between cocaine and the room and roamed freely around the cage.

Later in 2010, Deisseroth teamed with neuroscientist Anatol Kreitzer at the University of California, San Francisco, to investigate Parkinson's disease—an important step toward using optogenetics to target a neurodegenerative disease. The ultimate cause of Parkinson's is unknown but clearly involves the loss of a set of neurons that control voluntary movement.

The basal ganglia are the brain's action control center. One pathway there sends signals to "go," as in go ahead and perform this action, and one sends "stop" signals. In Parkinson's the pathways are thought to be out of balance, with interrupted motor cells causing the debilitating tremors and loss of movement control symptomatic of the disease.

Although this theory of Parkinson's had been widely considered since the 1980s, there was no way to probe the circuit directly until optogenetics came along. Working with mice, Deisseroth and Kreitzer activated the "go" and "stop" circuits with light, confirming that one in fact facilitates movement while the other inhibits it. Next they tested a more nuanced hypothesis: Might Parkinson's result from an overactive stop circuit? Deisseroth and Kreitzer tagged that circuit with ChR2 and delivered blue light directly into the brains of mice. When the light turned on, movement slowed and the mice had trouble walking, both symptoms of Parkinson's.

What the researchers really wanted, though, was insight into how to treat the disease. They thought activating the go pathway could rebalance the overactive stop network. When they targeted the go circuit, that approach worked even better than expected. The mice began walking normally again, their movement indistinguishable from the way they had moved in their healthy state. Today's leading treatment for Parkinson's—deep brain stimulation—involves inserting a large electrode deep within the patient's brain and zapping all surrounding tissue. Deisseroth hopes that his findings will bring a more targeted treatment soon.

Indeed, by combining opsins, including ChR2, which turns cells on, and halorhodopsin and bacteriorhodopsin, which turn cells off, Deisseroth can ask ever more nuanced questions about complex diseases: Epilepsy, autism, sleep disorders, and schizophrenia may all require this combination approach.

Turning cells on and off efficiently allows a whole range of new, more detailed experiments: Now Deisseroth can tell neurons to fire and shut down quickly, so they can be ready to receive the next signal telling them what to do. Using multiple opsins as well as blue, yellow, and green light, he can experiment with various combinations of activation in hopes of eliminating symptoms of disease.

Pacing the Heart with Light

Despite the fact that Deisseroth has focused on animal brains, the first optogenetic implants—which could be ready for human trials in as little as a decade—will almost surely focus on other organs, where applications are less risky. Early therapies could take the form of a heart pacemaker that uses light to activate heart cells and keep them firing on time. There has been talk of optogenetics for the blind, implanting opsins in vision cells and developing special glasses that shine light into them.

In the fall of 2011, Deisseroth cofounded a company in Menlo Park, around the corner from Stanford, dedicated to translating optogenetics research into therapies. One focus is peripheral nerve disorder, in which messages between the brain and the rest of the body are interrupted. It is often caused by spinal cord injuries, multiple sclerosis, and other nervous system disorders.

"It's not very glamorous, but there's a very large population of people who have peripheral nerve defects that keep them from having good bowel and bladder control," Deisseroth says. "And what's interesting is, if you ask the people who have paralysis if they could choose one thing, to be able to walk or to have bowel and bladder control, they essentially all pick bowel and bladder control, because it's the most limiting for them. It is a problem well suited to optogenetics." Bladder control requires both a contraction of the bladder and a relaxation of the sphincter, and optogenetics can both stimulate and inhibit those different neurons at the same time. Deisseroth hopes to introduce opsins to the crucial peripheral nerves outside the brain and then use simple LED implants to switch function back on.

Once someone has figured out how to get opsins inside the brains of primates and humans—Zhang at MIT is working on the problem now—optogenetic therapies targeting the brain can begin. The possibility also opens the door to Orwellian fears. If Deisseroth can control the brains of mice with light, what is to stop human mind control? The most cogent answer is this: Creating transgenic people by sending a retrovirus into healthy brains will never be allowed. Besides, the potential for healing is too great to ignore—starting with a better implant for those who suffer from Parkinson's, a neurodegenerative disease already treated with electrodes in the brain.

Getting into the Human Brain

Deisseroth's great insight has spawned research around the world. Every two weeks, scientists come from universities in the United States and abroad to spend a week at the D-lab learning the secrets of optogenetics, mastering everything from mouse surgery to cooking up viruses. At the end of the week they present their plans for research of their own. Deisseroth slouches in his seat, wearing coffee-stained jeans, clogs, and a short-sleeve button-down shirt that he has not tucked in. The laissez-faire demeanor is deceptive: Deisseroth is fully engaged and always on, often jumping in during a presentation to ask questions or offer suggestions. The waiting list to attend his workshop is more than a dozen labs long.

One notable alumna is Ana Domingos, who flew in from New York's Rockefeller University a few years back. She was investigating weight loss and wanted to use optogenetics to trigger dopamine, a mood-enhancing neurotransmitter, whenever mice drank water laced with an artificial sweetener, causing them to ignore their usual preference, a sugar-spiked drink. Domingos hopes to use her findings to develop weight loss therapies. "The first time I saw the mouse bingeing on water with sweetener, I got goosebumps," Domingos says. "I couldn't sleep. Karl gave me the tools to play god."

Following these presentations, Deisseroth grabs lunch before attending his weekly patient psychiatry sessions. He picks an outdoor seat at a nearby café swarming with people on a sunny, 75-degree day in mid-January. It's a rare moment of downtime for Deisseroth, who readily admits he needs to relax more.

Even with his lab in high gear, Deisseroth is constantly busy trying to help his psychiatry patients. One of them, Alicia A, has tried nearly every medication, ECT, and various electrical implants to keep her depression under control. She drives seven hours once a month to visit Deisseroth, and together they have found a successful combination of electrical nerve stimulation and antidepressant drugs that has allowed her to return to work and enjoy life. Yet she intently follows Deisseroth's optogenetics work and is adamant that if he ever starts human trials, she will be the first in line.

As much as Alicia A's life has improved from sessions with Deisseroth, the electrical stimulation is often uncomfortable, and her treatment requires constant monitoring. Deisseroth has an entirely different therapy possibility in mind for her. From his experience with ECT, he knows inducing a seizure with electricity resets individual neurons in the brain just like rebooting a computer, so those neurons fire all at once in a different order than before. But something peculiar and fascinating happens to the patient: When the therapy is over everything about the person—memories, priorities, the sense of self—comes back. Apparently these things are not generated by neurons but arise from the brain's physical structure and wiring. The wires are like superhighways, roads of activity where circuits of neurons constantly communicate, but sometimes the road might be gridlocked or icy, and the messenger can't get through.

At one level, optogenetics is nothing more than using light to control a targeted population of cells. But how these cells are wired up is a huge puzzle in itself and, to Deisseroth, one that lies at the true root of future psychiatric cures. To turn his wiring insights into therapy, he wants to use optogenetics to narrow down which circuits dictate which specific behaviors. Then, if he can determine whether the circuits are somehow impeded or blocked, he can try to physically shift them and normalize activity flow.

The Magnetic Cure

Deisseroth isn't certain which tools will allow him to study these connections—it's a capability beyond the reach of optogenetics—so he is once again on the edge of something big and unprecedented. A type of brain imaging, called diffusion tensor imaging, allows doctors to scan patients and produce vibrantly colored images of the brain's wiring. These connections vary from individual to individual. When abnormalities are detected, a machine therapy called transcranial magnetic stimulation (TMS) can send into the brain magnetic pulses powerful enough to shift and rewire those connections so their function is improved. TMS is already used to treat ailments like Parkinson's disease, migraines, and depression.

Years ago as a psychiatry resident, Deisseroth assisted with the clinical trial that got the therapy FDA-approved. He plans to continue using optogenetics to pin down circuits of brain cells responsible for disease and to combine that knowledge with the colorful circuit images to home in on which wires need to go where to establish normal communication. Then TMS can move the wires precisely where they need to go to cure any particular illness. If it works, scientists would have a complete understanding of an individual patient's brain.

The concept may sound extraordinary, too grand to work, but this is the type of challenge Deisseroth loves most. "I want to come up with totally new things, so I don't want to be affected by too many preconceptions," he says. Conveniently, Deisseroth's own brain is wired to generate its best ideas in moments of isolation. "I can remember a couple key insights just driving in my car. For me, that's meditative. I rarely solve a problem by thinking about it. The insights usually come from out of the blue, like a bolt."

Critical Thinking

1. Why do you think people with peripheral nerve defects would rather have good bowel and bladder control than be able to walk again?

2. Do you think the science of optogenetics will allow people to control others (e.g., mind control)? Why or why not?

3. Do you think great insights come "out of the blue" like a bolt, or from meditating on a problem? Why for either choice?

Create Central

www.mhhe.com/createcentral

Internet References

The Primary Structure of a Halorhodopsin
www.jbc.org/content/265/3/1253.abstract

Transcranial Magnetic Stimulation-Scholarpedia
www.scholarpedia.org/article/Transcranial_magnetic_stimulation

What Is Optogenetics?
http://optogenetics.weebly.com/what-is-it.html

AMY BARTH is an associate editor at *Discover*.

Article Prepared by: Claire N. Rubman, *Suffolk County Community College*

Anxiety Nation

Why are so many of us so ill at ease?

Sophie McBain

Learning Outcomes

After reading this article, you will be able to:

- Explain the term *pharmacological dissection.*
- Articulate the clinical definition of anxiety.
- Identify the World Health Organization's account of the country with the lowest reported level of anxiety.

For a condition that affects so many of us, there is very little agreement about what anxiety actually is. Is it a physiological condition, best treated with medication, or psychological—the product of repressed trauma, as a Freudian might suggest? Is it a cultural construct, a reaction to today's anomic society, or a more fundamental spiritual and philosophical reflection of what it means to be human? For most sufferers, the most pressing concern is whether drugs work, and if therapy is a good idea.

Our modern, medical definition of anxiety could be traced back to 1980 and the publication of the third edition of the *Diagnostic and Statistical Manual* (*DSM-III*), the doctor's and psychiatrist's bible for identifying mental illness. The authors of *DSM-III* suggested that, according to their new criteria, between 2 percent and 4 percent of the population would have an anxiety disorder. But three decades on, the *America's State of Mind Report* showed that one in every six people in the United States suffers from anxiety.

The most recent nationwide survey, which took place in 2007, found that three million people in the UK have an anxiety disorder. About 7 percent of UK adults are on antidepressants (often prescribed for anxiety, too) and one in seven will take benzodiazepines such as Xanax in any 1 year. Mental health charities warn that our anxiety levels are creeping even higher; they often blame our "switched-on" modern culture for this, or the financial crisis and the long recession that followed it.

And yet, it is difficult to quantify whether it is our feelings of anxiety that have changed, or whether it's just our perception of those feelings that is different: are we increasingly viewing ordinary human emotions as marks of mental illness? "In theory, it's possible that we've just watched too many Woody Allen films. That's a very difficult argument to definitively disprove," the clinical psychologist and author Oliver James told me.

If that seems like a slightly flippant way of framing the debate, that could be because James's books, including *The Selfish Capitalist and Britain on the Couch,* are premised on the idea that rates of depression and anxiety have reached record highs in the affluent consumer societies of the English-speaking world.

In January this year, Scott Stossel, who is the editor of the American magazine the *Atlantic,* published *My Age of Anxiety,* an account of his lifelong, debilitating battle with nerves. There has been a lot of interest in the book in both the United States and Europe. Stossel, who is 44, is a successful journalist and yet he is deeply insecure. He has been in therapy for three decades and has taken a cocktail of antidepressants, antipsychotic medications, and sedatives (not to mention more conventional cocktail ingredients such as gin, Scotch, and vodka) in an attempt to cope with any number of phobias, from the common (agoraphobia and fear of public speaking) to the more niche (turophobia: fear of cheese).

Stossel reveals in painful, intimate, and sometimes comical detail the humiliations of living with high anxious tension and very loose bowels. Despite the severity of his problems, he successfully concealed them from most of his friends and colleagues until the book was published. He told me when we spoke that in recent months co-workers have given him lots of hugs (which is sweet, but a little bit uncomfortable) and thousands of strangers have approached him because they so identify with the experiences he describes in the book.

"I was very nervous about coming out as anxious," Stossel says. "And now it's too late and I can't un-come out. It hasn't been a cure, but it has been something of a relief. I now feel there are practical things I can help with, like trying to reduce the stigma around anxiety."

He says we ought to view anxiety less as a "psychological problem" and more like a "medical condition, in the way gout or diabetes is. These are things that need to be managed and treated, and have an organic basis. It's not necessarily that you are weak, but that you have an illness."

Yet while we understand how our modern diet is making gout and diabetes more common, the causes of anxiety are more mysterious.

Anxiety has long been associated with depression, and often the two were subsumed under the notion of "melancholia": Robert Burton's great book *Anatomy of Melancholy* (1621) was as much about anxiety as sadness. But the *DSM-III* classified anxiety and depression as separate conditions: the former is related to feelings of worry, the latter to low mood, and loss of pleasure and interest. More often than not, however, the two occur together. The blurred lines between normality and illness, or depression and anxiety, make it very hard to grasp what it means to say that three million people in the UK suffer from anxiety.

If one in seven of us is taking pills to control or ward off anxiety, are we just medicalising an ordinary human emotion? Did the purveyors of the early antianxiety medicines such as Miltown—discovered in the 1940s, and the first in a line of blockbuster drugs including Prozac and Xanax—manage to create a new problem along with the solution they offered?

Stossel describes how in the 1950s a young psychiatrist called Donald Klein began randomly treating his patients with a new drug called imipramine. He noticed that patients on imipramine often remained very anxious but were less likely to suffer from acute paroxysms of anxiety. And so, having found a cure, he defined the problem—"panic attacks."

Until imipramine, panic attacks didn't "exist." This process of working backwards from new drugs to new illnesses is known as pharmacological dissection, and it is not uncommon. Yet even if modern drugs shaped our understanding of mental illness, that doesn't mean they made us sick.

As millions take pills, are we just medicalising an ordinary emotion?

Or maybe the UK's epidemic of anxiety isn't pathological at all but a product of historically unprecedented good health and affluence. Perhaps anxiety is a luxury that comes with wealth, freedom, and the privilege of having nothing fundamental to fear in our modern society.

This isn't an unpopular notion. A World Health Organization survey in 2002 found that, while 18.2 percent of Americans reported anxiety in any 1 year, south of the US border only 6.8 percent of Mexicans did. Of the 14 countries surveyed by WHO, Nigeria reported the lowest levels of anxiety, with only 3.3 percent of respondents experiencing anxiety in any year. Nigeria's per capita GDP is $2,690, about 6 percent that of the United States, and in 2010 84.5 percent of Nigerians were living on less than $2 a day, the international poverty line. Breaking out into a nervous sweat on the London Tube because you can't remember if you unplugged your hair straighteners is the kind of indulgence you can't afford if you're struggling to feed yourself, or so the argument goes.

However, it's not that simple. Again, it's very hard to tell whether feelings of anxiety vary internationally or if people label them differently. In countries with a large stigma against mental illness, people are less likely to report disorders, such as anxiety or depression. Yet the psychiatrist Vikram Patel, who recently featured on the BBC Radio 4 programme *The Life Scientific,* says his research in India and Zimbabwe has convinced him that rates of mental illness are the same all over the world.

The way we understand anxiety is cultural, says Beth Murphy, head of information at the mental health charity Mind. "If you're living on the breadline in a hand-to-mouth existence you might not recognise what you are feeling as anxiety, but it's quite probable that you're going to be pretty worried about where your next meal is coming from."

This raises another problem: if you are feeling anxious because it's very likely you could go hungry tomorrow, are you in any meaningful way unwell?

Just as sadness is natural but depression is an illness, most of the people I spoke to who suffered from anxiety instinctively drew a distinction between "good anxiety," the nervous adrenalin that helps you get stuff done and meet deadlines, and "bad anxiety," the destructive kind. Our common-sense interpretation of "bad anxiety" also suggests that the worries here should be disproportionate or irrational.

The *Diagnostic and Statistical Manual* used today identifies anxiety disorders according to how severe and persistent the feelings of worry are, and whether these feelings are accompanied by elements from a list of secondary symptoms, including sleep disturbance, muscle tension, poor concentration, and fatigue.

Although the anxiety should be "excessive" the focus is solely on the feelings, and not what caused them. This might go some way towards explaining the boom in prescriptions for mental illnesses; doctors sometimes prescribe antidepressants to someone who has suffered bereavement, something Oliver James described as "ludicrous." The counter-argument is: if a short course of drugs can make it easier to cope with the painful but completely healthy process of grieving, why not take them?

At its most extreme, anxiety is a debilitating, life-altering condition. I spoke to Jo, a volunteer at the charity Anxiety UK, and she told me that feelings of anxiety have "blighted" her life.

"It's stopped me from doing so many things that I would have liked to have been able to do and it's stopped me from living what I feel is a normal life, doing things like having relationships, perhaps getting married, having children, having a career. It's put paid to all that," she says bitterly.

Jo, who is in her fifties, has been overcome by anxiety since she was in her teens. She dropped out of school at 16, unable to cope with the pressure of exams, and when her anxiety peaks she is unable to work and is left isolated. Antianxiety drugs have helped ease the physical symptoms—such as headaches and irritable bowel syndrome—yet they've left her with "the same worries and fears."

What does anxiety feel like when it's at its worst? "It's an overwhelming feeling of being out of control, and overwhelmed by everything." Jo pauses, and then adds quietly, "It's not nice."

While researching this piece, I was struck by how many friends came forward with stories of anxiety-induced insomnia, phobias and stress, though mostly this didn't prevent them from working or socialising. I spent one strange dinner with a friend who is a lawyer. I noticed when we met that her hands were raw and bleeding slightly, and while we ate she repeatedly reached into her bag and disinfected them. Under stress from work, she had developed a huge fear of germs.

Another friend, a corporate lawyer, recently collapsed while out shopping after she suffered a panic attack. There's a recognisable stereotype of the neurotic, angst-filled high-flyer—and it has a historical precedent. In the 19th century, nervousness was seen as a mark of social standing, because only the new leisured classes could afford such sensibility. But how closely related are these manifestations of unease and anxiety to those feelings experienced by people who are incapacitated by their nerves or phobias?

The triggers for people's nervous complaints can be idiosyncratic. I chatted about this to Andy Burrows, a musician and the former drummer of the indie band Razorlight. He says he has never felt overly anxious about performing to huge crowds at Wembley or the O_2 Arena in London—a prospect that might make most people break into a sweat—but he has suffered from anxiety since his teens and is so freaked out by lifts and tunnels that he can recite from memory the average time that a London overground train spends underground. It takes 16 seconds to travel through the tunnel from Hampstead Heath to Finchley Road and Frognal Station "at regular speed," he says—and sometimes he just has to get off the train and walk between the two.

Of course, phobias can seem funny to an outsider. I can laugh with friends about the time I leapt up from my chair, tipped over my coffee and ran out of a café, because I suddenly couldn't cope with being in a confined space with a pigeon. And yet, for a brief few seconds, as someone with a fear of birds, I experienced a terror so profound that it overrode my usual instinct not to cause a scene.

In 2012, the National Health Service recorded 8,720 hospital admissions for acute anxiety. According to research for the Organisation for Economic Co-operation and Development, 40 percent of new claimants for disability benefits in the UK are suffering from mental illnesses, of which anxiety and depression are the most common. The effect of this is that Britain has a higher proportion of people claiming unemployment benefit for mental health conditions than any other developed nation. The estimated cost to the UK of mental illness is roughly 4.4 percent of GDP, through lost productivity and health-care costs.

What is going wrong? One problem is that we are not doing enough to support people with anxiety. The first port of call for most sufferers is their GP, and the response they get can vary. I know this because a few years ago, when I experienced a bereavement and a break-up in quick succession, I turned from a natural worrier into an unravelled bundle of nerves. I was unable to sleep, read, or concentrate.

Even sensitive GPs can be constrained in the solutions they can offer.

After a strange few months, spent mostly wandering aimlessly in London, as if somehow I might lose my panic down a backstreet, I burst into tears in front of my doctor. "Patient tearful but able to maintain eye contact," the GP typed on the large screen in front of us, leaving me feeling like some zoo exhibit. She advised me to book an appointment with someone who knew more about mental health.

In the end, I was lucky. The second doctor prescribed me a low dose of antidepressants (against his advice, I decided not to take these). Then, although the NHS waiting list for counselling was months long, my university counsellor could see me and within 2 months I felt almost normal again.

Even when they are very much aware of mental illness, GPs can often be constrained in the solutions they can offer. One in every 10 people in the UK has to wait more than a year for therapy and 54 percent have to wait for more than 3 months (people from black and ethnic-minority communities often wait the longest).

Anxiety is a broad, confusing label and is a condition with multiple causes. We are not the first generation to believe we live in an exceptionally anxious age, and yet in some ways, thanks to the development of drugs and talking therapies, anxiety is a peculiarly modern experience. Perhaps, at the very root of Britain's struggle with nerves—whether viewed in terms of its economic effects or from the perspective of plain, simple suffering, or whether one merely wonders why 3 million of us appear to be afflicted by a disorder we still can't quite define—is that we don't often talk about it.

In an odd way, it might be easier to admit in modern Britain that you're deeply sad than that you are anxious or scared. Collectively, we might be freaking out but most of us are suffering in silence.

Critical Thinking

1. Why do so many people suffer from anxiety in today's society?

2. How would our understanding of anxiety change if we viewed it as an illness instead of a psychological problem?

Create Central

www.mhhe.com/createcentral

Internet References

Anxiety Helpguide
http://www.helpguide.org/home-pages/anxiety.htm

Listening to Xanax
http://nymag.com/news/features/xanax-2012-3/

Medline Plus
http://www.nlm.nih.gov/medlineplus/anxiety.html

National Institute of Mental Health
http://www.nimh.nih.gov/health/publications/anxiety-disorders/index.shtml

Why Teenagers Act Crazy
http://www.nytimes.com/2014/06/29/opinion/sunday/why-teenagers-act-crazy.html?_r=0

Sophie McBain is a staff writer for the New Statesman.

McBain, Sophie. "Anxiety Nation." *New Statesman* 143. 14 (April, 11, 2014): 24–27.

Article

Prepared by: Claire N. Rubman,
Suffolk County Community College, Selden, NY

Is Facebook Making Us Lonely?

Social Media—From Facebook To Twitter—have made us more densely networked than ever. Yet for all this connectivity, new research suggests that we have never been lonelier (or more narcissistic)—and that this loneliness is making us mentally and physically ill. A report on what the epidemic of loneliness is doing to our souls and our society.

STEPHEN MARCHE

Learning Outcomes

After reading this article, you will be able to:

- Discuss the role of social media in terms of our social relationships.

- Talk about the role of Facebook and other social media in terms of our mental health.

Yvette vickers, a former *Playboy* playmate and B-movie star, best known for her role in *Attack of the 50 Foot Woman,* would have been 83 last August, but nobody knows exactly how old she was when she died. According to the Los Angeles coroner's report, she lay dead for the better part of a year before a neighbor and fellow actress, a woman named Susan Savage, noticed cobwebs and yellowing letters in her mailbox, reached through a broken window to unlock the door, and pushed her way through the piles of junk mail and mounds of clothing that barricaded the house. Upstairs, she found Vickers' body, mummified, near a heater that was still running. Her computer was on too, its glow permeating the empty space.

The *Los Angeles Times* posted a story headlined "Mummified Body of Former Playboy Playmate Yvette Vickers Found in Her Benedict Canyon Home," which quickly went viral. Within two weeks, by Technorati' count, Vickers's lonesome death was already the subject of 16,057 Facebook posts and 881 tweets. She had long been a horror-movie icon, a symbol of Hollywood's capacity to exploit our most basic fears in the silliest ways; now she was an icon of a new and different kind of horror: our growing fear of loneliness. Certainly she received much more attention in death than she did in the final years of her life. With no children, no religious group, and no immediate social circle of any kind, she had begun, as an elderly woman, to look elsewhere for companionship. Savage later told *Los Angeles* magazine that she had searched Vickers's phone bills for clues about the life that led to such an end. In the months before her grotesque death, Vickers had made calls not to friends or family but to distant fans who had found her through fan conventions and Internet sites.

Vickers's web of connections had grown broader but shallower, as has happened for many of us. We are living in an isolation that would have been unimaginable to our ancestors, and yet we have never been more accessible. Over the past three decades, technology has delivered to us a world in which we need not be out of contact for a fraction of a moment. In 2010, at a cost of $300 million, 800 miles of fiber-optic cable was laid between the Chicago Mercantile Exchange and the New York Stock Exchange to shave three milliseconds off trading times. Yet within this world of instant and absolute communication, unbounded by limits of time or space, we suffer from unprecedented alienation. We have never been more detached from one another, or lonelier. In a world consumed by ever more novel modes of socializing, we have less and less actual society. We live in an accelerating contradiction: the more connected we become, the lonelier we are. We were promised a global village; instead we inhabit the drab cul-de-sacs and endless freeways of a vast suburb of information.

At the forefront of all this unexpectedly lonely interactivity is Facebook, with 845 million users and $3.7 billion in revenue last year. The company hopes to raise $5 billion in an initial public offering later this spring, which will make it by far the largest Internet IPO in history. Some recent estimates put the company's potential value at $100 billion, which would make it larger than the global coffee industry one addiction preparing to surpass the other. Facebook's scale and reach are hard to comprehend: last summer, Facebook became, by some counts, the first website to receive 1 trillion page views in a month. In the last three months of 2011, users generated an average of 2.7 billion "likes" and comments every day. On whatever scale you care to judge Facebook—as a company, as a culture. as a country—it is vast beyond imagination.

Despite its immense popularity, or more likely because of it, Facebook has, from the beginning, been under something of a cloud of suspicion. The depiction of Mark Zuckerberg, in *The Social Network,* as a bastard with symptoms of Asperger's syndrome, was nonsense. But it felt true. It felt true to Facebook, if not to Zuckerberg. The film's most indelible scene, the one that may well have earned it an Oscar, was the final, silent shot of an anomic Zuckerberg sending out a friend request to his ex-girlfriend, then waiting and clicking and waiting and clicking—a moment of superconnected loneliness preserved in amber. We have all been in that scene: transfixed by the glare of a screen, hungering for response.

When you sign up for Google+ and set up your Friends circle, the program specifies that you should include only "your real friends, the ones you feel comfortable sharing private details with." That one little phrase, *Your real friends*—so quaint, so charmingly mothering—perfectly encapsulates the anxieties that social media have produced: the fears that Facebook is interfering with our real friendships, distancing us from each other, making us lonelier; and that social networking might be spreading the very isolation it seemed designed to conquer.

Facebook arrived in the middle of a dramatic increase in the quantity and intensity of human loneliness, a rise that initially made the site's promise of greater connection seem deeply attractive. Americans are more solitary than ever before. In 1950, less than 10 percent of American households contained only one person. By 2010, nearly 27 percent of households had just one person. Solitary living does not guarantee a life of unhappiness, of course. In his recent book about the trend toward living alone, Eric Klinenberg, a sociologist at NYU, writes: "Reams of published research show that it's the quality, not the quantity of social interaction, that best predicts loneliness." True. But before we begin the fantasies of happily eccentric singledom, of divorcees dropping by their knitting circles after work for glasses of Drew Barrymore pinot grigio, or recent college graduates with perfectly articulated, Steampunk-themed, 300-square-foot apartments organizing croquet matches with their book clubs, we should recognize that it is not just isolation that is rising sharply. It's loneliness, too. And loneliness makes us miserable.

We know intuitively that loneliness and being alone are not the same thing. Solitude can be lovely. Crowded parties can be agony. We also know, thanks to a growing body of research on the topic, that loneliness is not a matter of external conditions; it is a psychological state. A 2005 analysis of data from a longitudinal study of Dutch twins showed that the tendency toward loneliness has roughly the same genetic component as other psychological problems such as neuroticism or anxiety.

Still, loneliness is slippery, a difficult state to define or diagnose. The best tool yet developed for measuring the condition is the UCLA Loneliness Scale, a series of 20 questions that all begin with this formulation: "How often do you feel . . . ?" As in: "How often do you feel that you are 'in tune' with the people around you?" And: "How often do you feel that you lack companionship?" Measuring the condition in these terms, various studies have shown loneliness rising drastically over a very short period of recent history. A 2010 AARP survey found that 35 percent of adults older than 45 were chronically lonely, as opposed to 20 percent of a similar group only a decade earlier. According to a major study by a leading scholar of the subject, roughly 20 percent of Americans—about 60 million people—are unhappy with their lives because of loneliness. Across the Western world, physicians and nurses have begun to speak openly of an epidemic of loneliness.

The new studies on loneliness are beginning to yield some surprising preliminary findings about its mechanisms. Almost every factor that one might assume affects loneliness does so only some of the time, and only under certain circumstances. People who are married are less lonely than single people, one journal article suggests, but only if their spouses are confidants. If one's spouse is not a confidant, marriage may not decrease loneliness. A belief in God might help, or it might not, as a 1990 German study comparing levels of religious feeling and levels of loneliness discovered. Active believers who saw God as abstract and helpful rather than as a wrathful, immediate presence were less lonely. "The mere belief in God," the researchers concluded, "was relatively independent of loneliness."

But it is clear that social interaction matters. Loneliness and being alone are not the same thing, but both are on the rise. We meet fewer people. We gather less. And when we gather, our bonds are less meaningful and less easy. The decrease in confidants—that is, in quality social connections—has been dramatic over the past 25 years. In one survey, the mean size of networks of personal confidants decreased from 2.94 people in 1985 to 2.08 in 2004. Similarly, in 1985, only 10 percent of Americans said they had no one with whom to discuss important matters, and 15 percent said they had only one such good friend. By 2004, 25 percent had nobody to talk to, and 20 percent had only one confidant.

In the face of this social disintegration, we have essentially hired an army of replacement confidants, an entire class of professional carers. As Ronald Dworkin pointed out in a 2010 paper for the Hoover Institution, in the late '40s, the United States was home to 2,500 clinical psychologists, 30,000 social workers, and fewer than 500 marriage and family therapists. As of 2010, the country had 77,000 clinical psychologists, 192,000 clinical social workers, 400,000 nonclinical social workers, 50,000 marriage and family therapists, 105,000 mental-health counselors, 220,000 substance-abuse counselors, 17,000 nurse psychotherapists, and 30,000 life coaches. The majority of patients in therapy do not warrant a psychiatric diagnosis. This raft of psychic servants is helping us through what used to be called regular problems. We have outsourced the work of everyday caring.

We need professional carers more and more, because the threat of societal breakdown, once principally a matter of nostalgic lament, has morphed into an issue of public health. Being lonely is extremely bad for your health. If you're lonely, you're more likely to be put in a geriatric home at an earlier age than a similar person who isn't lonely. You're less likely to exercise. You're more likely to be obese. You're less likely to survive a serious operation and more likely to have hormonal imbalances. You are at greater risk of inflammation. Your memory may be worse. You are more likely to be depressed, to sleep badly, and to suffer dementia and general cognitive decline. Loneliness may not have killed Yvette Vickers, but it has been linked to a greater probability of having the kind of heart condition that did kill her.

And yet, despite its deleterious effect on health, loneliness is one of the first things ordinary Americans spend their money achieving. With money, you flee the cramped city to a house in the suburbs or, if you can afford it, a McMansion in the exurbs, inevitably spending more time in your car. Loneliness is at the American core, a by-product of a long-standing national appetite for independence: The Pilgrims who left Europe willingly abandoned the bonds and strictures of a society that could not accept their right to be different. They did not seek out loneliness, but they accepted it as the price of their autonomy. The cowboys who set off to explore a seemingly endless frontier likewise traded away personal ties in favor of pride and self-respect. The ultimate American icon is the astronaut: Who is more heroic, or more alone? The price of self-determination and self-reliance has often been loneliness. But Americans have always been willing to pay that price.

Today, the one common feature in American secular culture is its celebration of the self that breaks away from the constrictions of the family and the state, and, in its greatest expressions, from all limits entirely. The great American poem is Whitman's "Song of Myself." The great American essay is Emerson's "Self-Reliance." The great American novel is Melville's *Moby-Dick,* the tale of a man on a quest so lonely that it is incomprehensible to those around him. American culture, high and low, is about self-expression and personal authenticity. Franklin Delano Roosevelt called individualism "the great watchword of American life."

Self-invention is only half of the American story, however. The drive for isolation has always been in tension with the impulse to cluster in communities that cling and suffocate. The Pilgrims, while fomenting spiritual rebellion, also enforced ferocious cohesion. The Salem witch trials, in hindsight, read like attempts to impose solidarity—as do the McCarthy hearings. The history of the United States is like the famous parable of the porcupines in the cold, from Schopenhauer's *Studies in Pessimism*—the ones who huddle together for warmth and shuffle away in pain, always separating and congregating.

We are now in the middle of a long period of shuffling away. In his 2000 book *Bowling Alone,* Robert D. Putnam attributed the dramatic post-war decline of social capital—the strength and value of interpersonal networks—to numerous interconnected trends in American life: suburban sprawl, television's dominance over culture, the self-absorption of the Baby Boomers, the disintegration of the traditional family. The trends he observed continued through the prosperity of the aughts, and have only become more pronounced with time: The rate of union membership declined in 2011, again; screen time rose; the Masons and the Elks continued their slide into irrelevance. We are lonely because we want to be lonely. We have made ourselves lonely.

The question of the future is this: Is Facebook part of the separating or part of the congregating; is it a huddling-together for warmth or a shuffling-away in pain?

Well before Facebook, digital technology was enabling our tendency for isolation, to an unprecedented degree. Back in the 1990s, scholars started calling the contradiction between an increased opportunity to connect and a lack of human contact the "Internet paradox." A prominent 1998 article on the phenomenon by a team of researchers at Carnegie Mellon showed that increased Internet usage was already coinciding with increased loneliness. Critics of the study pointed out that the two groups that participated in the study—high-school journalism students who were heading to university and socially active members of community-development boards—were statistically likely to become lonelier over time. Which brings us to a more fundamental question: Does the Internet make people lonely, or are lonely people more attracted to the Internet?

The question has intensified in the Facebook era. A recent study out of Australia (where close to half the population is active on Facebook), titled "Who Uses Facebook?," found a complex and sometimes confounding relationship between loneliness and social networking. Facebook users had slightly lower levels of "social loneliness"—the sense of not feeling bonded with friends—but "significantly higher levels of family loneliness"—the sense of not feeling bonded with family. It may be that Facebook encourages more contract with people outside of our household, at the expense of our family relationships—or it may be that people who have unhappy family relationships in the first place seek companionship through other means, including Facebook. The researchers also found that lonely people are inclined to spend more time on Facebook: "One of the most noteworthy findings,' they wrote, "was the tendency for neurotic and lonely individuals to spend greater amounts of time on Facebook per day than non-lonely individuals." And they found that neurotics are more likely to prefer to use the wall, while extroverts tend to use chat features in addition to the wall.

Moira Burke, until recently a graduate student at the Human-Computer Institute at Carnegie Mellon, used to run a longitudinal study of 1,200 Facebook users. That study, which is ongoing, is one of the first to step outside the realm of self-selected college students and examine the effects of Facebook on a broader population, over time. She concludes that the effect of Facebook depends on what you bring to it. Just as your mother said: You get out only what you put in. If you use Facebook to communicate directly with other individuals—by using the "like" button, commenting on friends' posts, and so on—it can increase your social capital. Personalized messages, or what Burke calls "composed communication," are more satisfying than "one-click communication"—the lazy click of a like. "People who received composed communication became less lonely, while people who received one-click communication experienced no change in loneliness," Burke tells me. So, you should inform your friend in writing how charming her son looks with Harry Potter cake smeared all over his face, and how interesting her sepia-toned photograph of that tree-framed bit of skyline is, and how cool it is that she's at whatever concert she happens to be at. That's what we all want to hear. Even better than sending a private Facebook message is the semi-public conversation, the kind of back-and-forth in which you half ignore the other people who may be listening in. "People whose friends write to them semi-publicly on Facebook experience decreases in loneliness," Burke says.

On the other hand, non-personalized use of Facebook—scanning your friends' status updates and updating the world on your own activities via your wall, or what Burke calls "passive consumption" and "broadcasting"—correlates to feelings of disconnectedness. It's a lonely business, wandering the labyrinths of our friends' and pseudo-friends' projected identities, trying to figure out what part of ourselves we ought to project, who will listen, and what they will hear. According to Burke,

passive consumption of Facebook also correlates to a marginal increase in depression. "If two women each talk to their friends the same amount of time, but one of them spends more time reading about friends on Facebook as well, the one reading tends to grow slightly more depressed," Burke says. Her conclusion suggests that my sometimes unhappy reactions to Facebook may be more universal than I had realized. When I scroll through page after page of my friends' descriptions of how accidentally eloquent their kids are, and how their husbands are endearingly bumbling, and how they're all about to eat a home-cooked meal prepared with fresh local organic produce bought at the farmers' market and then go for a jog and maybe check in at the office because they're so busy getting ready to hop on a plane for a week of luxury dogsledding in Lapland, I do grow slightly more miserable. A lot of other people doing the same thing feel a little bit worse, too.

Still, Burke's research does not support the assertion that Facebook creates loneliness. The people who experience loneliness on Facebook are lonely away from Facebook, too, she points out; on Facebook, as everywhere else, correlation is not causation. The popular kids are popular, and the lonely skulkers skulk alone. Perhaps it says something about me that I think Facebook is primarily a platform for lonely skulking. I mention to Burke the widely reported study, conducted by a Stanford graduate student, that showed how believing that others have strong social networks can lead to feelings of depression. What does Facebook communicate, if not the impression of social bounty? Everybody else looks so happy on Facebook, with so many friends, that our own social networks feel emptier than ever in comparison. Doesn't that *make* people feel lonely? "If people are reading about lives that are much better than theirs, two things can happen," Burke tells me. "They can feel worse about themselves, or they can feel motivated."

Burke will start working at Facebook as a data scientist this year.

John cacioppo, the director of the Center for Cognitive and Social Neuroscience at the University of Chicago, is the world's leading expert on loneliness. In his landmark book, *Loneliness,* released in 2008, he revealed just how profoundly the epidemic of loneliness is affecting the basic functions of human physiology. He found higher levels of epinephrine, the stress hormone, in the morning urine of lonely people. Loneliness burrows deep: "When we drew blood from our older adults and analyzed their white cells," he writes, "we found that loneliness somehow penetrated the deepest recesses of the cell to alter the way genes were being expressed." Loneliness affects not only the brain, then, but the basic process of DNA transcription. When you are lonely, your whole body is lonely.

To Cacioppo, Internet communication allows only ersatz intimacy. "Forming connections with pets or online friends or even God is a noble attempt by an obligatorily gregarious creature to satisfy a compelling need," he writes. "But surrogates can never make up completely for the absence of the real thing." The "real thing" being actual people, in the flesh. When I speak to Cacioppo, he is refreshingly clear on what he sees as Facebook's effect on society. Yes, he allows, some research has suggested that the greater the number of Facebook friends a person has, the less lonely she is. But he argues that the impression this creates can be misleading. "For the most part," he says, "people are bringing their old friends, and feelings of loneliness or connectedness, to Facebook." The idea that a website could deliver a more friendly, interconnected world is bogus. The depth of one's social network outside Facebook is what determines the depth of one's social network within Facebook, not the other way around. Using social media doesn't create new social networks; it just transfers established networks from one platform to another. For the most part, Facebook doesn't destroy friendships—but it doesn't create them, either.

In one experiment, Cacioppo looked for a connection between the loneliness of subjects and the relative frequency of their interactions via Facebook, chat rooms, online games, dating sites, and face-to-face contact. The results were unequivocal. "The greater the proportion of face-to-face interactions, the less lonely you are," he says. "The greater the proportion of online interactions, the lonelier you are." Surely, I suggest to Cacioppo, this means that Facebook and the like inevitably make people lonelier. He disagrees. Facebook is merely a tool, he says, and like any tool, its effectiveness will depend on its user. "If you use Facebook to increase face-to face contact," he says, "it increases social capital." So if social media let you organize a game of football among your friends, that's healthy. If you turn to social media instead of playing football, however, that's unhealthy.

"Facebook can be terrific, if we use it properly," Cacioppo continues. "It's like a car. You can drive it to pick up your friends. Or you can drive alone." But hasn't the car increased loneliness? If cars created the suburbs, surely they also created isolation. "That's because of how we use cars," Cacioppo replies. "How we use these technologies can lead to more integration, rather than more isolation."

The problem, then, is that we invite loneliness, even though it makes us miserable. The history of our use of technology is a history of isolation desired and achieved. When the Great Atlantic and Pacific Tea Company opened its A&P stores, giving Americans self-service access to groceries, customers stopped having relationships with their grocers. When the telephone arrived, people stopped knocking on their neighbors' doors. Social media bring this process to a much wider set of relationships. Researchers at the HP Social Computing Lab who studied the nature of people's connections on Twitter came to a depressing, if not surprising, conclusion: "Most of the links declared with in Twitter were meaningless from an interaction point of view." I have to wonder: What other point of view is meaningful?

Loneliness is certainly not something that Facebook or Twitter or any of the lesser forms of social media is doing to us. We are doing it to ourselves. Casting technology as some vague, impersonal spirit of history forcing our actions is a weak excuse. We make decisions about how we use our machines, not the other way around. Every time I shop at my local grocery store, I am faced with a choice. I can buy my groceries from a human being or from a machine. I always, without exception, choose the machine. It's faster and more efficient, I tell myself, but the truth is that I prefer not having to wait with the other customers who are lined up alongside the conveyor belt: the hipster mom who disapproves of my high-carbon-footprint pineapple; the lady who tenses to the point of tears while she waits to see if the gods of the credit-card machine will accept or decline; the old man whose clumsy feebleness requires a patience that I don't possess. Much better to bypass the whole circus and just ring up the groceries myself.

Our omnipresent new technologies lure us toward increasingly superficial connections at exactly the same moment that they make avoiding the mess of human interaction easy. The beauty of Facebook, the source of its power, is that it enables us to be social while sparing us the embarrasing reality of society—the accidental revelations we make at parties, the awkward pauses, the farting and the spilled drinks and the general gaucherie of face-to-face contact. Instead, we have the lovely smoothness of a seemingly social machine. Everything's so simple: status updates, pictures, your wall.

But the price of this smooth sociability is a constant compulsion to assert one's own happiness, one's own fulfillment. Not only must we contend with the social bounty of others; we must foster the appearance of our own social bounty. Being happy all the time, pretending to be happy, actually attempting to be happy—it's exhausting. Last year a team of researchers led by Iris Mauss at the University of Denver published a study looking into "the paradoxical effects of valuing happiness." Most goals in life show a direct correlation between valuation and achievement. Studies have found, for example, that students who value good grades tend to have higher grades than those who don't value them. Happiness is an exception. The study came to a disturbing conclusion:

Valuing happiness is not necessarily linked to greater happiness. In fact, under certain conditions, the opposite is true. Under conditions of low (but not high) life stress, the more people valued happiness, the lower were their hedonic balance, psychological well-being, and life satisfaction, and the higher their depression symptoms.

The more you try to be happy, the less happy you are. Sophocles made roughly the same point.

Facebook, of course, puts the pursuit of happiness front and center in our digital life. Its capacity to redefine our very concepts of identity and personal fulfillment is much more worrisome than the data-mining and privacy practices that have aroused anxieties about the company. Two of the most compelling critics of Facebook—neither of them a Luddite—concentrate on exactly this point. Jaron Lanier, the author of *You Are Not a Gadget,* was one of the inventors of virtual-reality technology. His view of where social media are taking us reads like dystopian science fiction: "I fear that we are beginning to design ourselves to suit digital models of us, and I worry about a leaching of empathy and humanity in that process." Lanier argues that Facebook imprisons us in the business of self-presenting, and this, to his mind, is the site's crucial and fatally unacceptable downside.

Sherry Turkle, a professor of computer culture at MIT who in 1995 published the digital-positive analysis *Life on the Screen,* is much more skeptical about the effects of online society in her 2011 book, *Alone Together:* "These days, insecure in our relationships and anxious about intimacy, we look to technology for ways to be in relationships and protect ourselves from them at the same time." The problem with digital intimacy is that it is ultimately incomplete: "The ties we form through the Internet are not, in the end, the ties that bind. But they are the ties that preoccupy," she writes. "We don't want to intrude on each other, so instead we constantly intrude on each other, but not in 'real time.'"

Lanier and Turkle are right, at least in their diagnoses. Self-presentation on Facebook is continuous, intensely mediated, and possessed of a phony nonchalance that eliminates even the potential for spontaneity. ("Look how casually I threw up these three photos from the party at which I took 300 photos!") Curating the exhibition of the self has become a 24/7 occupation. Perhaps not surprisingly, then, the Australian study "Who Uses Facebook?" found a significant correlation between Facebook use and narcissism: "Facebook users have higher levels of total narcissism, exhibitionism, and leadership than Facebook non-users," the study's authors wrote. "In fact, it could be argued that Facebook specifically gratifies the narcissistic individual's need to engage in selfpromoting and superficial behavior."

Rising narcissism isn't so much a trend as the trend behind all other trends. In preparation for the 2013 edition of its diagnostic manual, the psychiatric profession is currently struggling to update its definition of narcissistic personality disorder. Still, generally peaking, practitioners agree that narcissism manifests in patterns of fantastic grandiosity, craving for attention, and lack of empathy. In a 2008 survey, 35,000 American respondents were asked if they had ever had certain symptoms of narcissistic personality disorder. Among people older than 65, 3 percent reported symptoms. Among people in their 20s, the proportion was nearly 10 percent. Across all age groups, one in 16 Americans has experienced some symptoms of NPD. And loneliness and narcissism are intimately connected: a longitudinal study of Swedish women demonstrated a strong link between levels of narcissism in youth and levels of loneliness in old age. The connection is fundamental. Narcissism is the flip side of loneliness, and either condition is a fighting retreat from the messy reality of other people.

A considerable part of Facebook's appeal terns from its miraculous fusion of distance with intimacy, or the illusion of distance with the illusion of intimacy. Our online communities become engines of self-image, and self-image becomes the engine of community. The real danger with Facebook is not that it allows us to isolate ourselves, but that by mixing our appetite for isolation with our vanity, it threatens to alter the very nature of solitude. The new isolation is not of the kind that Americans once idealized, the lonesomeness of the proudly nonconformist, independent-minded, solitary stoic, or that of the astronaut who blasts into new worlds. Facebook's isolation is a grind. What's truly staggering about Facebook usage is not its volume—750 million photographs uploaded over a single weekend—but the constancy of the performance it demands. More than half its users—and one of every 13 people on Earth is a Facebook user—log on every day. Among 18-to-34-year-olds, nearly half check Facebook minutes after waking up, and 28 percent do so before getting out of bed. The relentlessness is what is so new, so potentially transformative. Facebook never takes a break. We never take a break. Human beings have always created elaborate acts of self-presentation. But not all the time, not every morning, before we even pour a cup of coffee. Yvette Vickers's computer was on when she died.

Nostalgia for the good old days of disconnection would not just be pointless, it would be hypocritical and ungrateful. But the very magic of the new machines, the efficiency and elegance with which they serve us, obscures what isn't being served: everything that matters. What Facebook has revealed about human nature—and this is not a minor revelation—is that a connection is not the same thing as a bond, and that instant and total connection is no salvation, no ticket to a happier, better world or a more liberated version of humanity. Solitude used to be good for self-reflection and self-reinvention. But now we are left thinking about who we are all the time, without ever really thinking about who we are. Facebook denies us a pleasure whose profundity we had underestimated: the chance to forget about ourselves for a while, the chance to disconnect.

Critical Thinking

1. Why do some people find it easier to use social media than to physically interact in a social situation?
2. What are the advantages of social media such as Twitter and Facebook in relation to mental health?

Internet References

7 Ways Facebook Is Bad for Your Mental Health
    https://www.psychologytoday.com/blog/sex-murder-and-the-meaning-life/201404/7-ways-facebook-is-bad-your-mental-health

Does Facebook Make You Lonely?
    http://www.dailymail.co.uk/sciencetech/article-2791327/does-facebook-make-lonely-social-network-attracts-isolated-people-looking-friendship-study-claims.html

Why Social Makes Us Even More Lonely
    http://socialmediaweek.org/blog/2015/06/social-media-even-lonely

---

STEPHEN MARCHE, a novelist, writes a monthly column for Esquire. Naturally, you can friend him on Facebook or follow him on Twitter.

Article   Prepared by: Claire N. Rubman, *Suffolk County Community College*

Brutal Truths about the Aging Brain

A graying world will have more of the experience that comes with age. It will also be slower, fuzzier, more forgetful, and just a bit hard of hearing.

ROBERT EPSTEIN

Learning Outcomes

After reading this article, you will be able to:

- Describe the four cognitive systems that tend to decline with age.

- Explain why it is easier for elders to remember things from their 20s than from a month ago.

As a graduate student at Harvard University, I worked with one of the most influential behavioral scientists of all time, B. F. Skinner. Beginning in the summer of 1977, we worked together nearly every day for more than four years, designing experiments and chatting about literature, philosophy, and the latest research. Although we were 50 years apart in age, we were also friends. We saw *Star Wars* together, had lunch frequently in Harvard Square, and swam in his backyard pool each summer. "Fred" (from Burrhus Frederic) Skinner was the happiest, most creative, most productive person I have ever known. He was also, needless to say, quite smart.

But the septuagenarian I knew was well past his intellectual peak. One day he gave me a set of tapes of a famous debate he had had with psychologist Carl Rogers in 1962. The Skinner on those tapes seemed sharper, faster, and even wittier than the man I knew. Was I imagining this?

Recently, Gina Kirkish, a student at the University of California, San Diego, and I analyzed tapes of three comparable samples of Skinner's speech: that 1962 debate, a 1977 debate, and a speech he gave from notes shortly before he died in 1990 at age 86. We found that the speech rate dropped significantly over time, from 148 words per minute in the first sample to 137 in the second to 106 in the third—an overall decrease of more than 28 percent.

Skinner's memory and analytical skills were also declining during the years when I knew him. Sometimes he had no recollection of a conversation we had had only days before. When I tried to talk with him about technical papers he had published early in his career, he often didn't seem to understand what he had written. And he had no patience for anything mathematical, even his own equations. On the other hand, Skinner was still much smarter than most of the people I knew my own age. When you fall from a high enough cliff, you remain far above ground for a very long time.

The sad truth is that even normal aging has a devastating effect on our ability to learn and remember, on the speed with which we process information, and on our ability to reason. Recent studies suggest that the total loss in brain volume due to atrophy—a wasting away of tissue caused by cell degeneration—between our teen years and old age is 15 percent or more, which means that by the time we're in our seventies, our brains have shrunk to the size they were when we were between 2 and 3 years old. Unfortunately, most of the loss is in gray matter, the critically important part of the brain composed of neurons, the cells that transmit the signals that keep us breathing and thinking.

Contrary to what scientists long believed, only about 10 percent of our neurons die during adulthood. The real loss is in the network of connections—the "dendritic trees" that allow a single neuron to be connected to a thousand others. Over the years, 25 percent or more of this network disappears. According to William Jagust, a neuroscientist at the University of California, Berkeley, adults are also losing dopamine, a critical neurotransmitter (the type of chemical involved in transmitting signals between neurons), at the rate of 5 to 8 percent per decade. "By age 80," Jagust says, "you've lost 40 percent or so of dopamine function. When you think about it, it's remarkable that old people can do so well."

Shrinkage, dopamine depletion, and lost dendritic connections are not the only problems facing the aging brain. Myelin, a substance that insulates neurons, deteriorates, and the number of nerve fibers that carry messages throughout the central nervous system also decreases. Chemical problems—such as an increase in calcium conductance, which might impair neuronal communication—also become more common in older brains, as do problems with gene expression and protein production.

With the global population of people over 80 expected to more than quadruple to nearly 400 million by 2050, the aging brain will become an increasingly big headache for humankind. Here are four cognitive systems that tend to decline as we age. Get used to these changes. You'll be seeing a lot more of them in the future.

1. Senses

Our ability to learn and remember is limited by the accuracy of our senses, our points of contact with the world. But vision, hearing, touch, smell, and taste are not just detection systems. The sense organs also comprise a primitive kind of memory, a temporary storage system or "buffer" for the brain. Much of the input to our sense organs reverberates in receptors, and that reverberation allows even weak stimuli—for example, images flashed so quickly that we have no conscious awareness of them—to impact decisions we make later on. Without the buffering ability of our sense organs, a great deal of information about the world would be lost to us. Unfortunately, as we age, our sensory systems deteriorate, and at the extreme, we become completely insensitive to a wide range of input. For example, high-pitched tones that we can detect at a mere 30 decibels when we are young have to be boosted to an earsplitting 90 decibels for the elderly to hear. (Physics buffs: That's about a million times the energy intensity.) And pupil size decreases as we age, so when it is dim, the elderly person's eyes pick up about a third as much light as people in their prime. Because the deterioration of sense organs limits our access to critical information—speech, text, music, street signs—thinking itself is impaired.

And loss of information is just part of the problem. Research by psychologist Monica Fabiani and her colleagues at the University of Illinois at Urbana-Champaign suggests that in older people the main problem might not be that the sense organ is rejecting input but rather that the brain itself is having trouble filtering out irrelevant information. In a recent study, Fabiani had people of various ages read a book while trying to ignore auditory tones piped through headphones. Overall, the older the individual, the more trouble he or she had ignoring the tones. "The background stimuli may flood your thinking with things that are irrelevant and that you cannot inhibit," Fabiani says. As a result, "you basically lose the capacity to perform tasks."

How Some Brains Stay Razor Sharp

Facing the specter of Alzheimer's disease, the most devastating and widespread manifestation of brain deterioration in old age, worried baby boomers have inspired whole catalogs of brain-fitness books and services. That's good news for publishers, vitamin companies, and computer game designers, but probably bad news for boomers themselves. Elizabeth Zelinski, a gerontologist at the University of Southern California, told me she was appalled at the explosion of miracle cures on the market, adding bluntly, "There's no evidence that anything works." (There is some evidence that some interventions work very narrowly or for short periods of time, but generally speaking, the new industry makes outrageous claims.) And don't hold your breath waiting for neuroscience to rescue you from your upcoming decline. When I asked neuroscientist Eric Kandel, a Nobel Prize winner in medicine, how long it will be before we achieve some reasonable understanding of how memory actually works, he replied, "a hundred years."

On the bright side, some people appear to overcome the ravages of a rotting brain by recruiting new brain systems or structures to take over functions of old ones. Neuropsychologist Yaakov Stern of the Columbia University College of Physicians and Surgeons points out that upwards of 25 percent of people who function perfectly normally while alive have brains that show serious signs of Alzheimer's in autopsy. People with more education have lower rates of dementia, suggesting that brains that get more of a workout create reserves that kick in when frontline systems start to fail.

Kandel, now 82, appears to be one of those rare souls who has somehow managed to keep Father Time at bay. He remains active in research at Columbia University, and his extraordinary productivity and creativity are exemplified by his weighty 2012 book, *The Age of Insight: The Quest to Understand the Unconscious in Art, Mind, and Brain from Vienna 1900 to the Present.* Kandel's daughter, attorney Minouche Kandel, speculates that her father's clarity and energy result from an almost fanatical regimen of healthy food—mainly fish—and regular exercise. "He's lived this healthy lifestyle for as long as I can remember," she says, "and he was doing it long before it was popular."

Through some combination of luck, good genes, and a healthy lifestyle, it is possible, it seems, for a fortunate few to stay razor sharp well into old age.

R. E.

2. Memory

Most people think of human memory as a single system. But because different kinds of information are retained differently, experts speculate that distinct types of memory systems exist in the brain. Some information stays with us for only a short time—generally no more than a few seconds unless we do something with it. For example, if somebody tells you a phone number and you do not immediately repeat it, it will very likely disappear, never to return. Research suggests the existence of a short-term memory system, consisting in turn of two subsystems: immediate memory (the temporary storage system that holds on to information we don't process in some way) and working memory (a system that allows us to retain information as long as we keep using it).

As we age, our ability to process new information in working memory is severely compromised. In a typical test procedure for evaluating working memory, cognitive aging researcher Timothy Salthouse of the University of Virginia asked people to perform arithmetic computations while also trying to remember the last digit in each problem. People in their twenties were typically able to solve four or five of these problems in a row and still recall the final digits without error. With each decade, performance deteriorated; people in their seventies could typically solve no more than two such problems in a row and still get the final digits right.

One of the simplest ways to assess memory is to read test subjects a list of words and ask them, after a short time has passed, to repeat as many as they can. In a 1990 study, Hasker Davis and his colleagues at the University of Colorado found that people in their twenties could typically recall 90 percent of a list of 15 words after a short delay. With each additional decade of age, the percentage of words recalled decreased. People in their eighties could recall only about half the words.

3. Knowledge

Some information in our short-term memory system is consolidated into a long-term storage system, where it remains available to retrieve for months or years. If a memory of anything from a good meal to a coworker's name persists for 5 years, there is a good chance it will persist for another 40. But as we age, the degradation of sensory and working memory systems makes it increasingly difficult for us to transfer information into long-term storage. That's why, if you are over 50, you are more likely to remember the lyrics to a Beatles song than to any song you have heard in the past 20 years. To put this another way, our ability to learn new things is extraordinary when we are young and peaks in our teens. We can learn after that, but it becomes increasingly difficult. In

an early study by psychologist Jeanne Gilbert, English speakers of different ages were asked to learn Turkish vocabulary words. People in their sixties learned 60 percent fewer words than young adults in their twenties who spent equal time and effort on the task.

One of the most frustrating experiences we have as we age is accessing a particular word from long-term memory—the so-called "word-finding" or "tip-of-the-tongue" problem. Deborah Burke, a psychology professor at Pomona College who has studied this phenomenon for more than 20 years, explains that old people suffer from a disconnect between the meaning of a word—which presumably tells you that it is the correct word to say right now—and the sound of that word. It is, she says, "the most irritating and disturbing cognitive problem" reported by older adults. We do not know what causes the disconnect.

4. Intelligence

We also get dumber as we age. IQ remains fairly stable, but that is because it is a relative measure—a quotient (the Q) that shows where we stand relative to people our own age. The problem is that raw scores on intelligence tests actually peak in our teens, remain high for a few years, and then decline throughout life; IQ remains fairly stable only because people decline at roughly the same rate. And yes, even geniuses decline. I recently asked Nobel Laureate James Watson, 84, when he reached his intellectual peak, and he replied, "Twenty, maybe 21—certainly before we found the DNA structure." That seminal work had been done when he was 25.

Intelligence, like memory, is divided into types that decline somewhat differently. Factual information is the basis of what is called crystallized intelligence, and much of the crystallized knowledge we acquire stays fairly strong at least into our sixties. However, fluid intelligence—our ability to reason—declines dramatically in most people, in large part because we get *slow*. Generally speaking, on tasks involving reasoning, what a 20-year-old can do in about half a second takes a healthy 80-year-old more than two seconds—if, that is, he or she can do it at all. As Douglas Powell of the Harvard Medical School puts it in his recent book, *The Aging Intellect,* "No other single mental ability declines as rapidly during the adult years as processing speed."

Neuroscientists tackle the decline in reasoning and working memory under an umbrella concept called executive function. Somewhere in the brain there seems to be a coach: a system or structure that schedules and prioritizes, garnering resources, redirecting attention, or switching tasks as needed. Adam Gazzaley, a neurology professor at the University of California, San Francisco, has conducted research documenting how that coaching ability declines as we age. For example, older people are bad at multitasking, Gazzaley says, because they have trouble redirecting attention back to a task after it has been interrupted. On average, people in their seventies generally require twice as much time to do two things at once as do young adults, and they also make more errors on the tasks. That inability to focus takes its toll. "I would not be capable of doing groundbreaking work today," renowned physicist Freeman Dyson, 88, told me recently. When he was young, Dyson said, he could focus on a single problem nonstop for a week. "Today," he said, "I'm limited to two hours a day of serious work—which wouldn't be enough."

The deterioration of these four systems appears to be an inevitable part of normal, healthy aging, although the rate of decline varies among individuals. When you add disease to the picture, things truly look bleak. Half of Americans over 85 are suffering from Alzheimer's disease, which eventually robs people of their memories, identities, and the ability to function even minimally. Alzheimer's becomes increasingly common with age—so common that neurologist Gary Small of UCLA suggests that if we all lived to 110, we all would have it. These are the brutal truths we must face as we and our loved ones age.

Critical Thinking

1. What two processes are involved in the decline of the accuracy of the senses with age?
2. Why is crystallized intelligence much stronger than fluid intelligence in elders?

Create Central

www.mhhe.com/createcentral

Internet References

Changes in Cognitive Functioning in Human Aging
www.ncbi.nlm.nih.gov/books/NBK3885

Lifestyle Factors Affecting Late Adulthood
www.school-for-champions.com/health/lifestyle_elderly.htm

The Long Beach Longitudinal Study: USC Davis
http://gero.usc.edu/lbls/publications.shtml

What Happens to the Aging Brain?
www.psychologytoday.com/blog/memory-medic/201211

Article

Prepared by: Claire N. Rubman,
Suffolk County Community College, Selden, NY

Combat Age-Related Brain Atrophy

BARRY VOLK

Learning Outcomes

After reading this article, you will be able to:

- Describe how to avoid brain shrinkage.
- Discuss the role that the amino acid homocusteine plays in brain shrinkage.
- Explain the "therapeutic window of opportunity."

Even if you seem perfectly healthy, you may be losing as much as 0.4% of your *brain mass* every year.[1,2] The rate of brain shrinkage increases with age and is a major factor in early cognitive decline and premature death.[2–7]

Studies show that older adults with significant brain shrinkage are much more likely to have cognitive and movement disorders than similarly aged people with normal brain size. They are also at an increased risk of vascular death and ischemic stroke.[4, 8–10]

In addition, atrophy of specific brain regions has been associated with a variety of cognitive, behavioral, and mental health problems. Shrinkage of the temporal lobes, for example, is associated with a 181% increase in the risk of major depression.[7]

Perhaps most alarmingly, brain shrinkage sharply increases risk of early death:

- Younger individuals with overall brain shrinkage have as much as a 70% increase in the chance of dying,[5]
- In a study of people aged 85, temporal lobe atrophy is associated with a 60% increase in the risk of dying,[2]
- Severe atrophy of the frontal lobe (behind the forehead) increases the risk of death by 30%.[2]

Brains also shrink from the inside out, resulting in enlargement of the fluid-filled *ventricles,* or hollow spaces on the interior of the brain; such shrinkage has its own modest effect on early death.[2]

Even though brain shrinkage is progressive, a growing number of neuroscientists believe that brain shrinkage can be *slowed* or even *reversed.*[11–13] In this article, we will share with you how lifestyle changes and proper supplementation can help prevent this devastating cause of cognitive decline and premature death.

Brain Shrinkage Is Not Inevitable

Like so many of the symptoms of aging, brain shrinkage was long thought to be simply an inevitable consequence of growing older. However, we are learning that brain atrophy is by no means inevitable. A host of conditions—from cardiovascular disease and diabetes to sleep and anxiety disorders to lifestyle choices—have been associated with brain shrinkage. Since many of these are reversible or at least preventable, it's important to understand their impact on brain shrinkage, cognition, and life span.

The Connection Between Cardiovascular Disease and Brain Shrinkage

Although we don't often hear about this, there is a strong connection between cardiovascular disease and brain shrinkage.

Perhaps the most obvious connection is the one between blood vessel disease (atherosclerosis) and brain volume. Atherosclerosis occurs when plaque builds up inside your arteries and restricts blood flow throughout the body. Although we typically think of the negative effect atherosclerosis has on the heart, its effect on your brain can be equally devastating.

When blood flow to the brain is restricted, your brain receives less oxygen and fewer nutrients, causing it to shrink. Studies show that people with lower levels of blood flow to the brain have smaller total brain volumes and total thickness of the cortex (the active surface layer of the brain)—resulting in poorer performance on tests of cognitive function.[14]

In addition, disease of the coronary arteries (the arteries that feed the heart muscle) is also associated with decreased brain volume. When compared to healthy controls, patients with coronary artery disease had significantly smaller gray matter volume in several regions of their brains.[15] This is especially significant since gray matter is where all thinking, feeling, sensory, and motor function originates.

The relationship between cardiovascular disease and brain volume operates in both directions: People with smaller brain volumes have been found to have a 58% increase in the risk of death from all causes, a 69% increase in risk of vascular death, and a 96% increase in the risk of stroke, compared with those having normal brain volumes.[10]

Several other risk factors commonly associated with cardiovascular disease may also predict brain shrinkage. For example, people carrying the **ApoE4 gene variant** have significantly smaller overall brain size—with a specific decrease in brain areas that process memory and emotion.[16]

High levels of the amino acid **homocysteine**, another risk factor typically associated with heart disease, have now also been connected to brain shrinkage (independent of its impact on cardiovascular disease).

Specifically, studies have shown that people with high levels of homocysteine have smaller volumes of gray matter in the brain—and as a result, have worse scores on many tests of cognitive function.[17]

This was especially evident in a study of a group of people who had recently suffered strokes. The researchers found that those with the highest homocysteine levels had a tremendous **8.8-fold** increase in risk of brain shrinkage (compared with those having the lowest).[18] Other studies have demonstrated that the higher the level of plasma homocysteine, the greater the rate of brain atrophy and the risk for Parkinson's and Alzheimer's diseases.[19–22]

A deficiency of B vitamins has also been tied to brain shrinkage. This makes sense, since inadequate amounts of vitamins B6, B12, and folic acid can lead to elevated homocysteine levels. This occurs because these vitamins play a role in converting homocysteine into an important protein building block and when there's a shortage of B vitamins, that conversion process isn't as efficient, and homocysteine levels increase.[13,23]

Close associations have been found between low levels of folate, for example, and severe gray matter atrophy and atrophy of the hippocampus, a main memory-processing center in the brain.[24,25] Similarly, people with lower vitamin B12 levels have been shown to have progressive brain atrophy, with rates of brain volume loss 517% greater than those with higher levels.[13,26]

Remarkably, it has been found that brain shrinkage due to high homocysteine levels must reach a critical level before cognitive decline sets in.[21] This is another example of the "therapeutic window of opportunity" during which brain shrinkage may be prevented by adequate supplementation, as we'll see later.[27]

Protect Against Brain Shrinkage

- Your brain is shrinking as you age, costing you memories and mental sharpness.
- Worse, brain shrinkage has been directly associated with premature death.
- Causes of brain shrinkage are closely related to symptoms of aging, including cardiovascular disease, obesity, diabetes, and even poor sleep habits and distress.
- You may be able to prevent brain shrinkage by adopting healthy lifestyle habits and using supplements that target your own aging body's vulnerabilities.
- Supplements that reduce your cardiovascular risk, lower your blood sugar, or improve your sleep, for example, may do double duty in slowing or stopping brain shrinkage and improving your chances for a long, mentally fit life.

The Connection Between Diabetes and Brain Shrinkage

Diabetes is notorious for causing problems with the **peripheral nervous system**,[28] leading to conditions such as painful diabetic neuropathy and blindness-inducing diabetic retinopathy. New findings suggest that high blood sugar levels—and the *advanced glycation end products* (AGEs) that they produce—cause damage to the **central nervous system** as well, specifically neurodegeneration and brain atrophy.[29–31]

Studies have shown that, when compared to non-diabetic people of similar age, diabetics have an average of **4%** smaller hippocampal volume, a nearly 3% reduction in whole brain volume, and double the risk of mild cognitive impairment.[32,33]

In addition to causing brain shrinkage, studies now suggest that diabetes induces toxic, misfolded proteins quite similar to those found in neurodegenerative diseases such as Alzheimer's, pointing to yet another way that diabetes can damage brain cells.[34] Indeed, diabetes and Alzheimer's disease share many properties, including defective insulin release and signaling, impaired glucose uptake from the blood, increased oxidative stress, stimulation of brain cell death by apoptosis,[35,36] blood vessel abnormalities, and problems with energy production in mitochondria.[37,38]

Obesity and Your Brain

Like diabetes, obesity is a known cause of brain atrophy.[39] Even in people with normal cognition, higher body mass index (BMI, a measure of obesity) is associated with lower brain volume in obese and overweight people.[40]

Obesity and diabetes share many similar mechanisms, including insulin resistance and oxidative stress, both of which are known to contribute to brain atrophy.[38,41] In addition, fat deposits produce huge amounts of inflammatory signaling molecules (cytokines) that may contribute to brain cell death and brain volume loss.[39]

Additional links between obesity and brain shrinkage may be even more fundamental. About **46%** of Western Europeans and their descendants carry a gene variant called **FTO**, which is associated with fat mass and obesity. People who carry this gene weigh on average about **2.64 pounds** more and have an extra half-inch of waist circumference compared to those who lack the gene variant.[42] Recent findings show that carriers of the FTO gene variant have approximately 8% smaller frontal lobe volumes, and **12%** smaller occipital (back of the brain) volumes than people who don't carry this gene variant. These changes were **not** associated with differences in cholesterol levels or blood pressure, suggesting an independent relationship.[42]

Sleep Disruptions

Sleep disruptions and anxiety also contribute to loss of brain volume. Relatively healthy older adults with short sleep duration have significantly smaller brains than those with longer sleep duration. In addition, for every hour of reduced sleep duration, they experience a **0.59%** yearly increase in the size of the blood-filled ventricles, and a **0.67%** decrease in cognitive performance.[43] Similarly, increases in brain shrinkage are associated with decreased quality of sleep as well.[44]

Poor sleep and anxiety, of course, are related, and one study has shown that middle-aged women who have had longstanding psychological distress (based on a standard questionnaire) are at a **51%** increased risk of moderate-to-severe atrophy of the temporal lobes.[6]

Smoking and Drinking

Smoking has been recognized as a cause of brain shrinkage since at least 1987.[45,46] More recent studies have confirmed and extended this association, with evidence that any lifetime history of smoking (even if you currently do not smoke) is associated with faster brain shrinkage in multiple brain regions, compared with people who never smoked.[47]

Chronic alcohol consumption has also been associated with brain shrinkage, but in a dose-dependent way. While light-to-moderate drinkers have *larger* total brain volume than nondrinkers,[48] heavy drinkers are **80%** more likely than nondrinkers to sustain frontal lobe shrinkage, compared with nondrinkers,[49] and **32%** more likely to have enlargement of the ventricles, indicating shrinkage from within.[50] (A heavy drinker is defined as someone who consumes more than about **15 ounces** of pure alcohol per week. A standard drink is equal to **14.0 grams,** or **0.6 ounces,** of pure alcohol.)

Natural Supplements That Protect Brain Volume

Even though the array of factors that can cause brain shrinkage can be daunting, there is good news. Since brain shrinkage results from the same basic processes that cause other symptoms of aging, it's likely that brain shrinkage is preventable— *especially when caught early enough.*

That's why we want to provide you with information on key nutrients that have been shown to powerfully protect the brain. Here are four of the most potent brain-protecting nutrients.

B Vitamins

B vitamins are essential for supporting normal metabolic function, especially in the regulation of homocysteine[51] (and elevated homocysteine, as we have seen, leads to significant brain shrinkage and dementia, especially when B-vitamins are deficient).[18,27,52,53]

Elderly people are now generally advised to maintain optimal B-vitamin status—and for good reason.[13,54] Studies show that people with higher folate levels have slower rates of brain atrophy and a lower rate of conversion from mild cognitive impairment to actual dementia, and those who take folate or B12 have lower grades of brain white matter abnormalities.[53,55]

While each of these B vitamins provides its own unique benefits, several recent studies show why it's beneficial to supplement with a combination of folate, vitamin B6, and vitamin B12. This was clearly seen in a double-blind, placebo-controlled clinical trial in adults over age 70 who had mild cognitive impairment.[56]

For the study, one group of subjects took folate (**800 mcg/day**), vitamin B12 (**500 mcg/day**), and vitamin B6 (**20 mg/day**), while the other group took placebo.[56] After two years, supplemented patients' brains shrank at an annual rate that was **30%** slower than those taking the placebo. Supplemented patients whose homocysteine levels were abnormally high at baseline had a **53%** slower brain shrinkage rate than unsupplemented patients, showing that supplementing with B vitamins is especially important in people who have high homocysteine levels.

A follow-up study showed that brain areas most susceptible to atrophy in the early development of Alzheimer's disease are especially well-protected by the same B-vitamin regimen, with supplemented patients experiencing as much as a **7-fold** reduction in shrinkage of those regions.[57] Another study, using the same doses of B vitamins, found that supplemented patients had 30% lower mean plasma homocysteine levels, and slower rates of cognitive decline on multiple standard tests.[58]

Omega-3 Fatty Acids

Omega-3 fatty acids comprise a large and important portion of brain cell membranes, where they participate in a wide variety of cellular functions. Indeed, **30** to **50%** of the fatty acids in brain cell membranes are long-chain polyunsaturated fatty acids that include the vital *omega-3* group. Brain cell membranes are especially rich in **DHA,** an essential fatty acid derived only from the diet.[59,60]

Omega-3s have many functions that help protect brain cells. Omega-3 fats are known to enhance the brain's relaxing functions.[61] This protects brain cells from overexcitation, which is a major cause of brain cell damage that occurs with aging.[62] Omega-3s also help preserve brain cell function by increasing the production of anti-inflammatory signaling molecules in the brain.[59,63] Similarly, omega-3 fats in brain tissue protect cells from damage induced by stress and elevated stress steroids.[63]

The importance of this protection is especially seen when there's not enough of this vital nutrient. Indeed, abnormal distributions of fatty acids in brain cells are associated with a variety of mental health disorders, particularly major depression and bipolar disorder.[64]

It is not surprising, then, that age-related changes in brain cell omega-3 fat composition raise the risk of brain abnormalities as people age.[65] By contrast, studies show that a higher omega-3 index (which is the sum of the omega-3 fats EPA plus DHA), is correlated with larger brain volume.[66]

Unfortunately, aging is associated with a significant decline in DHA levels in the brain, a drop that is sharply worsened in Alzheimer's disease and possibly other neurodegenerative disorders.[67, 68] This highlights the importance of protecting your brain by supplementing with omega-3 fats.

Pomegranate

Pomegranates contain very high levels of polyphenols, which are plant-derived molecules with anti-inflammatory and neuroprotective properties.[69] Animal studies reveal that supplementing with pomegranate juice slows the development of Alzheimer-like disease, a major cause of brain atrophy.[69–71] This protection may arise from the ability of the polyphenols in pomegranate to slow or stop brain cell death.[72]

Human studies demonstrate significant improvements in cognition and memory with consumption of 8 ounces of pomegranate juice daily, and lab studies with human brain cells in culture show that pomegranate polyphenols protect cells against changes that occur in other neurodegenerative diseases.[73,74]

Resveratrol

Resveratrol is a major component of red grapes and certain other dark fruits; it has seen widespread use in preventing aging and age-related cardiovascular and neurologic conditions. Studies in a mouse model of chronic fatigue syndrome (which can produce brain shrinkage) show that four weeks of resveratrol therapy increased the animals' daily physical activity by more than **20%,** possibly as a result of reduced brain cell death.[75] In addition, the volume of the memory-intensive hippocampus was larger following supplementation.

Researchers are also exploring resveratrol as a potent neuroprotectant against the brain-shrinking effects of obesity and a high-fat diet. In studies of obese animals (obesity is a cause of brain shrinkage), resveratrol protected brain tissue from oxidative damage, a precursor to brain cell death.[76] And in mice fed a high-fat diet, resveratrol similarly protected against oxidative damage to the vital blood-brain barrier and decreased injury to the endothelial cells in the brain.[77]

These findings in animals may explain the results of a compelling human study in **2014,** which demonstrated that, in healthy overweight older adults, supplementing with **200 mg/day** of resveratrol improved the functional connections between the hippocampus and the frontal areas of the brain.[78] Such changes were accompanied by improved memory performance as well as better blood sugar control, again pointing to the complex interactions of metabolism and brain performance.

Summary

Brain shrinkage is a silent threat to our health and longevity. Loss of brain volume means loss of brain cells, which in turn means loss of memory and learning.

There are a myriad of threats to brain volume as we age. Virtually all of the chronic symptoms of aging have been associated with, and to some extent implicated in, brain shrinkage. In addition, lifestyle habits such as a high-fat diet, sedentary behavior, and smoking or excess drinking can further complicate matters.

Fortunately, like other symptoms of aging, brain shrinkage appears to be preventable through a combination of lifestyle changes and sensible supplementation. Start by identifying which aging symptoms most directly affect you, and then focus your supplement regimen on controlling or reversing those factors. With proper care, your brain can maintain its youthful volume and function for years to come.

References

1. Enzinger C, Fazekas F, Matthews PM, et al. Risk factors for progression of brain atrophy in aging: six-year follow-up of normal subjects. *Neurology.* 2005 May 24;64(10):1704–11.

2. Hedman AM. Human brain changes across the life span: a review of 56 longitudinal magnetic resonance imaging studies. *Human Brain Mapping.* 2012;33:1987–220.

3. Olesen PJ, Guo X, Gustafson D, et al. A population-based study on the influence of brain atrophy on 20-year survival after age 85. *Neurology.* 2011 Mar 8;76(10):879–86.

4. Guo X, Steen B, Matousek M, et al. A population-based study on brain atrophy and motor performance in elderly women. *J Gerontol A Biol Sci Med Sci.* 2001 Oct;56(10):M633–7.

5. Henneman WJ, Sluimer JD, Cordonnier C, et al. MRI biomarkers of vascular damage and atrophy predicting mortality in a memory clinic population. *Stroke.* 2009 Feb;40(2):492–8.

6. Johansson L, Skoog I, Gustafson DR, et al. Midlife psychological distress associated with late-life brain atrophy and white matter lesions: a 32-year population study of women. *Psychosom Med.* 2012 Feb-Mar;74(2):120–5.

7. Olesen PJ, Gustafson DR, Simoni M, et al. Temporal lobe atrophy and white matter lesions are related to major depression over 5 years in the elderly. *Neuropsychopharmacology.* 2010 Dec;35(13):2638–45.

8. Debette S, Seshadri S, Beiser A, et al. Midlife vascular risk factor exposure accelerates structural brain aging and cognitive decline. *Neurology.* 2011 Aug 2;77(5):461–8.

9. Stoub TR, Detoledo-Morrell L, Dickerson BC. Parahippocampal white matter volume predicts Alzheimer's disease risk in cognitively normal old adults. *Neurobiol Aging.* 2014 Aug;35(8):1855–61.

10. van der Veen PH, Muller M, Vincken KL, Mali WP, van der Graaf Y, Geerlings MI. Brain volumes and risk of cardiovascular events and mortality. The SMART-MR study. *Neurobiol Aging.* 2014 Jul;35(7):1624–31.

11. Draganski B, Lutti A, Kherif F. Impact of brain aging and neuro-degeneration on cognition: evidence from MRI. *Curr Opin Neurol.* 2013 Dec;26(6):640–5.

12. Akinyemi RO, Mukaetova-Ladinska EB, Attems J, Ihara M, Kalaria RN. Vascular risk factors and neurodegeneration in ageing related dementias: Alzheimer's disease and vascular dementia. *Curr Alzheimer Res.* 2013 Jul;10(6):642–53.

13. Grober U, Kisters K, Schmidt J. Neuroenhancement with vitamin B12-underestimated neurological significance. *Nutrients.* 2013 Dec;5(12):5031–45.

14. Alosco ML, Gunstad J, Jerskey BA, et al. The adverse effects of reduced cerebral perfusion on cognition and brain structure in older adults with cardiovascular disease. *Brain Behav.* 2013 Nov;3(6):626–36.

15. Anazodo UC, Shoemaker JK, Suskin N, St Lawrence KS. An investigation of changes in regional gray matter volume in cardiovascular disease patients, pre and post cardiovascular rehabilitation. *Neuroimage Clin.* 2013;3:388–95.

16. Cherbuin N, Leach LS, Christensen H, Anstey KJ. Neuroimaging and APOE genotype: a systematic qualitative review. *Dement Geriatr Cogn Disord.* 2007;24(5):348–62.

17. Ford AH, Garrido GJ, Beer C, et al. Homocysteine, grey matter and cognitive function in adults with cardiovascular disease. *PLoS One.* 2012;7(3):e33345.

18. Yang LK, Wong KC, Wu MY, Liao SL, Kuo CS, Huang RF. Correlations between folate, B12, homocysteine levels, and radiological markers of neuropathology in elderly post-stroke patients. *J Am Coll Nutr.* 2007 Jun;26(3):272–8.

19. Narayan SK, Firbank MJ, Saxby BK, et al. Elevated plasma homocysteine is associated with increased brain atrophy rates in older subjects with mild hypertension. *Dement Geriatr Cogn Disord.* 2011;31(5):341–8.

20. Rajagopalan P, Hua X, Toga AW, Jack CR, Jr., Weiner MW, Thompson PM. Homocysteine effects on brain volumes mapped in 732 elderly individuals. *Neuroreport.* 2011 Jun 11;22(8):391–5.

21. de Jager CA. Critical levels of brain atrophy associated with homocysteine and cognitive decline. *Neurobiol Aging.* 2014 Sep;35 Suppl 2:S35–9.

22. Sapkota S, Gee M, Sabino J, Emery D, Camicioli R. Association of homocysteine with ventricular dilatation and brain atrophy in Parkinson's disease. *Mov Disord.* 2014 Mar;29(3):368–74.

23. Herrmann W, Obeid R. Homocysteine: a biomarker in neurodegenerative diseases. *Clin Chem Lab Med.* 2011 Mar;49(3):435–41.

24. Gallucci M, Zanardo A, Bendini M, Di Paola F, Boldrini P, Grossi E. Serum folate, homocysteine, brain atrophy, and auto-CM system: The Treviso Dementia (TREDEM) study. *J Alzheimers Dis.* 2014;38(3):581–7.

25. Squire LR. Memory and the hippocampus: a synthesis from findings with rats, monkeys, and humans. *Psychol Rev.* 1992 Apr;99(2):195–231.

26. Vogiatzoglou A, Refsum H, Johnston C, et al. Vitamin B12 status and rate of brain volume loss in community-dwelling elderly. *Neurology.* 2008 Sep 9;71(11):826–32.

27. Nachum-Biala Y, Troen AM. B-vitamins for neuroprotection: narrowing the evidence gap. *Biofactors.* 2012 Mar-Apr;38(2):145–50.

28. Cade WT. Diabetes-related microvascular and macrovascular diseases in the physical therapy setting. *Phys Ther.* 2008 Nov;88(11):1322–35.

29. Toth C, Martinez J, Zochodne DW. RAGE, diabetes, and the nervous system. *Curr Mol Med.* 2007 Dec;7(8):766–76.

30. Biessels GJ, Reijmer YD. Brain changes underlying cognitive dysfunction in diabetes: what can we learn from MRI? *Diabetes.* 2014 Jul;63(7):2244–52.

31. Moran C, Munch G, Forbes JM, et al. Type 2 diabetes mellitus, skin autofluorescence and brain atrophy. *Diabetes.* 2014 Jul 22.

32. Roberts RO, Knopman DS, Przybelski SA, et al. Association of type 2 diabetes with brain atrophy and cognitive impairment. *Neurology.* 2014 Apr 1;82(13):1132–41.

33. Wisse LE, de Bresser J, Geerlings MI, et al. Global brain atrophy but not hippocampal atrophy is related to type 2 diabetes. *J Neurol Sci.* 2014 Sep 15;344(1–2):32–6.

34. Ashraf GM, Greig NH, Khan TA, et al. Protein misfolding and aggregation in Alzheimer's disease and type 2 diabetes mellitus. *CNS Neurol Disord Drug Targets.* 2014;13(7):1280–93.

35. Britton M, Rafols J, Alousi S, Dunbar JC. The effects of middle cerebral artery occlusion on central nervous system apoptotic events in normal and diabetic rats. *Int J Exp Diabesity Res.* 2003 Jan-Mar;4(1):13–20.

36. Smale G, Nichols NR, Brady DR, Finch CE, Horton WE Jr. Evidence for apoptotic cell death in Alzheimer's disease. *Exp Neurol.* 1995 Jun;133(2):225–30.

37. Adeghate E, Donath T, Adem A. Alzheimer disease and diabetes mellitus: do they have anything in common? *Curr Alzheimer Res.* 2013 Jul;10(6):609–17.

38. Moroz N, Tong M, Longato L, Xu H, de la Monte SM. Limited Alzheimer-type neurodegeneration in experimental obesity and type 2 diabetes mellitus. *J Alzheimers Dis.* 2008 Sep;15(1):29–44.

39. Kiliaan AJ, Arnoldussen IA, Gustafson DR. Adipokines: a link between obesity and dementia? *Lancet Neurol.* 2014 Sep;13(9):913–23.

40. Raji CA, Ho AJ, Parikshak NN, et al. Brain structure and obesity. *Hum Brain Mapp.* 2010 Mar;31(3):353–64.

41. Fotuhi M, Hachinski V, Whitehouse PJ. Changing perspectives regarding late-life dementia. *Nat Rev Neurol.* 2009 Dec;5(12):649–58.

42. Ho AJ, Stein JL, Hua X, et al. A commonly carried allele of the obesity-related FTO gene is associated with reduced brain volume in the healthy elderly. *Proc Natl Acad Sci U S A.* 2010 May 4;107(18):8404–9.

43. Lo JC, Loh KK, Zheng H, Sim SK, Chee MW. Sleep duration and age-related changes in brain structure and cognitive performance. *Sleep.* 2014 Jul;37(7):1171–8.

44. Sexton CE, Storsve AB, Walhovd KB, Johansen-Berg H, Fjell AM. Poor sleep quality is associated with increased cortical atrophy in community-dwelling adults. *Neurology.* 2014 Sep 3.

45. Kubota K, Matsuzawa T, Fujiwara T, et al. Age-related brain atrophy enhanced by smoking: a quantitative study with computed tomography. *Tohoku J Exp Med.* 1987 Dec;153(4):303–11.

46. Durazzo TC, Meyerhoff DJ, Nixon SJ. Chronic cigarette smoking: implications for neurocognition and brain neurobiology. *Int J Environ Res Public Health.* 2010 Oct;7(10):3760–91.

47. Durazzo TC, Insel PS, Weiner MW. Greater regional brain atrophy rate in healthy elderly subjects with a history of cigarette smoking. *Alzheimers Dement.* 2012 Nov;8(6):513–9.

48. Gu Y, Scarmeas N, Short EE, et al. Alcohol intake and brain structure in a multiethnic elderly cohort. *Clin Nutr.* 2014 Aug;33(4):662–7.

49. Kubota M, Nakazaki S, Hirai S, Saeki N, Yamaura A, Kusaka T. Alcohol consumption and frontal lobe shrinkage: study of 1432 nonalcoholic subjects. *J Neurol Neurosurg Psychiatry.* 2001 Jul;71(1):104–6.

50. Mukamal KJ, Longstreth WT, Jr., Mittleman MA, Crum RM, Siscovick DS. Alcohol consumption and subclinical findings on magnetic resonance imaging of the brain in older adults: the cardiovascular health study. *Stroke.* 2001 Sep;32(9):1939–46.

51. Varela-Moreiras G. Nutritional regulation of homocysteine: effects of drugs. *Biomed Pharmacother.* 2001 Oct;55(8):448–53.

52. Polyak Z, Stern F, Berner YN, et al. Hyperhomocysteinemia and vitamin score: correlations with silent brain ischemic lesions and brain atrophy. *Dement Geriatr Cogn Disord.* 2003;16(1):39–45.

53. Blasko I, Hinterberger M, Kemmler G, et al. Conversion from mild cognitive impairment to dementia: influence of folic acid and vitamin B12 use in the VITA cohort. *J Nutr Health Aging.* 2012 Aug;16(8):687–94.

54. Smith AD, Refsum H. Vitamin B-12 and cognition in the elderly. *Am J Clin Nutr.* 2009 Feb;89(2):707s–11s.

55. Healthy Quality Ontario. Vitamin B12 and cognitive function: an evidence-based analysis. *Ont Health Technol Assess Ser.* 2013;13(23):1–45.

56. Smith AD, Smith SM, de Jager CA, et al. Homocysteine-lowering by B vitamins slows the rate of accelerated brain atrophy in mild cognitive impairment: a randomized controlled trial. *PLoS One.* 2010;5(9):e12244.

57. Douaud G, Refsum H, de Jager CA, et al. Preventing Alzheimer's disease-related gray matter atrophy by B-vitamin treatment. *Proc Natl Acad Sci U S A.* 2013 Jun 4;110(23):9523–8.

58. de Jager CA, Oulhaj A, Jacoby R, Refsum H, Smith AD. Cognitive and clinical outcomes of homocysteine-lowering B-vitamin treatment in mild cognitive impairment: a randomized controlled trial. *Int J Geriatr Psychiatry.* 2012 Jun;27(6):592–600.

59. Singh RB, Gupta S, Dherange P, et al. Metabolic syndrome: a brain disease. *Can J Physiol Pharmacol.* 2012 Sep;90(9):1171–83.

60. Nguyen LN, Ma D, Shui G, et al. Mfsd2a is a transporter for the essential omega-3 fatty acid docosahexaenoic acid. *Nature.* 2014 May 22;509(7501):503–6.

61. Sagduyu K, Dokucu ME, Eddy BA, Craigen G, Baldassano CF, Yildiz A. Omega-3 fatty acids decreased irritability of patients with bipolar disorder in an add-on, open label study. *Nutr J.* 2005 Feb 9;4:6.

62. Scrable H, Burns-Cusato M, Medrano S. Anxiety and the aging brain: stressed out over p53? *Biochim Biophys Acta.* 2009 Dec;1790(12):1587–91.

63. Hennebelle M, Champeil-Potokar G, Lavialle M, Vancassel S, Denis I. Omega-3 polyunsaturated fatty acids and chronic stress-induced modulations of glutamatergic neurotransmission in the hippocampus. *Nutr Rev.* 2014 Feb;72(2):99–112.

64. Tatebayashi Y, Nihonmatsu-Kikuchi N, Hayashi Y, Yu X, Soma M, Ikeda K. Abnormal fatty acid composition in the frontopolar

cortex of patients with affective disorders. *Transl Psychiatry.* 2012;2:e204.

65. Virtanen JK, Siscovick DS, Lemaitre RN, et al. Circulating omega-3 polyunsaturated fatty acids and subclinical brain abnormalities on MRI in older adults: the Cardiovascular Health Study. *J Am Heart Assoc.* 2013 Oct;2(5):e000305.

66. Pottala JV, Yaffe K, Robinson JG, Espeland MA, Wallace R, Harris WS. Higher RBC EPA + DHA corresponds with larger total brain and hippocampal volumes: WHIMS-MRI study. *Neurology.* 2014 Feb 4;82(5):435–42.

67. Torres M, Price SL, Fiol-Deroque MA, et al. Membrane lipid modifications and therapeutic effects mediated by hydroxydocosahexaenoic acid on Alzheimer's disease. *Biochim Biophys Acta.* 2014 Jun;1838(6):1680–92.

68. Zhang C, Bazan NG. Lipid-mediated cell signaling protects against injury and neurodegeneration. *J Nutr.* 2010 Apr;140(4):858–63.

69. Hartman RE, Shah A, Fagan AM, et al. Pomegranate juice decreases amyloid load and improves behavior in a mouse model of Alzheimer's disease. *Neurobiol Dis.* 2006 Dec;24(3):506–15.

70. Kumar S, Maheshwari KK, Singh V. Protective effects of Punica granatum seeds extract against aging and scopolamine induced cognitive impairments in mice. *Afr J Tradit Complement Altern Med.* 2008;6(1):49–56.

71. Rojanathammanee L, Puig KL, Combs CK. Pomegranate polyphenols and extract inhibit nuclear factor of activated T-cell activity and microglial activation in vitro and in a transgenic mouse model of Alzheimer disease. *J Nutr.* 2013 May;143(5):597–605.

72. Choi SJ, Lee JH, Heo HJ, et al. Punica granatum protects against oxidative stress in PC12 cells and oxidative stress-induced Alzheimer's symptoms in mice. *J Med Food.* 2011 Jul-Aug;14(7–8):695–701.

73. Bookheimer SY, Renner BA, Ekstrom A, et al. Pomegranate juice augments memory and FMRI activity in middle-aged and older adults with mild memory complaints. *Evid Based Complement Alternat Med.* 2013;2013:946298.

74. Forouzanfar F, Afkhami Goli A, Asadpour E, Ghorbani A, Sadeghnia HR. Protective effect of Punica granatum L. against serum/glucose deprivation-induced PC12 cells injury. *Evid Based Complement Alternat Med.* 2013;2013:716730.

75. Moriya J, Chen R, Yamakawa J, Sasaki K, Ishigaki Y, Takahashi T. Resveratrol improves hippocampal atrophy in chronic fatigue mice by enhancing neurogenesis and inhibiting apoptosis of granular cells. *Biol Pharm Bull.* 2011;34(3):354–9.

76. Rege SD, Kumar S, Wilson DN, et al. Resveratrol protects the brain of obese mice from oxidative damage. *Oxid Med Cell Longev.* 2013;2013:419092.

77. Chang HC, Tai YT, Cherng YG, et al. Resveratrol attenuates high-fat diet-induced disruption of the blood-brain barrier and protects brain neurons from apoptotic insults. *J Agric Food Chem.* 2014 Apr 16;62(15):3466–75.

78. Witte AV, Kerti L, Margulies DS, Floel A. Effects of resveratrol on memory performance, hippocampal functional connectivity, and glucose metabolism in healthy older adults. *J Neurosci.* 2014 Jun 4;34(23):7862–70.

Critical Thinking

1. How are middle aged men and women addressing the issues associated with brain shrinkage in their everyday lives?

2. What could we change in our daily diet to impact our brains as we age?

3. Is brain shrinkage an inevitable aspect of aging?

Internet References

Brain Food: 6 Snacks That Are Good for the Mind
http://www.telegraph.co.uk/news/science/science-news/11364896/Brain-food-6-snacks-that-are-good-for-the-mind.html

Brain Shrinkage
http://www.mayoclinic.org/diseases-conditions/mild-cognitive-impairment/multimedia/brain-shrinkage/img-20006725

Eat Smart for a Healthier Brain
http://www.webmd.com/diet/eat-smart-healthier-brain

Frontotemporal Dementia
http://www.alz.org/dementia/fronto-temporal-dementia-ftd-symptoms.asp

Study: 4 Factors That May Shrink Your Brain
http://healthland.time.com/2011/08/03/study-4-factors-that-may-shrink-your-brain/

Protect Your Brain Against Aging
http://alzdiscovery.org/cognitive-vitality

Article   Prepared by: Claire N. Rubman, *Suffolk County Community College*

Age-Proof Your Brain
10 Easy Ways to Stay Sharp Forever

Beth Howard

learning new is better!

Learning Outcomes

After reading this article, you will be able to:

- Tell an elder how to delay memory loss and/or dementia.
- Predict which chronic health impairments lead to an early dementia and explain why.

Alzheimer's isn't inevitable. Many experts now believe you can prevent or at least delay dementia—even if you have a genetic predisposition. Reducing Alzheimer's risk factors like obesity, diabetes, smoking and low physical activity by just 25 percent could prevent up to half a million cases of the disease in the United States, according to a recent analysis from the University of California in San Francisco.

"The goal is to stave it off long enough so that you can live life without ever suffering from symptoms," says Gary Small, M.D., director of the UCLA Longevity Center and coauthor of *The Alzheimer's Prevention Program: Keep Your Brain Healthy for the Rest of Your Life.* Read on for new ways to boost your brain.

Get Moving

"If you do only one thing to keep your brain young, exercise," says Art Kramer, professor of psychology and neuroscience at the University of Illinois. Higher exercise levels can reduce dementia risk by 30 to 40 percent compared with low activity levels, and physically active people tend to maintain better cognition and memory than inactive people. "They also have substantially lower rates of different forms of dementia, including Alzheimer's disease," Kramer says.

Working out helps your hippocampus, the region of the brain involved in memory formation. As you age, your hippocampus shrinks, leading to memory loss. Exercise can reverse this process, research suggests. Physical activity can also trigger the growth of new nerve cells and promote nerve growth.

How you work up a sweat is up to you, but most experts recommend 150 minutes a week of moderate activity. Even a little bit can help: "In our research as little as 15 minutes of regular exercise three times per week helped maintain the brain," says Eric B. Larson, M.D., executive director of Group Health Research Institute in Seattle.

Pump Some Iron

Older women who participated in a yearlong weight-training program at the University of British Columbia at Vancouver did 13 percent better on tests of cognitive function than a group of women who did balance and toning exercises. "Resistance training may increase the levels of growth factors in the brain such as IGF1, which nourish and protect nerve cells," says Teresa Liu-Ambrose, head of the university's Aging, Mobility, and Cognitive Neuroscience Laboratory.

Seek Out New Skills

Learning spurs the growth of new brain cells. "When you challenge the brain, you increase the number of brain cells and the number of connections between those cells," says Keith L. Black, M.D., chair of neurosurgery at Cedars-Sinai Medical Center in Los Angeles. "But it's not enough to do the things you routinely do—like the daily crossword. You have to learn new things, like sudoku or a new form of bridge."

UCLA researchers using MRI scans found that middle-aged and older adults with little Internet experience could trigger brain centers that control decision-making and complex reasoning after a week of surfing the net. "Engaging the mind can help older brains maintain healthy functioning," says Cynthia R. Green, Ph.D., author of *30 Days to Total Brain Health*.

Say "Omm"

Chronic stress floods your brain with cortisol, which leads to impaired memory. To better understand if easing tension changes your brain, Harvard researchers studied men and women trained in a technique called mindfulness-based stress reduction (MBSR). This form of meditation—which involves focusing one's attention on sensations, feelings and state of mind—has been shown to reduce harmful stress hormones. After eight weeks, researchers took MRI scans of participants' brains that showed the density of gray matter in the hippocampus increased significantly in the MBSR group, compared with a control group.

Eat Like a Greek

A heart-friendly Mediterranean diet—fish, vegetables, fruit, nuts and beans—reduced Alzheimer's risk by 34 to 48 percent in studies conducted by Columbia University.

"We know that omega-3 fatty acids in fish are very important for maintaining heart health," says Keith Black of Cedars-Sinai. "We suspect these fats may be equally important for maintaining a healthy brain." Data from several large studies suggest that older people who eat the most fruits and vegetables, especially the leafy-green variety, may experience a slower rate of cognitive decline and a lower risk for dementia than meat lovers.

And it may not matter if you get your produce from a bottle instead of a bin. A study from Vanderbilt University found that people who downed three or more servings of fruit or vegetable juice a week had a 76 percent lower risk for developing Alzheimer's disease than those who drank less than a serving weekly.

Spice It Up

Your brain enjoys spices as much as your taste buds do. Herbs and spices such as black pepper, cinnamon, oregano, basil, parsley, ginger and vanilla are high in antioxidants, which may help build brainpower. Scientists are particularly intrigued by curcumin, the active ingredient in turmeric, common in Indian curries. "Indians have lower incidence of Alzheimer's, and one theory is it's the curcumin," says Black. "It bonds to amyloid plaques that accumulate in the brains of people with the disease." Animal research shows curcumin reduces amyloid

plaques and lowers inflammation levels. A study in humans also found those who ate curried foods frequently had higher scores on standard cognition tests.

Find Your Purpose

Discovering your mission in life can help you stay sharp, according to a Rush University Medical Center study of more than 950 older adults. Participants who approached life with clear intentions and goals at the start of the study were less likely to develop Alzheimer's disease over the following seven years, researchers found.

Get a (Social) Life

Who needs friends? You do! Having multiple social networks helps lower dementia risk, a 15-year study of older people from Sweden's Karolinska Institute shows. A rich social life may protect against dementia by providing emotional and mental stimulation, says Laura Fratiglioni, M.D., director of the institute's Aging Research Center. Other studies yield similar conclusions: Subjects in a University of Michigan study did better on tests of short-term memory after just 10 minutes of conversation with another person.

Reduce Your Risks

Chronic health conditions like diabetes, obesity and hypertension are often associated with dementia. Diabetes, for example, roughly doubles the risk for Alzheimer's and other forms of dementia. Controlling these risk factors can slow the tide.

"We've estimated that in people with mild cognitive impairment—an intermediate state between normal cognitive aging and dementia—good control of diabetes can delay the onset of dementia by several years," says Fratiglioni. That means following doctor's orders regarding diet and exercise and taking prescribed medications on schedule.

Check Vitamin Deficiencies

Older adults don't always get all the nutrients they need from foods, because of declines in digestive acids or because their medications interfere with absorption. That vitamin deficit—particularly vitamin B_{12}—can also affect brain vitality, research from Rush University Medical Center shows. Older adults at risk of vitamin B_{12} deficiencies had smaller brains and scored lowest on tests measuring thinking, reasoning and memory, researchers found.

Critical Thinking

1. Name three categories of foods that are heart friendly.
2. Identify five herbs or spices that are antioxidants.
3. Why are friends important to brain health?
4. Which exercise stimulates brain circuits more: a daily crossword puzzle or learning something new?

Create Central

www.mhhe.com/createcentral

Internet References

Aging in Different Ways
www.brainfacts.org/across-the-lifespan/agingarticles/2012

Alzheimer's Disease Research Center
http://alzheimer.wustl.edu

AARP
www.aarp.org

Stockholm Gerontology Research Center
www.aldrecentrum.se/Havudmeny/English

Vitamin B12 Deficiency in the Elderly
www.ncbi.nlm.nih.gov/pubmed/10448529

BETH HOWARD last wrote for *AARP The Magazine* about medical breakthroughs, in the September/October 2011 issue.

Article

Prepared by: Claire N. Rubman,
Suffolk County Community College, Selden, NY

The Shock of Elder Abuse in Assisted Living

If you're like many recently surveyed, what you don't know may surprise you.

LOIS A. BOWERS

Learning Outcomes

After reading this article, you will be able to:

- Describe the nature of abuse in assisted living environments including medication errors and inappropriate sexual behavior.

- Discuss the discrepancy between nurse aides and executive directors with regard to rates of abuse.

- Articulate preventative measures suggested by the author.

Executive directors of assisted living communities may not be aware of all of the cases of elder abuse—especially sexual incidents—occurring in their communities. That's the conclusion of Marguerite "Marti" DeLiema, a doctoral candidate at the University of Southern California's (USC's) Davis School of Gerontology.

DeLiema discussed elder abuse with the more than 100 people attending the Assisted Living Federation of America (ALFA) Executive Director Leadership Institute (EDLI), held in conjunction with ALFA's annual meeting in May.

As part of her session, she polled attendees about their observations or suspicions of staff members' physical mistreatment of residents, mismanagement of resident medication (stealing residents' medication for themselves, giving medication intended for one resident to another resident or withholding medication from a resident) and inappropriate sexual behavior with residents within the past year.

When it came to physical mistreatment of residents or mismanagement of medication, EDLI participants' reporting of observed or suspected incidents was similar to that of assisted living nurse aides surveyed by Nicholas Castle, PhD, and Scott Beach, PhD, for a large study published in the *Journal of Applied Gerontology*. Concerning sexually inappropriate behavior between a staff member and a resident, however, the executive directors reported a much lower frequency of this type of abuse than did the nurse aides, DeLiema says.

All but one responding executive director said they had never observed or suspected a staff member of such behavior, she says; one reported observing or suspecting one case. By comparison, the Castle and Beach study of nurse aides, DeLiema says, had "a lot more shocking results." For instance, three percent of the nurse aides surveyed said they knew of staff members' "unwelcome fondling" of a resident, and seven percent said they were aware of staff members who had exposed a resident's body part as a form of abuse.

"What really surprised me was the reaction of the audience to the Castle and Beach study results" related to sexual abuse, DeLiema says of EDLI participants. "They were really shocked by how high those rates were. They were shaking their heads and putting their hands over their mouths. They were really surprised. So that speaks to the fact that they just are not aware that this is going on in their communities."

Why does this apparent discrepancy exist between executive directors and nurse aides? One possibility, she says, is that the aides are closer to the delivery of care and so may see more incidents of inappropriate sexual interaction.

"It's my guess that it's just that [the executive directors are] further removed," DeLiema says. "These nursing aides are literally with [residents] 24/7, and they are the ones who have to manage the more difficult behaviors and do all of the personal care work. You would hope that the executive director would hear about these things if they're being reported, but perhaps not."

Also, DeLiema adds, perhaps some incidents of abuse are handled within the nursing department and are not communicated to the executive director. Or perhaps the EDLI survey-takers hesitated to respond honestly to the question, even though they were submitting their answers electronically and anonymously during the EDLI session.

Elder abuse takes many forms—financial, sexual, physical and emotional/psychological abuse as well as neglect. What can be done to prevent and address such abuse in long-term care (LTC) settings, whether it be perpetrated by a staff member, a family member or another resident? Increased awareness—through educational programs such as the EDLI and events such as World Elder Abuse Awareness Month, observed every June, and World Elder Abuse Awareness Day, observed every year on June 15—is one solution. Others, according to DeLiema:

- Develop and maintain a good working relationship with the LTC ombudsman in your state. "Sometimes, the cases we see, the facility can only do so much. They really need to pull someone in from the outside, and sometimes, the best option is more of a mediator than the police or adult protective services," she says, noting that ombudsmen usually take a person-centered approach.

- Educate residents, family and staff members that reporting abuse is a good thing. "You really need buy-in from the older adults if you're going to try to 'protect' them," DeLiema says. "And the same with physicians, getting them to feel that reporting is the best option" rather than trying to address incidents directly themselves.

- Train direct care staff who work with combative residents so that they don't react in an abusive way to

behaviors that, because of a cognitive disease process, may be beyond a resident's control. "It's important that they have a good understanding of the disease process," DeLiema says. Training, she adds, can answer these questions: "What is cognitive impairment, how does it manifest, what kind of behaviors can they expect?"

- Establish a system to address suspected or confirmed incidents of staff mistreatment of residents to ensure that such incidents don't recur.

The USC Davis School of Gerontology touts that it is the oldest and largest such school in the world. DeLiema also points executive directors and others to the school's website (gero. usc.edu) and its Guide for Elder Abuse Response (GEAR) app (guideforelderabuse.org) as additional resources. The app, she notes, has some elements of particular interest to those working in California, but it also contains information of wide potential interest.

Critical Thinking

1. Do families recognize when abuse may be occurring in assisted living homes?

2. Under what circumstances does a family use an assisted living facility for their loved one?

3. Are families generally satisfied with the quality of care at assisted living facilities?

Internet References

Elder Abuse
   http://www.cdc.gov/violenceprevention/elderabuse/index.html

Elder Abuse
   https://www.nia.nih.gov/health/publication/elder-abuse

What is Elder Abuse?
   http://www.aoa.gov/AoA_programs/Elder_Rights/EA_Prevention/whatIsEA.aspx

Article   Prepared by: Claire N. Rubman, *Suffolk County Community College*

Elder Abuse Identification: A Public Health Issue

HELEN SORENSON

Learning Outcomes

After reading this article, you will be able to:

- Identify six ways in which elders can be abused.

- Describe some of the warning signs of elder abuse.

Elder abuse wears many hats. As defined by the World Health Organization, elder abuse is a single or repeated act or lack of appropriate action occurring within any relationship where there is an expectation of trust that causes harm or distress to an older person.[1] It can be manifested as physical, mental, financial, emotional, sexual, or verbal abuse. Abuse can also be in the form of passive or active neglect. Elder abuse is not confined to any country, any culture, or any age group (young-old to old-old). However, the very old seem to be most vulnerable. Determining the extent of elder abuse in any specific population is difficult, as much of it is unreported. There is a stigma associated with being abused that affects both the victim and the perpetrator, especially when it occurs within the family. Fear, loyalty, and/or shame may prevent the abused from taking any action to stop it. Suffering in silence for some seems to be a badge of honor. For those brave enough to report the abuse, it may not be considered a legitimate complaint coming from someone who has been diagnosed with delirium or dementia or from someone who is judged to "just be senile."

In all likelihood, respiratory therapists unknowingly care for patients who are or who have been abused. Unless questioned, the victim will usually not share information about the mistreatment. Brief encounters may not elicit information. Established relationships can develop between therapists/patients in smaller community hospitals, in home care, or in rehabilitation settings. These may be instances in which abusive situations can be addressed and stopped. Awareness of the possibility is the key.

Scenario

Doris and Frank live in a small house in the rural Midwest. Doris is 72, Frank is 84, and both are retired. Two years ago their daughter, who lives nearby, decided that Mom didn't really need all the "stuff" she had collected over the years. When Doris and Frank were away, she disposed of many items. After repeatedly asking her not to do this to no avail, they changed the locks on the house. Not deterred by this action, the daughter broke the window, got inside the house, and threatened to "burn the house down" if they ever locked her out again. When they disagreed, she struck Frank.

Will they report this? No, because she is their daughter, and it wouldn't be right. Are her actions justified? Is she legitimately concerned about their safety, or is this elder abuse? This is a difficult situation. Elderly individuals can be institutionalized (for their safety) after reporting abuse. Since most older adults prefer to remain in their homes, they do not report abuse. Another option is to take out a restraining order against their child, which may also have adverse consequences. What is needed is counseling for both the victims and the offender, which is a complex process and involves the local Department of Social Services. There are no easy answers.

Incidence of Abuse

Elder abuse is a public health issue that affects a significant percentage of the population and in the future is likely to get worse. A systematic review of studies by Cooper et al measuring the prevalence of elder abuse or neglect was published in 2008.[2] This summary of the best evidence determined the following: 25% of dependent older adults reported significant levels of psychological abuse, and 1% reported physical abuse. Twenty percent of the older adults who presented to the emergency department were experiencing neglect, and the incidence of financial abuse has been estimated to be about 6%–18%.[2] Another prevalence survey published in 2010 included data from 5,777 (60.2% female) respondents.[3] Abuse during a one-year period was as follows: 4.6% emotional abuse, 1.6% physical abuse, 0.6% sexual abuse, 5.1% potential neglect, and 5.2% financial abuse. Overall, 10% of those interviewed reported abuse of some kind. Factoring in demographic information, women and frail elders were more likely to experience verbal abuse. African-Americans were more likely to experience financial abuse, and Latinos were less likely than respondents from any other ethnic group to report any form of abuse. Overall, low social support increased the risk for suffering any form of mistreatment, and relatively little of this abuse was reported to the authorities.[3]

Understanding that abuse and mistreatment of older adults happens is the easy part of the dilemma. Determining the form of abuse, who is at risk, who is doing the abusing, and how it can be stopped is more difficult. The National Center on Elder Abuse (NCEA), in conjunction with the Administration on Aging, has provided a list of warning signs (see Table 1).[4] While one sign does not necessarily indicate abuse, it may raise a red flag that other signs may be present but not yet assessed. There may be many other logical reasons for the presence of the warning signs, but awareness of potential abuse is key to prevention.

Identification of Abuse

Warning signs of abuse may not be readily apparent to the RT providing routine therapy on a newly admitted patient. Respiratory therapists who work in intensive care may be more likely to notice bruises and burns, but their focus is generally on ventilation and respiration. RTs who work in home care or rehabilitation may be the most likely to pick up on the fact that "something is just not quite right" with their elderly patient. If during the course of a visit or an examination, any of the warning signs of abuse are noticed, it is time to ask questions. Any licensed health care provider is qualified to ask questions. Respiratory therapists routinely ask about shortness of breath, quality of sleep, and frequency of cough. If bruises are noted, asking "has someone hurt you" or "did someone do this to you" are not unusual questions.

To increase the odds of getting an honest response, it may be necessary to interview the older adult without others present. If family members or caregivers seem reluctant to leave you alone with the individual in question, this may also be a potential "red flag." If the patient seems afraid to answer two simple questions or seems elusive with a response, contact your hospital social worker or case worker for a follow-up. Respiratory therapy education does not always cover assessing for abuse; but despite lack of training, awareness is vital. Educators could add a unit on elder abuse to a disease management course or give reading assignments to students to increase their awareness of the problem. Classroom discussions can and often do result in attitudinal changes not measurable by examinations.

Questions for the RT to Ask

Questions that may elicit a response to warning signs or bruises include:[5]

- ? *Has someone hurt you?*
- ? *Did someone do this to you?*
- ? *Has anyone ever touched you without your consent?*
- ? *Does anyone yell at you or threaten you?*
- ? *Who cares for you at home?*
- ? *Are you afraid of your caregiver?*
- ? *Do you feel safe where you live?*
- ? *Who manages your finances?*
- ? *What happens when you and your caregiver disagree?*

Table 1   Warnings of Potential Elder Abuse

Warning Signs	Potential Causes
Bruises, pressure marks, broken bones, abrasions and burns	Physical abuse, neglect, or mistreatment
Unexplained withdrawal from normal activities, new onset of depression, change in alertness	Emotional abuse
Bruises around breasts, genitalia	Sexual abuse
Sudden change in financial status	Financial exploitation
Bed sores, unattended medical needs, poor hygiene, unusual weight loss	Neglect
Controlling spouses/caregivers, threats, belittling comments	Verbal/Emotional abuse
Frequent arguments between caregiver/older adult, tense relationships	Emotional abuse

Source: National Center on Elder Abuse, U.S. Administration on Aging, www.ncea.aoa.gov

Keep in mind that skin tears and bruises in older adults are not always the result of abuse, but assuming that they are "just signs of old age" may be doing a disservice to the patient.

Elder Abuse Screening Instruments

In an effort to facilitate early identification of elder abuse, a number of screening instruments have been created to help nurses detect mistreatment.[6-9] One of the more current instruments, the Geriatric Mistreatment Scale, is available in both Spanish and English versions and screens for five different types of elder mistreatment.[9] While useful, it is also important to realize that even when assessed, many older adults will not report and will not admit that they are the victims of abuse. Another screening instrument published by the American Medical Association and available at www.centeronelderabuse.org/docs/AMA_Screening_Questions.pdf suggests questions that physicians should incorporate into their daily practice. While presenting all aspects of elder abuse is beyond the scope of this article, a chapter authored by Tom Miller in "Elder Abuse: A Public Health Perspective" contains a very useful algorithm for elder abuse intervention designed for health professionals.[10] Unfortunately, sometimes it is the caregiver who is abusive.

Abuse at the Hands of Caregivers

In response to an increased awareness of elder abuse, in 1987 the Omnibus Budget Reconciliation Act (OBRA) enacted major reforms that ultimately led to improved training of caregivers working with elderly clients.[11] Additional initiatives across the country have attempted to address the problem in a variety of ways. An earlier publication estimated that at least 4% of elderly people are maltreated by their caregivers.[12] Reasons cited have been stress, dependency of the caregiver on the abused older adult for finances and living arrangements, and social isolation.[13] Marshall et al have offered that caregiver stress, rather than malicious intent, is often the cause of abuse.[14] Considering that neglect is also considered a form of abuse, how many patients develop bedsores for lack of being turned or have their call-lights ignored because they are "needy patients who whine a lot"?

Recognizing and Reporting Abuse

Health care professionals need to be able to recognize the "at-risk" factors for elder mistreatment. It is imperative to abide by all reporting laws and equally important is to maintain a therapeutic relationship with the potential victim. Communication and trust issues can make a big difference in the cooperation and willingness of older adults to share incidences of abuse.

Legislatures in all 50 states have passed some form of elder abuse prevention laws. In March of 2011 Congress passed a comprehensive federal elder abuse prevention law.[15] Help for our older adults is out there; but first, abuse must be recognized. While not a comfortable situation to address, there are ways to let authorities know of a potential problem without violating the Health Insurance Portability and Accountability Act (HIPAA) rules and regulations. Anyone can report a case of elder abuse in good faith. The Elder Abuse and Neglect Act provides that people—who in good faith report suspected abuse or cooperate with an investigation—are immune from criminal or civil liability or professional disciplinary action. It further provides that the identity of the reporter shall not be disclosed except with the written permission of the reporter or by order of a court. Anonymous reports are accepted. While not easy to do, these actions may be as important as starting an IV, delivering a medication, or viewing an x-ray to get at the root of what is causing the older adult to suffer.

The following are resources that one can refer to for help if abuse is suspected or confirmed:

- Eldercare Locator: (800) 677-1116. Monday–Friday, 9 A.M. to 8 P.M. EST. Trained operators will refer you to a local agency that will help.
- The National Domestic Violence Hotline: (800) 799-SAFE (800-799-7233).
- National Committee for the Prevention of Elder Abuse: www.preventelderabuse.org.
- National Center on Elder Abuse/Administration on Aging: www.ncea.aoa.gov.
- Center of Excellence on Elder Abuse & Neglect: www.centeronelderabuse.org.

References

1. McAlpine CH. Elder abuse and neglect. Age Ageing 2008; 37(2):132–133.
2. Cooper C, Selwood A, Livingston G. The prevalence of elder abuse and neglect: a systematic review. Age Ageing 2008; 37(2):151–160.
3. Acierno R, Hernandez MA, Amstadter AB, et al. Prevalence and correlates of emotional, physical, sexual, and financial abuse and potential neglect in the United States: the National Elder Mistreatment Study. Am J Public Health 2010; 100(2):292–297.
4. National Center on Elder Abuse (NCEA), Administration on Aging website. www.ncea.aoa.gov.
5. Gray-Vickrey P. Combating elder abuse. Nursing 2004; 34(10): 47–51.
6. Yaffe MJ, Wolfson C, Lithwick M, Weiss D. Development and validation of a tool to improve physician identification of elder abuse: the Elder Abuse Suspicion Index (EASI). J Elder Abuse Negl 2008; 20(3):276–300.

7. Neale AV, Hwalek M, Scott R, Stahl C. Validation of the Hwalek-Sengstock elder abuse screening test. J Appl Gerontol 1991; 10(4):406–418.

8. Schofield MJ, Mishra GD. Validity of self-report screening scale for elder abuse: Women's Health Australia Study. Gerontologist 2003; 43(1):110–120.

9. Giraldo-Rodriguez L, Rosas-Carrasco O. Development and psychometric properties of the Geriatric Mistreatment Scale. Geriatr Gerontol Int 2012; June 14 [Epub ahead of print].

10. Summers RW, Hoffman AM, editors. Elder abuse: a public health perspective. Washington DC: American Public Health Association; 2006.

11. Hawes C, Mor V, Phillips CD, et al. The OBRA-87 nursing home regulations and implementation of the Resident Assessment Instrument: effects on process quality. J Am Geriatr Soc 1997; 45(8):977–985.

12. Pillemer K, Finkelhor D. The prevalence of elder abuse: a random sample survey. Gerontologist 1988; 28(1):51–57.

13. Penhale B. Responding and intervening in elder abuse and neglect. Ageing Int 2010; 35:235–252.

14. Marshall CE, Benton D, Brazier JM. Elder abuse. Using clinical tools to identify clues of mistreatment. Geriatrics 2000; 55(2):45–53.

15. The Elder Justice Coalition EJA Update, May 20, 2012. Available at: www.elderjusticecoalition.com *Accessed Sept. 11, 2012.*

Critical Thinking

1. How can a health-care worker maintain a therapeutic relationship with an elder who is being abused but does not want the abuse reported?

2. Why are people who report elder abuse immune from criminal or civil liability, even if they have betrayed their elder person's confidentiality and trust?

3. Under what conditions would you report suspected elder abuse?

Create Central

www.mhhe.com/createcentral

Internet References

Center of Excellence on Elder Abuse and Neglect
www.centeronelderabuse.org

Eldercare Locator
www.eldercare.gov

Eldercare Locator Resource Center
www.n4a.org/programs/eldercare-locator

National Center on Elder Abuse/Administration on Aging
www.ncea.aoa.gov

National Committee for the Prevention of Elder Abuse
www.preventelderabuse.org

HELEN SORENSON, MA, RRT, FAARC, is adjunct faculty and an associate professor (retired) with the department of respiratory care at the University of Texas Health Science Center at San Antonio, TX.

Sorenson, Helen. From *AARC Times*, November 2012, pp. 12–14, 16. Copyright © 2012 by AARC Times, Daedalus Enterprises, Inc., a publication of the American Association for Respiratory Care, Irving, TX. Used with permission.